Luka Biong Deng Kuol is Professor of Practice, Africa Center for Strategic Studies, National Defense University, Washington, USA, and Global Fellow, Peace Research Institute Oslo, Norway.

Sarah Logan is a Policy Economist at the International Growth Centre (IGC) at the London School of Economics and Political Science. She is a qualified lawyer with significant policy experience in sub-Saharan Africa.

D08786618

'This book is a remarkable story of the South Sudanese struggle. It appears at a critical time in our history, as our political and social concerns are further mitigated by the eminent threat to our communities' safety and survival. The present crisis of war, economic down-turns, human-rights violations, state fragility and internally displaced persons in the country has reached a critical point. The beauty of this book is that it also provides details of local solutions through the real intellectual experience and exposure of Kuol, Logan and their contributors. To those interested in the South Sudanese story – I highly recommend this book.'

PROFESSOR JULIA DUANY
Vice Chancellor of Dr John Garang Memorial University of Science and Technology

Edited by Luka Biong Deng Kuol and Sarah Logan

The Struggle for South Sudan

Challenges of Security and State Formation

I.B. TAURIS
LONDON · NEW YORK

Published in 2019 by
I.B.Tauris & Co. Ltd
London • New York
www.ibtauris.com

ISBN (HB): 978 1 78831 517 3
ISBN (PB): 978 1 78831 518 0
eISBN: 978 1 78672 575 2
ePDF: 978 1 78673 575 1

A full CIP record for this book is available from the British Library
A full CIP record is available from the Library of Congress

Library of Congress Catalog Card Number: available

Typeset by Tetragon, London
Printed and bound in Great Britain

Contents

List of Figures and Tables

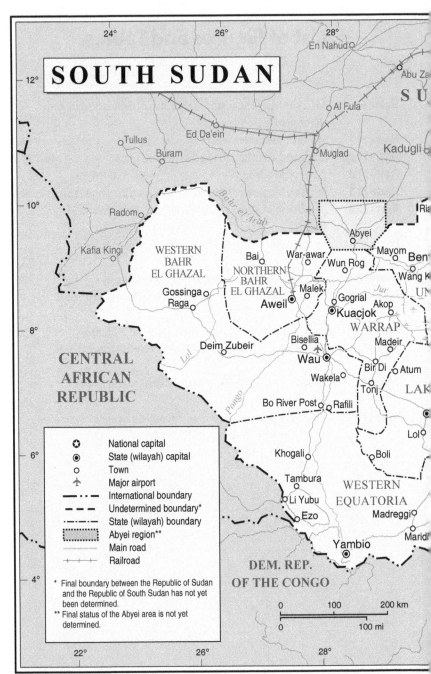

The boundaries and names shown and the designations used on this map do not imply official endorsement or acceptance by the United Nations.

Department of Field Support
Cartographic Section

Acknowledgements

We would like to thank the International Growth Centre (IGC) at the London School of Economics and Political Science, the Africa Center for Strategic Studies at the National Defense University and Richard Newfarmer, former IGC Country Director for South Sudan, for their support.

Contributors

Luka Biong Deng Kuol is Professor of Practice for Security Studies at the Africa Center for Strategic Studies (ACSS), National Defense University, Washington, DC. He is also associate professor at the University of Juba, South Sudan, and a Global Fellow at the Peace Research Institute Oslo (PRIO) in Norway. He has been resident fellow at the Harvard Kennedy School, director of the Institute of Peace, Development and Security Studies at the University of Juba, and academic staff at the University of Gezira, Sudan. He has served as a Minister of Presidency of Southern Sudan and as a National Minister of Cabinet Affairs of Sudan. He has also worked as a Senior Economist for the World Bank in Southern Sudan and was a founding member of the South Sudan National Bureau of Statistics.

Lovise Aalen is a political scientist and research director at the Chr. Michelsen Institute. Her research interest is institutional solutions in divided societies, including power-sharing, federalism and decentralisation, with a particular focus on South Sudan, Sudan and Ethiopia. Her publications include *The Politics of Ethnicity in Ethiopia: Actors, Power and Mobilisation Under Ethnic Federalism* (2011), *Considering the State: Perspectives on South Sudan's Subdivision and Federalism Debate* (co-edited with Mareike Schomerus, 2016) and *Manipulating Political Decentralisation: Africa's Inclusive Autocrats* (co-authored with Ragnhild L. Muriaas, 2018).

Lotjie de Vries is an assistant professor at the Sociology of Development and Change Group at Wageningen University. Her research focuses on local dynamics of (in)security, transnational security governance in peripheries and at borders, and state–society relations in (post-)conflict settings. She works mainly in South Sudan and the Central African Republic.

Alex de Waal is executive director of the World Peace Foundation and research professor at the Fletcher School of Law and Diplomacy, Tufts University. He has worked extensively on the Horn of Africa, and served with the African Union High-Level Implementation Panel for Sudan and South Sudan from 2009–2012. He is the author *of The Real Politics of the Horn of Africa: Money, War and the Business of Power* (2015) and *Mass Starvation: The History and Future of Famine* (2018).

Daniel J. M. Deng began working in Africa in 1998 as a project manager for peace programmes in the Democratic Republic of Congo. In 1999 he transferred to Zimbabwe, where he covered eight southern African countries. Since 2003, he has worked in strategic planning, management, monitoring and evaluation for UN agencies, international NGOs and government ministries. He served as senior advisor to the Japan International Cooperation Agency (JICA) and on the Development Advisory Council for South Sudan of the US Agency for International Development (USAID). He is now Chief of Party for Management Systems International (MSI), South Sudan office.

Francis M. Deng is South Sudan's Roving Ambassador and was its first Permanent Representative to the UN. He served as the UN Secretary-General's Special Advisor on the Prevention of Genocide, and before that as Representative of the Secretary-General on Internally Displaced Persons. He was Sudan's Ambassador to Canada and the US, and Sudan's Minister of State for Foreign Affairs. He has held a series of positions at leading think-tanks and universities in the US. He holds an LLM and a JSD from Yale Law School, and has authored and edited over 30 books.

Nora Dihel is a senior economist at the World Bank. Prior to joining the Bank, she worked in the Chief Economist Unit of the Directorate General for Trade of the European Commission and the OECD Trade Directorate. She has published extensively on the economic impact of service reforms, regional integration and South–South linkages. Nora has a doctorate in Economics from the Helmut Schmidt University, Germany.

Douglas H. Johnson is the author and editor of many works of South Sudanese history, including *South Sudan: A New History for a New Nation* (2016), *The Root Causes of Sudan's Civil Wars: Peace or Truce?* (2011), *When Boundaries Become Borders: The Impact of Boundary-Making in Southern Sudan's Frontier Zones* (2010), *Sudan: British Documents on the End of Empire; Series B, 5* (1998) and *Nuer Prophets: A History of Prophecy From the Upper Nile in the Nineteenth and Twentieth Centuries* (1994). He is a fellow of the Rift Valley Institute.

Peter Hakim Justin is a PhD candidate at Wageningen University and affiliated with the African Studies Centre in Leiden. His research project falls under the programme entitled *Grounding Land Governance – Land*

Conflicts, Local Governance and Decentralization in Post-Conflict Uganda, Burundi and South Sudan.

Daniel M. Kammen is chair of the Energy and Resources Group, and a professor in the Goldman School of Public Policy at the University of California, Berkeley. He served as science envoy for the US State Department in 2016 and 2017.

Sarah Logan is a lawyer and economist who has worked on South Sudan for several years. She is currently a policy economist at the International Growth Centre (IGC) at the London School of Economics and Political Science. She has an LLB from the University of Cape Town and a Master of Public Administration from Columbia University's School for International and Public Affairs (SIPA).

David Mozersky is the co-founder of Energy Peace Partners and the founding director of the Program on Conflict, Climate Change and Green Development at the University of California, Berkeley's Renewable and Appropriate Energy Lab. He has been involved with peace-building and conflict-resolution efforts in South Sudan for more than 15 years.

Barbara Nunberg is a visiting scholar at New York University's Wagner Graduate School of Public Service. She was previously Professor of Professional Practice at Columbia University's School for International and Public Affairs (SIPA), and earlier served in a series of senior positions at the World Bank, including as head of Public Sector Reform and Governance for the East Asia and Pacific Region. She has also held visiting appointments at Georgetown University, the University of California, Berkeley and Duke University, and was a visiting fellow at the University of California, Los Angeles, and at Harvard University, as well as a Social Science fellow at USAID. She has extensive experience in research, policy development and implementing operational programmes on governance and public management in developing countries.

Patrick O'Mahony has managed USAID and UN-funded reconstruction and governance programmes in conflict-affected, fragile and transition states for over 20 years. He is currently managing a USAID-funded programme to support social cohesion and reconciliation in Sri Lanka.

Utz Pape works as senior economist in the Poverty and Equity Global Practice at the World Bank, currently based in Nairobi. His work experience in post-conflict countries contributes to his research agenda, which includes the design of methodologies for poverty measurement in fragile settings. He holds a PhD from the International Max Planck Research School and the Free University of Berlin, and was a post-doctoral associate at Harvard University. He also holds a Master of Public Administration / International Development from the London School of Economics and Political Science and Columbia University's School for International and Public Affairs (SIPA).

Naomi Pendle is a post-doctoral researcher in the Firoz Lalji Centre for Africa at the London School of Economics and Political Science (LSE). She has lived, worked and researched in South Sudan since 2009. She is actively engaged in various research programmes focusing on South Sudan, including the Conflict Research Programme and the Centre for Public Authority and International Development, both of which are based at LSE.

Joseph Siegle directs the Africa Center for Strategic Studies' research programme at the National Defense University in Washington, DC. His research focuses on the relationship between governance, security and economic development. He has been, among others, a Douglas Dillion Fellow at the Council on Foreign Relations, a senior research scholar at the Centre for International Security Studies at the University of Maryland, and country director for World Vision.

John Young is a Canadian who has lived in Africa for 20 years, largely in the countries of the Horn, where he has held various positions. He has a PhD in Political Science, and his interests have largely focused on armed groups, peace processes and governance. As well as writing numerous articles he is the author of two books: *Peasant Revolution in Ethiopia: Tigray Peoples' Liberation Front 1975–1991* (1998) and *The Fate of Sudan: Origins and Consequences of a Flawed Peace Process* (2012). Another book, *South Sudan's Civil War: Violence, Insurgency and Failed Peacemaking,* is forthcoming in 2018, and he is co-authoring two other books on, respectively, the failure of the western-modelled nation-state in the Horn of Africa, and the failure of the western model of democracy in the Horn of Africa.

List of Abbreviations

ANC	African National Congress
ANDM	Amhara National Democratic Movement
ARCSS	Agreement on the Resolution of the Conflict in the Republic of South Sudan
AU	African Union
AUBP	African Union Border Programme
BSS	Bank of South Sudan
CANS	Civil Authority of the New Sudan
CES	Central Equatoria State
CFSAM	Crop and Food Security Assessment Mission
CPA	Comprehensive Peace Agreement
CPI	Consumer Price Index
DDR	Demobilisation, Disarmament and Reintegration
DFG	German Research Foundation
EAC	East African Community
ELF	Eritrean Liberation Front
EPLF	Eritrean Peoples' Liberation Front
EPRDF	Ethiopian Peoples' Revolutionary Democratic Front
ERBS	Exchange Rate-Based Stabilisation
FAO	UN Food and Agriculture Organization
FRELIMO	Mozambique Liberation Front
FY	Fiscal Year
GOS	Government of Sudan
GPAA	Greater Pibor Administrative Area
GRSS	Government of the Republic of South Sudan
HLRF	High Level Revitalisation Forum
HRMIS	Human Resources Management Information System
ICC	International Criminal Court
ICCPR	International Covenant on Civil and Political Rights
ICESCR	International Covenant on Economic, Social and Cultural Rights
ICG	International Crisis Group
ICSS	Interim Constitution of South Sudan
IDP	Internally Displaced Persons
IEA	International Energy Agency

IGAD	Inter-Governmental Authority on Development
KANU	Kenyan African National Union
MBS	Money-Based Stabilisation
NIF	National Islamic Front
NPG	Nile Provisional Government
NUP	National Unionist Party
OAU	Organisation of African Unity
OLF	Oromo Liberation Front
OPDO	Oromo Peoples' Democratic Organisation
PFM	Public Financial Management
POC	Protection of Civilians
PREC	Peace Renewable Energy Credit
PRMA	Petroleum Revenue Management Act
PV	(Solar) photovoltaics
REC	Renewable Energy Credit
RENAMO	Mozambican National Resistance
SANU	Sudan African National Union
SPLA	Sudan People's Liberation Army
SPLM	Sudan People's Liberation Movement
SPLM-IO	Sudan People's Liberation Movement (in Opposition)
SPLM/A(-IO)	Sudan People's Liberation Movement/Army(-in-Opposition)
SSDF	South Sudan Defence Forces
SSEPS	South Sudan Electronic Payroll System
SSLA	South Sudan Liberation Army
SSLM	Southern Sudan Liberation Movement (until 1999); South Sudan Liberation Movement (thereafter)
SSP	South Sudanese Pound
SSPD	South Sudanese Professionals in Diaspora
TCSS	Transitional Constitution of the Republic of South Sudan
TFA	Transitional Financial Arrangement
TPLF	Tigray Peoples' Liberation Front
UNDP	UN Development Programme
UNECA	United Nations Economic Commission for Africa
UNMIS	UN Mission in Sudan
UNMISS	UN Mission in South Sudan
UNOCHA	UN Office for the Coordination of Humanitarian Affairs
UNODC	UN Office on Drugs and Crime
USAID	US Agency for International Development
WDI/WB	World Development Indicators/World Bank
WFP	World Food Programme

Foreword

Paul Collier

I first visited Southern Sudan in 2008, during the interim period between the signing of the Comprehensive Peace Agreement and independence. Leaders were exuberantly hopeful and expansive: oil and aid were set to pour money into government coffers. I have never been served so much champagne. Yet a decade later, the country has become the emblematic instance of social implosion, and in the process its economy has been wrecked. By the time I returned in 2012, shortly after independence, the symptoms were already detectable: leaders were talking the language of division and belligerence, instead of unity and purpose.

What happened in South Sudan was entirely avoidable and is still rectifiable. But the longer a conflict is maintained, the deeper the cleavages and the more bitter the hatreds. Resetting the society onto the path from impoverished violence to secure prosperity becomes ever more difficult, yet correspondingly ever more urgent.

South Sudan has its own unique history and characteristics, but it is not alone in facing this transition. Recently, Professor Sir Tim Besley and I jointly directed a commission on precisely this theme, under the auspices of the British Academy and the International Growth Centre (IGC). Our report, *Escaping the Fragility Trap*, has much relevance for South Sudan. We highlight the need for both the leaders in fragile societies and international actors to change their approach: fragility is not the result of fate, but of mistaken choices.

There has been far too much faith put in elections as instant means of creating legitimate and trusted government. In fragmented societies, elections, with their winner–loser outcome, breed arrogance and grievance, not unity of purpose. The only legitimacy that matters is that between government and citizens, and in a fragmented society with a new state this can only be built gradually. Trust will depend upon inclusion in power: what will such a government look like? Lebanon provides one viable model: a government of national unity, with effective checks and balances on the abuse of power, whether by individuals or groups. Belgium and Nigeria provide another: decentralization of budgets and political authority, with each region controlled by a different identity group. These, or some hybrid of them, are the realistic political options for a reset in South Sudan.

The international community has an important role to play in brokering such a peace agreement, and in maintaining it. Brokering means just that: international actors should not be demanding specific outcomes, and least of all that the result should be frozen into a complex new constitution and blessed by an election. A broker helps the parties to negotiate a mutually satisfactory deal, rather than insisting that they sign up to yet another international dream. Credible guarantees can maintain peace agreements, often in the form of international security arrangements.

This book brings together a wide range of perspectives to provide a comprehensive and insightful analysis of South Sudan's past and present, as well as recommendations for realistic, homegrown and context-specific reforms that could promote sustainable peace and enable a brighter future for the country. Luka Biong Deng Kuol is an old friend of the IGC's South Sudan programme, and Sarah Logan has been part of the IGC South Sudan team for several years. In putting this volume together, they have assembled the expertise that is now needed for change.

South Sudan has been thrust back into the international limelight by the mistakes of both its own leaders and the international community. Each of these actors should read this book from cover to cover with a sense of chastened humility and a determination to do better.

PAUL COLLIER

Director, the International Growth Centre,
and Professor of Economics and Public Policy,
Blavatnik School of Government, University of Oxford

Introduction

Luka Biong Deng Kuol and Sarah Logan

It's been a tragic start for South Sudan, the world's youngest country. Less than three years after gaining independence in 2011 after a violent liberation war, the country slid back into conflict. In the wake of infighting among the ruling Sudan People's Liberation Movement (SPLM), violence erupted in the South Sudanese capital, Juba, in December 2013. The conflict pitted President Salva Kiir's predominantly Dinka presidential guard against Nuer fighters loyal to the former vice-president Riek Machar. As fighting spread across the country, it has taken on an increasingly ethnic nature. Ceasefires have been agreed in the August 2015 Agreement on the Resolution of the Conflict in the Republic of South Sudan (ARCSS), as well as the December 2017 Agreement on the Cessation of Hostilities and Protection of Civilians and Humanitarian Access, but there have been repeated ceasefire violations by all sides and the conflict continues unabated.

The humanitarian situation in South Sudan grows ever more urgent. Over a third of the country's population has been displaced, fleeing either to refugee camps in neighbouring countries or to the protection of civilian sites within South Sudan (Reuters, 2018). Tens of thousands have died in the conflict or as a result of the conflict, and food scarcity is placing two-thirds of South Sudanese at risk of extreme hunger in 2018 (Bariyo, 2018). Soldiers on all sides of the conflict continue to recruit children, rape and kill civilians, and plunder civilian property. Civilians have been attacked while sheltering inside UN bases. And while South Sudan has slipped into famine and economic collapse, the government has continued to spend millions of dollars buying weapons. Indeed, while addressing an African Union summit earlier this year, UN Secretary General António Guterres stated that he has 'never seen a political élite with so little interest in the well-being of its own people' (News24, 2018).

After little implementation of ARCSS to date, the Intergovernmental Authority on Development (IGAD), the eight-member trade bloc in north-eastern Africa, has established the High Level Revitalisation Forum (HLRF). The HLRF is tasked with undertaking a new round of peace talks aimed at restoring a permanent ceasefire, fully implementing ARCSS and revising certain ARCSS provisions to reflect the change in circumstances since August 2015. These talks remain ongoing at the time of writing.

In the context of South Sudan's seemingly intractable conflict and dire humanitarian situation, this book is an attempt to analyse the crisis and some of its contributing factors. It aims to serve as a starting point for an honest reflection on what went wrong, and a collective search for realistic, homegrown, and context-specific solutions within South Sudan's capability to adopt and implement. It hopes to prompt discussions for change and to mobilise a concerted effort towards building a more peaceful and democratic South Sudan.

The contributors to this book have worked on South Sudan for a number of years, and bring a wealth of knowledge and different perspectives to this discussion. As a result of the quality and variety of these contributions, this book represents possibly the most comprehensive analysis to date of South Sudan's social and political history, post-independence governance systems and necessary reforms for rebuilding the country.

The initial chapters examine the impact of colonial rule and customary law on identity, belonging and ethnic conflict in southern Sudan and, later, in South Sudan. In Chapter 1, Naomi Pendle looks at South Sudan's history from the condominium era onwards, exploring the role of colonially imposed customary law in differentiating between ethnic groups, and also at the commonality that customary law established across groups. Through examples, she demonstrates the relationship between legal systems and ethnic and national identity in South Sudan.

Then, in Chapter 2, Peter Hakim Justin and Lotje de Vries consider how rounds of reshuffling of the political system, internal borders and power relations have been a source of confusion, élite manipulation and conflict in South Sudan. They demonstrate how the mobilisation of ethnic identities has become central to territorial claims and the creation of territorial borders, and warn that the proliferation of states and further manipulation of borders and identities could exacerbate ethnic-based conflict in the country.

In Chapter 3, Francis and Daniel Deng examine the difficulties around African countries inheriting constitutions modelled on those of their colonial powers, which tended to be ill-suited to managing Africa's ethnic diversity and are often beyond post-independence governments' capacity to implement. They argue that western-oriented constitutions fostered homogeneous, centralised states intolerant of differing political and cultural aspirations, and have been used by some African leaders to bolster their authoritarian governments under the guise of consolidating unity. A new, more inclusive constitutionalism is needed to balance national unity and self-determination, to achieve a degree of group autonomy without perpetuating the identity conflicts witnessed in Sudan and South Sudan.

Sarah Logan extends this constitutionalism analysis in Chapter 4 to consider to what extent electoral systems and systems of government support or undermine power-sharing and group autonomy in diverse and divided countries such as South Sudan. She shows that the strong presidential system adopted in South Sudan has made the government more vulnerable to collapse than would have been the case under a parliamentary system, with its multi-agent executive and stronger checks and balances. She also considers the advantages that establishing a House of Nationalities, along the lines of Ethiopia's House of Federation, may have on resolving inter-ethnic conflict and managing ethnic diversity in the country.

In Chapter 5, Luka Biong Deng Kuol examines the link between conflict and systems of government, looking at federalism and decentralisation and the ability of these systems to safeguard minority interests, manage diversity and reduce the risk of conflict. He finds that there is growing evidence to suggest that federal systems outperform unitary systems in managing diversity and reducing conflict, and that decentralisation can be seen to be more effective than federalism not only in managing diversity and reducing conflict, but also in delivering public goods.

Douglas H. Johnson expands on federalism in Chapter 6, drawing on rich, informative conference accounts to trace the role of federalism in the history of South Sudanese political thought from the early 1950s onwards. He notes that a federal Sudan was the primary goal of the southern Sudanese, and only when federalism efforts failed was the idea of an independent South Sudan pursued. The federalism debate has continued in South Sudan post-independence, as many continue to view it as a way to manage the country's ethnic diversity.

John Young, in Chapter 7, outlines Ethiopia's ethnic federalism model, designed to overcome ethnic-based conflicts similar to those which afflict South Sudan. Ethiopia's constitution gives ethnic communities the right to self-determination and secession, which many believed would lead to the country's disintegration. However, this has not yet happened. Young finds that while South Sudan could learn from Ethiopia's experience, it is necessary for South Sudan to develop its own governance model out of its unique circumstances and experience.

In Chapter 8, Joseph Siegle and Patrick O'Mahony shift the focus to decentralisation, which has emerged as a highly popular strategy for improving government efficiency and responsiveness, as well as social and political stability in developing countries. They review the theory and empirics of the intersection between decentralisation and internal conflict, finding that decentralisation has highly differentiated effects on ethnic conflict. Notably in countries with greater sub-national autonomy, histories of previous ethnic conflict and weak central governments lacking a monopoly on the use of force, decentralisation may make a country more vulnerable to ethnic conflict. Thus, it's imperative that South Sudan undertakes a comprehensive risk assessment before opting for a decentralised system.

Alex de Waal and Naomi Pendle consider the political arena in which decentralisation generally takes place in Chapter 9. Power is contested between central state authorities and provincial élites, with the technocratic logic of decentralised government, including greater public participation and increased service delivery efficiency, often being secondary to political contests over power. Proliferation of administrative units is frequently designed to serve the political purposes of the central government, increasing patronage scope and weakening regional blocs. Central government and provincial élites tussle over power in decentralised systems, particularly if local authorities possess greater legitimacy, resilience and capacity, leading to a varied political terrain. This is demonstrated using several case studies from South Sudan.

Lovise Aalen, in Chapter 10, looks at why, despite decentralisation's claims to bring government closer to the people, improve service delivery and better manage diversity, it has not led to improved governance or economic performance or to a deepening of democracy in Africa. She finds that the main reason for the failure is not the idea of decentralisation itself, but the lack of proper implementation, which is frequently intentional. She argues that decentralisation reforms are most likely to be implemented and sustained by regimes that are able to use local government structures as a tool for consolidating the regime's control at the local level.

With reflections on federalism and decentralisation complete, the final chapters of this book look at other key reforms necessary for reconstruction and development in South Sudan. These include reforms needed to achieve economic stability and poverty alleviation, civil service reform, and better utilisation of South Sudan's resources, such as notable solar potential, for short- and long-term development gains. Nora Dihel and Utz Pape outline the challenges of macroeconomic stabilisation and poverty alleviation in South Sudan in Chapter 11. They show that South Sudan displays all the signs of macroeconomic collapse, with contracting output, spiralling inflation and divergence between the official and black market exchange rates. Low oil production, agricultural disruptions and continued high recurrent spending on the security sector has driven the economy into decline. Moving forward, curbing inflation and stabilising the economy should be key policy priorities, and strong political will is needed to adhere to any stabilisation plan.

In Chapter 12, Barbara Nunberg looks at the civil service reform needs in South Sudan. She identifies short- and long-term bottlenecks to building civil service capacity in the country and draws on similar experiences from elsewhere to provide appropriate recommendations. These include the need to reduce the civil service wage bill through voluntary and involuntary retrenchment programmes (likely requiring external financing), and the redeployment of security personnel to dedicated public works projects that would address short-term recovery needs, such as infrastructure rehabilitation or community-based services.

Finally, David Mozersky and Daniel Kammen provide an example of how South Sudan's abundant renewable energy resources could be better used for the country's development in Chapter 13. They argue that transitioning international organisations' operations from diesel to renewable energy would unlock numerous short- and long-term benefits that could help expand and diversify South Sudan's energy sector and lessen its crippling dependence on fossil fuel. Given the higher upfront costs of large infrastructure purchases, new innovative financing mechanisms may be required to facilitate this transition. Coupled with local training and capacity building, South Sudanese communities could be empowered to maintain, support and grow the sector well beyond the current crisis.

Many of South Sudan's challenges do not lend themselves to clear, prescriptive solutions. Nevertheless, this book attempts to build a framework within which these challenges can be considered. The diversity of contributors' perspectives means some contradictions between chapters may exist. As much as possible, terminology has been standardised throughout the book, for example, 'southern Sudan' is used for pre-2005 references, 'Southern Sudan' for the interim 2005–2011 period, and 'South Sudan' for the country's post-2011 independence period.

The editors are indebted to the many researchers who have contributed to this book, and to all those who read it. We hope it provokes readers to reflect on what has gone wrong in South Sudan, and the realistic solutions that exist to help move South Sudan into a sustainable and peaceful post-conflict period and put it back on the path to growth and development.

References

Bariyo, Nicholas (2018), 'Hunger woes escalate in war-torn South Sudan', *Wall Street Journal*, 26 February, https://www.wsj.com/articles/hunger-woes-escalate-in-war-torn-south-sudan-1519674389.

News24 (2018), 'US pushes UN to consider arms embargo on South Sudan', 8 March, https://www.news24.com/Africa/News/us-pushes-un-to-consider-arms-embargo-on-south-sudan-20180308.

Reuters (2018), 'U.S., Britain and Norway warn South Sudan parties over ceasefire violations, 2 January, https://www.reuters.com/article/us-southsudan-unrest/u-s-britain-and-norway-warn-south-sudan-parties-over-ceasefire-violations-idUSKBN1ER0LM.

CHAPTER 1

Learning from Customary Law

Forging Ethnic and National Identities in South Sudan

Naomi Pendle

Introduction

The 2005 Comprehensive Peace Agreement of the Government of Sudan (GOS) and the Sudan People's Liberation Army (SPLA) resulted in the formation of the new state of South Sudan in 2011. In this context, national leaders and international observers called for the South Sudanese to start nation-building to accompany the state-building project (Jok, 2011). Throughout the 22-year war that led to the CPA, southern Sudanese had fought each other. This fractured trust in a common southern Sudanese identity, militarised relationships and carved out new group boundaries and perceived divisions between groups.

Since the CPA, the new national government's attempts to centralise power have prompted protests on the periphery, and opposition leaders have often shaped their mobilisation strategies around more localised identities such as ethnicity (Thomas, 2015). South Sudanese have asserted sub-national identities as an expression of exclusion from the state, thereby further fragmenting identities. For a short time after the December 2013 conflict erupted, commanders and political leaders in the armed opposition were able to coalesce a common Nuer identity, in response to the apparent targeting of Nuer by government soldiers in Juba. This was in contrast to previous decades, when Nuer leaders had found the Nuer notoriously difficult to unify politically (Johnson, 2003). This common Nuer political identity has not lasted. Other broad identities such as 'Equatorian' have similarly only had a fragile political weight. Yet people have increasingly relied on more fragmented, localised identities to survive the war and have distanced themselves from larger notions of a community, such as belonging to a South Sudanese nation.

Since the Anglo-Egyptian condominium in the early nineteenth century, and throughout the episodes of war in southern Sudan, customary courts have operated and have been a dominant source of public authority. Chiefs have kept order through customary courts, even when national politics have changed in times of war, peace or regime change. Customary law advocates have sometimes imagined southern Sudan as a single legal community, to the extent that it has a shared jurisprudence and experience that values the use of the customary law. This perspective has created discourses of commonality and a southern Sudanese sense of belonging. Customary laws were upheld in the south, sometimes through government policy and sometimes despite government rulings. This created a shared jurisprudence, procedure and legal language across very different southern legal regimes. This commonality exists alongside a more detailed landscape of contested and contrasting identity, seen in customary law's horizontal plurality and the variety between groups' substantive laws. While the common use of customary laws helps people imagine South Sudan as a shared legal body, it masks the diversity of substantive customary law, thereby permitting simultaneously both unity and diversity of law, culture and identity.

Proponents of federalism, especially ethnic federalism, appear to imagine that South Sudanese society is structured into a plurality of discrete ethnic groups over which an administrative structure can be neatly layered. For some policymakers, there are similar assumptions behind customary law. They assume the unity of socio-political groups (along tribal or ethnic lines) and imagine that there is a common moral code reflecting this unity, which serves as the foundation of the group's customary law. The law itself often claims its authority through its association with a specific moral community (Rangelov, 2014).

However, studies have long noted that a unified legal system can become the cause, as well as the consequence, of a group's unity (Kuper and Kuper, 1965). As Assaf Likhovski notes, 'law is not merely a way to enhance separate, oppositional identities. Law can also serve as a common ground, a mediating factor in the conflict between [...] norms, a way to express heterogeneous, hybrid, impure forms of the self' (Likhovski, 2006: 214). Laws, including customary laws, not only resemble but also (re)imagine and constitute communities and ideas of belonging. Through customary laws and customary courts, governments, chiefs and South Sudanese citizens have reimagined and recreated both real and fictitious legal communities and ideas of identity. Lessons can be learnt from the experience of customary law in South

Sudan about how a perception of shared identity can be maintained while other identities and notions of community can still be valued.

This chapter explores examples of how chiefs, judges and governments have used customary law not simply to reflect pre-existing layers, but also to remake them through constitution, co-option and contestation by local actors. It will provide, first, a brief introduction to customary law in southern Sudan and, second, discuss ideas of identity in dominant government discourses about southern Sudanese customary laws during the Anglo-Egyptian government, under the SPLA and into the post-CPA era. Customary law simultaneously promoted ideas of being southern and (re) created a diversity of moral and legal communities within this national identity. In the post-CPA era, the central government has attempted, but often failed, to control ideas of identity in customary law. The example of the Dinka laws of *Wathalel* will then be discussed; these have served as a mantra for a common western Dinka identity and a common southern Sudanese identity, while at the same time protecting the *de facto* diversity of substantive law. The Dinka laws of Bahr el Ghazal have a common name in the discourse, but have variation that has persisted because this commonality has not been constituted as a reality in the courts. *Wathalel* also gives us insights into how the law and local governance has, in fact, been shaped from the bottom up as much as by the decisions of national governments.

Customary law during the condominium years

In Anglo-Egyptian condominium Sudan in the 1920s, the government was moving formally from military campaigns of pacification into a civil administration, which included indirect rule and promotion of the rule of law. One of the most profound contributions of the condominium government in Sudan was its law and law courts, predominantly in the form of the chiefs' courts and customary law (Johnson, 2003). Through the courts, the government hoped to increase public security (Howell, 1954) and enforce acceptance of the government (Johnson, 1986). Adherence to the courts was presented as synonymous with recognition of the government's authority to settle disputes (Johnson, 1986), and of government authority more broadly.

The British use of customary law in southern Sudan reflected a mid-nineteenth-century shift in British jurisprudence which recognised the rules of the 'native' as laws, and which cautioned against the rapid application of western law in the colonies. The Sudan government, in the Chiefs'

Courts Ordinance of 1931, formally established the customary courts as a dominant form of legal and political authority across southern Sudan. Yet the apparently acephalous societies of southern Sudan offered the British no obviously recognisable, pre-existing legal authorities to co-opt as public authorities over the 'native' law (Johnson, 2003).

The government appointed as chiefs a diverse collection of individuals who had often gained authority through their ability to deal with government (Leonardi, 2013). The substance of the customary law was negotiated between the government and these chiefs, and it merged southern Sudanese ideas and practices with British notions of justice (Leonardi et al., 2010). After the nineteenth-century shift towards native law, the British government was hesitant to impose the entire substance of English law. Some Anglicisation of procedure was, however, imposed (Likhovski, 2006), encouraging a degree of commonality across chiefs' courts.

Southern Sudanese distinctiveness

From early in the twentieth century, customary law became part of the Anglo-Egyptian government's understanding of southern Sudan as distinct from northern Sudan, and government support for customary law reflected official ideas about the nature of the southern Sudanese and strategies for control.

After the Egyptian Revolution of 1919 and the White Flag mutiny of 1924, the Sudanese government was increasingly concerned about rebellions among the educated classes of Egypt and northern Sudan. An interventionist British 'Southern Policy' sought to separate southern Sudan as an administrative entity, preserving its assumed pre-modern, 'primordialist' character to reduce its vulnerability to anti-British revolutionary ideas from an educated, modern class in Egypt and northern Sudan (Vaughan et al., 2013; Leonardi, 2013). British government officials perceived the danger of a 'civilised' western system of government in southern Sudan (Rahim, 1966). Southerners were perceived by some government officials as a 'backward race',[1] 'savages'[2] and like other African peoples (Westermann, 1935). Although some committed, long-serving district commissioners and anthropologists from the 1930s reshaped perceptions of the southern Sudanese as rational, they were still seen as being at an early stage of legal development. For example, even in the 1940s scholarly British works still described the Nuer as a 'primitive people' (Evans-Pritchard, 1954), with their custom evolving slowly into law with the introduction of sanction by British officials. Paul Howell (1949) explicitly cautioned against an imposition of European concepts of law 'likely to cause indigestion' in the 'boiling pot' of the law, as it could risk disintegration.

Customary law in southern Sudan imagined the south as a community distinct from the north, and constituted this discourse through the practice of the courts. The government presented the south as a tribal African society needing its own legal system, one that differed from the Sharia-influenced law in the north (Deng, 2009). Yet for the south, the government's promotion of customary law free of Sharia law emphasised a separate southern identity. The government codified this separation by issuing two different ordinances to govern the native courts in Sudan: the 1931 Chiefs' Courts Ordinance for the south and the 1932 Native Courts Ordinance for the rest of Sudan.

By the late 1940s, rapid shifts in geopolitics unsettled political support for ideas of southern belonging, and by 1947 Sudan faced imminent independence as a united country and preparation for independence dominated government business (Johnson, 1986). Many British officials privately disapproved of this policy and continued to warn of the need to safeguard the south from the rapid incorporation of northern laws.[3] After independence, new Sudanese officials, trained under the British, initially provided some continuity of customary law use. However, Khartoum's post-independence power over law and legal community would prompt disagreement in later decades.

Colonial authorities' construction of ethnic identities

The condominium government's creation of distinct legal regimes helped construct a common vision of being southern. Yet, the content of customary law was not the same across the south, as customary courts continued to adjudicate based on a plurality of customary laws, thus strengthening people's visions of smaller, salient, legal communities.

Chiefdoms were a key unit in customary law. District commissioners had responsibility to oversee customary courts and to hear appeals from customary courts. They varied widely in their level of activity and legal intervention, and they did not always harmonise customary law within their districts (Johnson, 1986). British anthropological and legal studies, however, encouraged government officials to imagine that most substantive customary law was common within tribal groupings. The Sudan government assumed some commonality in legal ontology and substance within a tribal group, based on a perceived common culture, despite detailed commentaries reflecting variance within tribal groups regarding substantive law, court structures and compensation rates (Johnson, 1986). Much of the study of law in the condominium era focused on recording the customary laws of a specific tribe (Lugard, 1965). For example, in *A Manual of Nuer Law*, Edward Evans-Pritchard and Paul Howell describe Nuer law in general, assuming a commonality within the customary law of the Nuer, although they recognise some variance across Nuer communities where Howell had worked.

In the 1940s, some condominium government officials became actively involved in making common substantive legal codes along ethnic lines, as they believed that creating a common legal community across an ethnic group would reinforce the political unity of that ethnic group and help them gain a political voice in national politics. For example, in Upper Nile Province, the district commissioners decided that 'the Nuer had reached a stage in their development when concerted planning for Nuerland [...] was necessary'.[4] Unifying the court system in Nuerland and creating a common Nuer customary law was seen as the efficient 'machinery' for forming a Nuer political confederation.[5] The district commissioners disagreed on whether 'pockets of variant law' should be allowed to remain,[6] and it was concluded that standardisation should not be enforced.[7] Attempts at some degree of standardisation of Nuer customary law also provided an opportunity for the government to review and change the law based on its own ideas of equity, despite the rhetoric of preservation of tradition.[8]

Yet even among government officials, the need for tribal, political confederations was not uncontested (Johnson, 1986). 'Tribes' were not static, moral and legal communities were not bounded, and there were no pre-existing, unchanging legal codes, let alone a common code across a whole tribe. For example, in 1944, Dinka in east and west Gogrial, despite having a common language and similar cultures, and having lived through decades of common British government, were still applying different rules to divorce, children and *arueth* (the number of cattle payable to the husband's kin after the completion of the bridewealth payments to the bride's family).

During these processes of codification, British officials were frustrated when the 'true' tribal law could not be remembered, and when there was local variance in customary law within a tribe or a lack of variance between tribes. Government officials often used chiefs' meetings to reshape the content of customary law, but justified these changes as a way to reinstate tradition. For example, the Tonj District Annual Chiefs Meeting in 1938 repealed a law on the basis that it was 'contrary to Dinka custom'.[9] The apparent paradox that customary law was both pre-existing and not in use was explained by the suggestion that the Turkish and early condominium governments had been the cause of the loss of memory of customary laws.[10] The British colonial government often insisted that the 'true' law was the pre-condominium law, supporting the idea of a pre-existing, static set of established laws which gained their authority from antiquity and which complied with a more essentialist understanding of the nature of law. This mimics the legal fictions and jurisprudence of the English common law itself, which upholds precedent and the idea that law gains authority by being based on old principles. The government further entrenched customary law by upholding rulings if they were in conformity with the tribal law.[11]

Government officials also conjured up various theories to explain the apparent breakdown of tribal groupings. One official attributed it to the waning need for corporate self-defence due to the existence of government.[12] Evans-Pritchard explained that, prior to government sanction, customary norms had been upheld through a 'balanced opposition' between groups, but that by the 1940s the government's introduction of the threat of force had reduced the need for larger groups to balance opposition, thereby encouraging social disintegration (Howell, 1954). Douglas Johnson (1986) later attributed societal breakdown among the Nuer to the chiefs' courts beginning to enforce full payment of compensation; previously, outstanding obligations between individuals and sub-groups had been a key mechanism to maintaining community bonds.

Changes in Nuer law during the condominium era altered inter-ethnic relations, and attempts to make common Nuer laws created differences between Nuer laws and the laws of other ethnic groups. In certain localities, communities had previously had close, inter-ethnic relationships regarding trade and marriage, and had shared grazing for many years. These close relationships had been governed by local, shared, inter-ethnic legal codes that were specific to those communities. The government's attempts to make common ethnic laws threatened to dismantle these legal relationships (OLS Southern Sector, n.d.). Courts and legal relations, however, continued to operate across tribal divisions and, in some ways, were even supported by the British. For example, border courts became key mechanisms for the British for the enforcement of peaceful relationships between Dinka and Nuer communities.

Customary law during the SPLA war years

In 1983, Sudan's September Laws imposed Islamic laws on all peoples in Sudan, and were used to partly justify the southern rebellions of the Anyanya II and SPLA (Leonardi, 2013). John Garang, the SPLA's leader and founding member, had adopted a Marxist, developmentalist vision for Sudan from the SPLA's inception in 1983. This political theory would have opposed both Sharia law and customary law. Similarly, many left-wing African leaders in the twentieth century pushed back against customary law as a colonial construct and a means of despotism (Mamdani, 1996).

However, reality demanded a cheap means of local governance. In practice, the SPLA had little option but to use customary law, as this was the main form of governance available in rural areas. Sudan state laws applied in GOS-held urban areas, but customary law operated in SPLA-held areas. The SPLA had no capacity to implement the different laws they authored in the early years, even among their own military personnel. The SPLA would occasionally suspend parts of customary law when there were fears this would prompt violence, but these occasions were rare.[13] Additionally, southerners who were displaced, either within Sudan or outside the country, often maintained social relations with their southern homelands through using customary law and preserving a common legal community despite spatial distance. Court rulings among displaced southerners were often administered by chiefs' courts in the homelands. The common law and jurisdiction enabled people to imagine an ongoing commonality between people hundreds of miles apart, allowing them to retain a sense of identity despite being dispersed.

There were also varied political visions in the SPLA. In the 1970s and the 1980s, southern Sudanese academics began to use customary law to emphasise southern identity (Deng, 1971) and to demarcate the north–south division (Deng, 1987). Southern Sudanese thinkers emphasised that the north and south had ontologically different socio-legal systems and that customary law was a crucial element of their southern identity. Customary law was the alternative moral and legal framework that differentiated southerners from the north and Sharia law (Mijak, 1999; Thiik, quoted in Fadlalla, 2009), and which provided a discourse of southern Sudanese unity that contrasted with a Sudanese identity (Jok et al., 2004).

In the 1980s, customary law was also used to try to reduce tribal divisions and construct a common identity amongst the SPLA-supporting areas of the south. For example, between the Western Dinka and Nuer there had been significant violent clashes and a lack of access to judicial redress. By the mid-1980s, they were under the common governance of the SPLA. In 1987, the Mal Tribal Conference established a common Nuer–Dinka customary court to end the conflict and solve new cases. The *mal*, or blood compensation for people killed, was reduced to 15 cattle to create a common substantive law across the Nuer–Dinka boundary, promoting the idea of being part of the same legal and political system. With the SPLA split between the leadership of John Garang and Riek Machar in 1991, one consequence was the end of inter-Nuer–Dinka justice and opportunities for peaceful redress of grievances.

Even in post-CPA Southern Sudan, interviewees in rural areas continue to see non-customary law as not being Southern law but a product of Khartoum. Many of the statutory lawyers operating in Southern government courts since the CPA were trained outside southern Sudan, often in Khartoum. As these lawyers were absent from the south during the war while they sought training and employment elsewhere, some Southern Sudanese accused them of having failed to make a contribution to the southern liberation struggle and of imposing ideas from the north.[14] In contrast, interviewees noted the continued presence of chiefs administering customary law throughout the SPLA war, and it was common for people to describe a chief's authority as being partly based on his contribution to the SPLA war effort.

Garang's public political vision for the SPLA had been to overthrow the Khartoum government while maintaining a united New Sudan. This was generally seen as a call to overhaul the Khartoum government rather than split Sudan. To make this work, however, the SPLA needed to construct a vision of a common Sudanese identity separate from customary law, as customary law implied a distinct southern identity. Fadlalla (2009) describes the customary rules as unifying Sudan by reflecting ancient history and ethnic groups, not only in the south, but across Sudan. In this imagining, customary law becomes a legal system passed down through generations, in contrast to the laws of various governments. By the late 1990s, SPLA discourse was describing customary law as an African (including Sudanese) alternative to imposed ideas from the west and Islam (Mijak, 1999), and the SPLA and its New Sudan vision claimed to protect the customary law of the whole of Sudan (Lueth, 1999).

In 1994, more formal construction of civil authority by the SPLA began. The SPLA Penal Code explicitly stated that 'the provisions of this law shall not prejudice the application of the existing customary laws and practices prevailing in each area' (Section 6). Similarly, the Civil Procedure Act of 1994 also entrenched customary law's authority. However, some of the SPLA's intellectual leadership still expressed dissatisfaction with the defence of customary law. The movement was eager to present itself as a body capable of governance in the modern era, and customary law carried connotations of preserving what had been considered 'primitive' during colonial rule (Deng, 1987). The attempts in the 1970s, 1980s and 1990s to write down certain customary laws by Deng (1971), Makec (1988) and Mijak (1999) can be seen as a response to the codified nature of Sharia law, countering claims of dichotomy between customary law and modernity.

During the 1990s, the SPLA began to call for the codification and harmonisation of customary laws in view of the diversity of customary practices in the New Sudan. In April 1999, a workshop on law and legal reform conducted by the Sudan People's Liberation Movement (SPLM) recommended that the SPLM 'reconcile the various customary laws through inter-ethnic chiefs' meetings at county, regional and, eventually, national levels' (Lueth, 1999: 11). The SPLM leadership imagined that the construction of a nationwide common customary law could help construct a clear vision of a united New Sudan and a viable legal system for a modern state. In practice, it would also give the SPLM power to influence customary law content.

Customary law during the post-CPA era

The GOS and SPLA tentatively brought their war to an end with the 2005 CPA and the 2006 Juba Declaration, which incorporated into the SPLA the largest SPLA-opposing southern militia, the South Sudan Defence Forces (SSDF). However, violence continued across the south and national unity remained fragile. During the previous decades of war, élites had militarised ethnic boundaries (Jok and Hutchinson, 1999), brought division within ethnic communities (Johnson, 2003), and left local administrative structures subject to military might. After the death of Garang in 2005 and the integration of the SSDF, the SPLM/A increasingly supported Southern separation, and by the 2011 referendum on Southern independence a vote in favour of the creation of the new nation-state of South Sudan seemed inevitable. South Sudan became an independent state-in-waiting.

This new context prompted questions concerning South Sudan's legal system, the jurisprudence that would be the legal system's foundation, and the identity of the legal community that would be governed by the laws of this new state. It was also unclear what authority the South Sudanese government would have over its territory in practice, and whether centrally conceived ideas of the law would be enforceable in the rural, extensive periphery due to inadequate capacity and lack of trust in the central government.

The SPLM proclaimed customary law to be the ideological foundation of South Sudan's legal system. The 2011 Transitional Constitution of the Republic of South Sudan (TCSS) entrenched customary law in the nation's justice system and made the 'customs and traditions of the people' a source of legislation (Article 5(b)). The Local Government Act of 2009 empowered customary law courts to decide cases within their jurisdiction based on 'the customs, traditions, norms and ethics of the communities' (Article 98(1)). This promotion of customary law aligned with a renewed international consensus in favour of customary law in Africa, after its initial post-colonial decline in popularity in the 1960s and 1970s.

In practice, recognition was not just about entrenching customary law, but also about the new central government trying to capture some of the legitimacy and authority of the customary law courts. As the SPLA had found in the 1980s, the nascent Government of the Republic of South Sudan (GRSS) needed to rely on the customary courts to preserve law and order across much of the country. Yet statutory provisions limited the jurisdiction of the customary courts and created an opportunity for new statutory courts to capture some jurisdiction from the customary law courts. In the post-CPA era, chiefs competed with statutory judges for judicial power, with the latter claiming expanded powers over statutory and constitutional provisions.[15]

The statutory provisions are ambiguous, however. For example, GRSS changed the jurisdiction of customary courts to exclude criminal cases unless there was a 'customary interface'. As customary law historically dealt with all types of cases, including those usually classified as criminal, all criminal cases could be argued to have a customary interface. Additionally, the involvement of cattle in many criminal cases raises problems as chiefs claim a historic governance role over cattle camps.[16] In practice, the distinction between criminal and civil cases is often ignored in the workings of the courts, or chiefs intentionally interpret cases as not being criminal in order to maintain their jurisdiction.

In turn, statutory courts have repeatedly criticised customary courts' procedure to justify their authority to hear appeals of decisions based on customary law. Statutory courts have often demanded unrealistic standards of procedure and evidence, almost guaranteeing that parties can use statutory courts to overturn any customary law decision where evidence may be considered insufficient. Some judicial authorities have even threatened chiefs with criminal prosecution, and accused chiefs of misusing their power when they have not applied procedures as dictated by the statutory courts, despite a lack of consensus on procedure.[17]

Yet customary law courts remain popular and are used more regularly by communities than statutory courts (Makec, 2007). Much of the competition has therefore been between the local government and the judiciary over control of customary courts. The government has used new statutory powers to declare some courts illegal if they are not established by the South Sudanese judiciary, and some courts have been closed on this basis (Mayom, 2010b). For example, in 2013 the Warrap State government reshuffled customary courts and chiefs on the basis that they needed warrants of establishment. Reshuffled chiefs applied customary law in unfamiliar and sometimes controversial ways, prompting local protest. Elsewhere in South Sudan, the national judiciary and state-level governments have disagreed over warrants of establishment and chiefs' appointments as they squabble for control of the customary law. Some county commissioners have also asserted that customary courts can only operate with their explicit permission.[18]

As in the past, some government leaders continue to try to capture control of the content of customary law by claiming the need for a common South Sudanese customary law to construct a unified legal community and South Sudanese nation. As Chief Justice Makec explained in 2010, 'the English common law – the model that South Sudan is adopting now – was originally a customary law and became the custom of all tribes in England and all the tribes became a nation: such a development is ideal for South Sudan as it is moving towards nationhood' (Mayom, 2010).

Makec referred to the eleventh- and twelfth-century construction of an English common law, which homogenised the various laws that had existed in pockets across England. However, English common law was not achieved through codification, but was constructed through a common appeal to the monarch at a time of the political centre's growth in influence. Nonetheless, Makec hoped a common law in South Sudan would similarly help construct South Sudan as a nation.

Such sentiment encouraged calls for harmonising South Sudanese customary laws, with diversity seen as a problem.[19] Mennen argued that 'the first step in developing a legal pluralist system in Southern Sudan is to begin documentation of all customary law and to create a legal clearinghouse for judicial decisions by tribe' (Mennen, 2007: 65). UNDP implemented a project post-CPA to record customary law, to facilitate harmonisation (UNDP,

2016).[20] Its method assumed that interviewing even one official from an ethnic group could produce an account of the customary law of the whole group.[21] Such an approach made the assumption of standardised content and failed to recognise the complexity of customary law. Cherry Leonardi et al. (2010) highlight the political nature of codification of customary law in South Sudan, as attempting to develop a common South Sudanese customary legal code might not only reimagine South Sudan as a single legal community, but also draw power to the centre through the centre's writing of this code.

The *Wathalel* example

Chiefs' meetings during the condominium-era attempted to standardise laws of the western Dinka known as *Wathalel*, leading to their codification in 1975 and 1984 (Leonardi et al., 2010). As with the Nuer laws of Fangak, *Wathalel* was presented as a static, bounded body of laws that was hoped would encourage Dinka unity. The laws reflected a common government sentiment at the time that each ethnic group should be subject to its own laws. As one district commissioner explained in 1946,

> the most important thing about any new warrant is that it should give legal recognition to the universal Dinka feeling that Dinka law, though liable to minor local variations, is essentially one and that as a corollary a Dinka judge's opinion is legally valid anywhere in Dinkaland and not only in his own court area.[22]

Dinka judges were thus free to move between courts in different Dinka districts due to the commonality of the law, a practice that emphasised the common legal standards and legal community of the Dinka.

Yet in practice, *Wathalel* is an example of law as disputed process. It highlights that there is much variation in the way that these discourses are constituted in practice. While it promotes common substantive law to ease judicial redress of grievances, and appeals to the notion of belonging to the western Dinka, it often conceals an ongoing fluidity and political dialogue, thereby also allowing for diversity and contest.

Local memory attributes *Wathalel* to a specific incident of government pressure for conflict resolution. Elopement between the Dinka of Tonj and Dinka of Agar had prompted violent conflict, and compensation variance between these groups prevented easy judicial redress. *Wathalel* constructed a common code and levels of compensation between these groups. In the context of chiefs' meetings in the 1940s, the content of the common Dinka law was constructed through dialogue between the government and chiefs. The Re-Statement of Bahr el Ghazal Region Customary Law (Amendment) Act of 1984 was a codified expression of *Wathalel* which sought to preserve customary law in the context of Sharia, and it was the dominant legal provision in SPLA areas of the western Dinka (Kuol, 1997). It envisioned a common Dinka belonging during a season of wartime uncertainty.

Across the western Dinka in the post-CPA era, chiefs still cite *Wathalel* as the basis of their court decisions, and statutory courts also reference this law.[23] As one official in the Warrap State Ministry of Justice explained: '*Wathalel* is our customary law and it is fixed. John Makec wrote it down. This is the law and it cannot be changed and we rule based on this.'[24] Many western Dinka cite *Wathalel* as the source of customary law and frequently used elements of the law can be quoted by many in the population. More educated segments of the Dinka population have been accused of being less familiar with *Wathalel* due to their absence from the community while furthering their education or working elsewhere.[25] Consequently, those returning from elsewhere have sometimes adopted highly conservative customary law in order to demonstrate that they belong.

Yet despite making reference to a common code, the law's substance is not consistent across the western Dinka, as customary laws have often been remade at a local level. SPLA commanders during the war and politicians post-CPA have altered certain provisions of *Wathalel* in their own territories, creating variety in the substantive law. For example, in the early post-CPA years in Lakes State, the governor increased compensation for murder from 31 to 51 head of cattle. Common customary laws are also still subject to diverse interpretations by chiefs.

The following example highlights the complexity of cases where interpretation of *Wathalel* is disputed: during the SPLA war, a trader and a tea-lady eloped to Khartoum. Another man had already paid a dowry of 50 cattle for the tea-lady. According to *Wathalel*, this gave him the right to the woman and any children she had. Since the destination of the eloping couple was unknown, the man who had paid the dowry could not reclaim the woman. While in Khartoum, the eloped couple had four children. The woman later died and her husband gave the children to his uncle to look after. At the end of the war, the uncle returned to South Sudan with the four children, and this alerted the tea-lady's family to the existence of the four children. As the children's father had never paid a dowry, the women's family claimed the children based on *Wathalel*. Chiefs in the initial case awarded the children to the woman's family. Her family then passed the children on to the family of the man who had paid the woman's dowry. Other chiefs contested the case's outcome, also using *Wathalel*. One chief argued that, for the dowry to carry legal meaning, it should have been enforced years before and the dowry returned, especially as no children had come from the marriage. Therefore, the man who paid the dowry had no legal claim over the children. This alternative interpretation of *Wathalel* arose in the context of pressure to find a ruling that would take into account the children's rights after an NGO got involved.[26] Another chief opined that not reclaiming the 50 cows may have been the act of a man in support of a poorer family and that his act of generosity should be honoured. A ministry official argued that the elopement was a crime and that the family should not be allowed to keep the children as they would then benefit from this crime.

This case highlights that in many legal decisions *Wathalel* itself is contested and reinterpreted, to allow it consistency with other norms and legal provisions. In these contestations, various legal authorities grapple to assert their rulings and power. The substance of the law, therefore, is often made from the bottom up, yet even in this contestation, the various perspectives and authorities referred to the authority of *Wathalel*.

Even the ontology of *Wathalel* varies. For example, some Rek Dinka courts describe *Wathalel* as being applied in all cases as the underlying legal foundation, whereas in some Agar Dinka courts, *Wathalel* is described as merely one of several legally permissible options. Others have understood *Wathalel* as the principle of living subject to the law or being governed.[27] *Wathalel* prohibits taking justice into one's own hands, instead asserting that justice should be sought through the courts. One chief described *Wathalel* as follows:

All these rules have an opposite: if your cows are stolen, don't go to steal someone's cows or you will be killed. Come to the government to bring out your cows. If the sister elopes, don't run to the husband, run to the Chief. And if your brother is killed, you come to the government. And don't go to see the person who killed someone there, because you will become part of the problem. Revenge will keep going. If you kill, you will be killed also. If someone spoils your things, you should not go to revenge it. You should ask the government to do it. If you revenge it, it will cause conflict amongst people and it can spoil the government.

Possibly a more significant consequence of a common western Dinka customary law was the introduction of a division between those who were Dinka and those who were not. Enforcing different customary laws within each tribe complicated inter-tribal relations and introduced division, creating dissonance where there had previously been consistency. The lack of an explicit common legal community implied a difference in moral frameworks and norms, and a cultural and normative division between communities. It also made conflicts harder to resolve, creating enmity between groups (OLS Southern Sector, n.d.).

In the post-CPA years, some attempts have been made to preserve the western Dinka as a legal community. During various episodes of inter-clan violence in Lakes State, chiefs from Warrap State have been invited to sit on special courts to settle post-conflict cases. People in Lakes State viewed these chiefs as outsiders and often resisted this. However, the government insisted that Warrap State chiefs could legitimately rule on cases in Lakes State based on the commonality of the laws among the western Dinka, and it was also hoped that, as relative outsiders, the chiefs would be a more neutral voice.

Conclusion

Over time, political actors at local and national levels have used discourses of customary law in what is today South Sudan to contribute to ideas of identity and belonging, including by shaping ideas about 'southern' identity and common ethnic (or sub-ethnic) identities. Common legal communities are imagined through an appeal to shared customary law. For various governments in southern Sudanese history, customary law has conveyed a shared underlying jurisprudence and political philosophy based on custom. In practice, customary law, as it has been constituted in the courts, has showed great variance and flexibility across South Sudan and within ethnic groupings, and the fiction of a common substantive law often persists despite diversity. Customary law has consistently resisted the central government's imposition of its own preferred notions of identity, instead creating a sphere in which ideas of identity can be peacefully contested.

As South Sudanese policymakers and members of the international community grapple with strategies and normative models to build a new sense of a South Sudanese community, there are lessons to be learnt from the histories of customary law in southern Sudan. Fictions and apparent paradoxes have often been key to making things work.

Notes

1   E. G. Coryton, 'Governor Upper Nile Province draft of letter by Governor to Civil Secretary which is not being sent but retained in the file', South Sudan National Archive (SSNA) UNP/41. A.6., Juba.

2   C. C. G. Cumings (Chief Justice) (1946), 'Flogging as a Court Punishment for Adults', 25 August 1946, SSNA CS/41. A.19/3, Juba.

3   James W. Robertson (1947), Letter from J. E. Robertson (Civil Secretary), SSNA Z.D. 1.A.S., Juba.

4   Paul P. Howell, Notes on Nuer District Commissioners Meeting: 1–5 February 1943, Sudan Archive, GB-0033-767/2/18, Durham.

5   Ibid.

6   Ibid.

7   Memorandum of Nuer Laws and Customary Payments Discussed by Chiefs, Sudan Archive, Durham, GB-0033-SAD 767/2/31, Durham.

8   Ibid.

9   Official correspondence to Paul P. Howell, Tonj District Annual Chiefs' Meeting 1938, Sudan Archive, Durham, SAD.767/11/1–32.

10 For example the Governor's Speech at Nuer Chiefs' Meeting, Sudan Archive, Durham; and Notes on Dinka Social Structure and Laws, Tonj File, Sudan Archive, Durham.

11 John Deng, Letter to The Honorable Chief Justice of the Sudan, 15 November 1960, SSNA UNP. 40. C.62., Juba.

12 C. G. Davies, Letter to Paul P. Howell from Syd C. G. Davies, 4 May 1949, SSNA UNP. 66.G.3/3, Juba.

13 Author interview, chief, Kuajok, January 2013 (in Dinka).

14 Author interview, woman, Kuajok, January 2012 (in Dinka).

15 Author interview with Ministry of Justice, Public Prosecutor, Lakes State, 2012 (in English).

16 Speech by chief, Lakes State, 2012 (in Dinka).

17 Author interview with Ministry of Justice, Public Prosecutor, Lakes State, 2012 (in English).

18 Speech by County Commissioner, Warrap State, February 2012.

19 Author interview with UN Consultant 2, August 2012, Juba (in English).

20 Author interview with UN Consultant 1, August 2012, Juba (in English).

21 Author interview with UN Consultant 2, August 2012, Juba (in English).

22 A court warrant, February 1946, Sudan Archive, Durham, GB-0033-SAD 767/8/45.

23 Focus group discussion with members of the *Akutdhiëc/payam*-level Customary Court, May 2012, Greater Gogrial (in Dinka); discourse at Chiefs' Meeting, Lietnhom, June 2012 (in Dinka).

24 Discussion with official in the Warrap State Ministry of Justice, Kuajok (Warrap State), January 2013 (in English).

25   Focus group discussion with members of the *Akutdhiëc / payam*-level Customary Court, May 2012, Greater Gogrial (in Dinka).
26   Discourse at an NGO-organised workshop, Warrap State, January 2013 (in Dinka and English).
27   Author interview with executive chief, Luonyaker, Warrap State, 2012 (in Dinka).

References

Bahr el Ghazal Regional Customary Law (Amendment) Act of 1984.

Boone, Catherine (2007), 'Property and constitutional order: Land tenure reform and the future of the African state', *African Affairs* 106, no. 425: 557–86.

Branch, Adam and Zachariah C. Mampilly (2005), 'Winning the war, but losing the peace? The dilemma of SPLM/A civil administration and the tasks ahead', *The Journal of Modern African Studies* 43, no. 1: 1–20.

Chiefs' Courts Ordinance of 1931.

Civil Justice Ordinance of 1929.

Civil Procedure Act of 1983.

Civil Procedure Act of 1994.

Comaroff, John L. (2002), 'Governmentality, materiality, legality and modernity: On the colonial state in Africa', in Jan-Georg Deutsch et al. (eds), *African Modernities: Entangled Meanings in Current Debate* (Oxford: James Currey).

Deng, Francis M. (1987), *Tradition and Modernization: A Challenge for Law Among the Dinka of the Sudan*, 2nd edn (New Haven, CT: Yale University Press).

— (2009), *Customary Law in the Modern World: The Crossfire of Sudan's War of Identities* (Oxford: Routledge).

— (1971), *Tradition and Modernization: A Challenge for Law Among the Dinka of Sudan* (New Haven: Yale University Press).

Evans-Pritchard, Edward E. (1954), 'Introduction', in Paul P. Howell, *A Manual of Nuer Law: Being an Account of Customary Law, Its Evolution and Development in the Courts Established by the Sudan Government* (London: Oxford University Press).

Fadlalla, Mohamed (2009), *Customary Laws in Southern Sudan: Customary Laws of the Dinka and Nuer* (New York, NY: iUniverseInc).

Garland, P. S. (1954), Letter from Garland (Western Nuer District Commissioner) to the Governor, Bentiu, 4 September 1954, South Sudan National Archive, UNP/ 39. L.1., Juba.

Hancock, G. M. (1945), *Records of an interesting case in Yirol*, 16 November 1945 (official record), Sudan Archive, Durham, GB-0033-SAD. 767/8/5.

Howell, Paul P. (1949), Letter from Howell (Secretary, Nuer District Commissioners' Meeting, Fangak) to J. S. R. Duncan, 11 May 1949, South Sudan National Archive, UNP/66. E.6/8, Juba.

— (1954), *A Manual of Nuer Law: Being an Account of Customary Law, Its Evolution and Development in the Courts Established by the Sudan Government* (London: Oxford University Press).

— (n.d.), Notes on Dinka Social Structure and Laws, Tonj File – 66.A, Sudan Archive, GB-0033-(767/8/5), Durham.

Interim Constitution of Southern Sudan of 2005.

Isser, Deborah (2011), 'Customary justice and the rule of law in war-torn societies', *The George Washington International Law Review,* 44(3): 573–575.

Johnson, Douglas H. (1986), 'Judicial regulation and administrative control: Customary law and the Nuer, 1898–1954', *The Journal of African History* 27, no. 1: 59–78.

— (2003), *The Root Causes of Sudan's Civil War* (Oxford: James Currey).

Jok, Aleu Akechak Robert A. Leitch and Carrie Vandewint (2004), *A Study of Customary Law in Contemporary Southern Sudan*, World Vision International and the South Sudan Secretariat of Legal and Constitutional Affairs.

Jok, Jok Madut (2011), *Diversity, Unity and Nation Building in South Sudan: United States Institute of Peace Special Report No. 287*, https://www.usip.org/sites/default/files/Diversity,%20Unity,%20and%20Nation%20Building%20in%20South%20Sudan%20(Jok).pdf.

Jok, Jok Madut and Sharon E. Hutchinson (1999), 'Sudan's prolonged civil war and the militarization of the Nuer and Dinka ethnic identities', *African Studies Review* 42, no. 2: 125–45.

Judiciary Act of 2008.

Kuol, Monyluak Alor (1997), *Administration of Justice in the (SPLM/A) Liberated Areas: Court Cases in War-Torn Southern Sudan* (Oxford, United Kingdom: University of Oxford Refugee Studies Programme).

Kuper, Hilda and Leo Kuper (1965), *African Law: Adaption and Development* (Berkeley, CA: University of California Press).

Lakes State Customary Law Act of 2010.

Leonardi, Cherry (2013), *Dealing With Government in South Sudan: Histories in the Making of Chiefship, Community and State* (Woodbridge, UK: James Currey).

Leonardi, Cherry et al. (2010), *Local Justice in Southern Sudan*, Peaceworks, https://www.usip.org/sites/default/files/PW66%20-%20Local%20Justice%20in%20Southern%20Sudan.pdf.

Lienhardt, Godfrey (1961), *Divinity and Experience: The Religion of the Dinka* (London: Oxford University Press.

Likhovski, Assaf (2006), *Law and Identity in Mandate Palestine* (Chapel Hill, NC: University of North Carolina Press).

Local Government Act of 2009.

Lueth, M. (1999), *Workshop on Rehabilitation and Restructuring of Legal Institutions and Other Law Enforcement Agencies in New Sudan, New Cush 20th April 1999*. Available in the Sudan Open Archive.

Lugard, Frederick D. (1922), *The Dual Mandate in British Tropical Africa* (London: Blackwood and Sons).

Maine, Henry J. S. (1861), *Ancient Law: Its Connection With the Early History of Society* (London: Oxford University Press).

Makec, John Wuol (1988), *Customary Law of the Dinka People of Sudan in Comparison With the Aspects of Western and Islamic Laws* (London: Afroworld).

— (2007), *Access to Justice in Africa and Beyond: Making the Rule of Law a Reality*, Penal Reform International and Bluhm Legal Clinic of the Northwestern University School of Law, book freely available at http://www.etc-graz.at/typo3/fileadmin/user_upload/ETC-Hauptseite/Menschenrechte_lernen/POOL/AcesstoJusticeAfirca.PDF.

Mamdani, Mahmood (1996), *Citizen and Subject: Contemporary Africa and the Legacy of Late Colonialism* (Princeton, NJ: Princeton University Press).

Mayom, Manyang (2010), 'Interview: Avoid taking law in own hands, says S. Sudan chief justice', *Sudan Tribune*, 8 January, http://www.sudantribune.com/spip.php?page=imprimable&id_article=33722.

— (2010b), 'Lakes state caretaker closes down all illegal courts in Sudan's Rumbek state', *Sudan Tribune*, 6 March, http://www.sudantribune.com/spip.php?article34344.

— (2011), 'Lakes state officials says men, imprisoned for making girls pregnant, should be released', *All Africa*, 10 March, http://allafrica.com/stories/201103141217.html.

Mennen, Tiernan (2007), 'Legal pluralism in Southern Sudan: Can the rest of Africa show the way?', *Africa Policy Journal* 3: 49–73.

Mijak, D. B. (1999), *Save Our Customary Laws Now: SPLM Workshop on the Rehabilitation and Restructuring of Legal Institutions and Law Enforcement Agencies*, New Cush, 20 April 1999, Sudan Open Archive.

OLS Southern Sector (n.d.), *Introduction to Sudanese Cultures: Participants Manual*.

Rahim, M. Abdel (1966), 'The development of British policy in Southern Sudan 1899–1947', *Middle Eastern Studies* 2, no. 3: 227–49.

Rangelov, Iavor (2014), *Nationalism and the Rule of law: Lessons from the Balkans and Beyond* (Cambridge: Cambridge University Press).

SPLA Penal Code.

Thiik, Ambrose Riiny (Former Chief Justice) (2013), Rift Valley Institute / Juba University Lectures, Juba.

Thomas, Edward (2015), *South Sudan: A Slow Liberation* (London: Zed Books).

Transitional Constitution of the Republic of South Sudan of 2011.

UNDP (2016), *Study on the Harmonisation of Customary Laws and the National Legal System in South Sudan*, http://www.ss.undp.org/content/dam/southsudan/library/Rule%20of%20Law/DLD345%20UN_HCLR_FA.pdf.

Vaughan, Christopher, Marieke Schomerus and Lotje de Vries. (2013), *The Borderlands of South Sudan: Authority and Identity in Contemporary and Historical Perspectives* (New York, NY: Palgrave Macmillan).

Westermann, Diedrich (1939), *The African Today and Tomorrow* (London: Oxford University Press).

CHAPTER 2

Governing Unclear Lines

Local Boundaries as a (Re)source of Conflict in South Sudan[1]

Peter Hakim Justin and Lotje de Vries

Introduction

In October 2015, the South Sudanese president, Salva Kiir, announced the annulment of the ten states that had existed since 1992 and decreed the creation of 28 new ones (Sudan Tribune, 2015), a decision that provoked mixed reactions across the country. Changes to the administrative structures in South Sudan, and opposition to those changes, are not new. Before Sudanese independence in 1956, southern élites lobbied for a federal system as an acceptable alternative to southern independence, which northern political élites rejected (Johnson, 2014). The call for federalism and the further division of the country into 32 states has created tensions within South Sudan between different levels of government and political élites (de Vries, 2014; Schomerus and Aalen, 2016). Kiir's unilateral decision superficially responded to some of his critics' demands without actually addressing most of the fundamental governance issues that fuelled political contestation and continued demand for federalism in the country. This chapter illustrates how confusion over levels of authority and the absence of clear boundaries between administrative units have contributed to tensions between communities, risking escalation into conflict along ethnic lines.

This chapter draws on extensive socio-anthropological fieldwork that was carried out in Central Equatoria State during three visits (November 2011–June 2012, September 2012–April 2013 and January–February 2015), and analyses literature and historical documents to understand the linkages between local government, internal borders and conflicts. Studying internal boundary conflicts in Central Equatoria State is of methodological and theoretical relevance for two reasons. First, most writings on peace and conflict in South Sudan tend to pay little attention to the relationship between territories and internal borders, which, this chapter argues, is crucial to understanding the increasing levels of 'ethnic conflict'. Second, Central Equatoria State was initially relatively peaceful compared to other states in the country, which may offer insight into the relationship between political manipulation and violent contestation. Using three case studies, this chapter demonstrates how ethnic identity or sense of belonging is used by élites as a strategy to make claims on political, economic and socio-cultural aspects of land.

The first section gives some insights into colonial intervention in Africa and shows how this contributed to linking identity to territories. The second section gives an overview of the historical development of internal borders in South Sudan and puts this in the context of Central Equatoria State. The subsequent sections examine the three case studies and discuss how socio-cultural, political and economic interests are stirring up conflicts over internal boundaries in the state.

The colonial legacy of linking ethnicity to territory

In 1964, the Organisation of African Unity (OAU) adopted the *uti possidetis* principle, which committed newly independent states to respecting national borders established under colonial rule. Although South Sudan's independence may seem to diverge from this principle, the new border between Sudan and South Sudan is in fact based on the border created by the British colonial authorities and both countries recognise it as it existed at Sudanese independence on 1 January 1956. Within South Sudan, internal borders as they stood on 1 January 1956 were also used as the reference for initial state borders (see Figure 2.1).

Many boundaries between African states remain disputed, despite some degree of demarcation at independence (Asiwaju, 2012; AUBP, 2014). This is the case for the Sudan–South Sudan border, as evidenced by the ongoing disputes over the border town of Abyei (Craze, 2013). According to Andrew Natsios, the former US Special Envoy to Sudan, 'the exact demarcation of what is now a heavily militarised border had not been agreed on by the two countries and will continue to be a source of considerable tension' (Natsios, 2015: 419; see also Schomerus et al., 2013; Copnall, 2014). Higlig (known as Panthou in South Sudan), another disputed border town, became

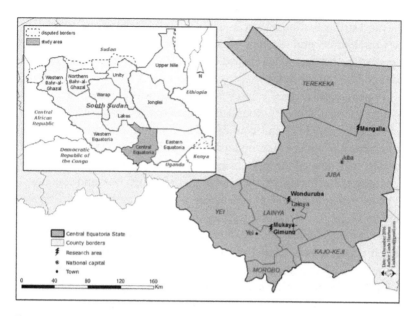

Figure 2.1 Map showing the former ten states of South Sudan and the research area

the cause of military confrontations between the two countries in 2012 (Johnson, 2012).

Border contestation in Sudan and South Sudan can be traced back to the pre-independence period. This points to an important aspect of the colonial heritage of African boundaries that is little studied, namely that most post-colonial governments not only inherited the national borders imposed on them, but also the internal boundaries (Hamid, 2002). As a result, the link between identity and territories is fundamental in determining how landownership claims are made and land access regulated. In turn, this determines how borders between communities are negotiated (Berry et al., 2013; Lund and Boone, 2013). As discussed below, borders are a source of an increasing number of conflicts. But to what extent are those conflicts related to the question of landownership or internal borders? What has caused this increase in conflict? What is the relationship between local conflicts and national politics, and how are these related to the issue of land? Lastly, and this has become all the more pertinent after recent administrative reshuffles, what impact could these changes have on the establishment of local government in South Sudan? As the three case studies will show, the legacies of those boundaries continue to play a major role in shaping everyday manifestations of power and authority. Perhaps the most striking of those legacies in South Sudan is the strong correlation between identity and territory, which has become instrumental in defining relations between the state and society on the one hand, and between communities on the other.

Prior to colonial intervention, many African societies were characterised by a great deal of mobility. Boundaries were not fixed and shifted between overlapping networks and communities. Communities were based on proximity, kinship or common loyalty to a king (Lentz, 2000). Territorial borders were defined through alliances between leaders, and could change according to fluctuations in those relations or through wars and conquests. With extremely low population densities, power and authority were organised and legitimised around people rather than territories. As a result, leaders were to some extent accountable to their subjects as people could simply decide to move elsewhere (Englebert, 2009). Colonial intervention radically changed most of those dynamics. Borders became fixed lines with administrative powers attached to them. As Jeffrey Herbst notes, boundaries became the mechanism for 'determining who is a citizen and who not', giving meaning to 'the cadastral boundary lines originally created by the Europeans' (Herbst, 2000: 231). The internal borders created by colonial administrations laid the foundations for the establishment of provinces and districts. However, many of these internal boundaries are undefined and unmarked, as are some of the national borders. Zoe Cormack (2016) refers to such borders as a constellation of 'points' such as trees, streams and hills, which may well have different meanings to different people. Nonetheless, by attaching political power to territorial boundaries, the creation of those territories strengthened or 'constructed' ethnic identities.

There is consensus among scholars that the colonial intervention in sub-Saharan Africa resulted in the creation of territories inhabited along ethnic lines (Lentz, 2000; Leonardi and Santschi, 2016; Mamdani, 1996). More contested, however, is whether the colonial intervention contributed to the 'construction' or 'invention' of ethnic identities (Lentz et al., 2000). Contrary to the pre-colonial structure of leadership, which depended on a set of traditional leaders, the colonial approach was to select an individual chief from the majority group in a new territory, or from those claiming to be autochthonous to the area (Mamdani, 2001). This forced groups to abide by the powers of autochthons or majority groups (Lentz, 2013; Leonardi, 2013). Over time, those policies contributed to the reinforcement of ethnicity or even the construction of new identities that became strongly linked to the territories inhabited. In the case of South Sudan, the increased connection between identity and territories has provided élites with tools of manipulation with which to consolidate territorial claims.

Internal borders in South Sudan

The establishment of new states and counties along identity lines (autochthonous groups or majority groups) is a typical South Sudanese governance strategy. In combination with increased interest in political, economic and land resources following the 2005 Comprehensive Peace Agreement (CPA), this approach facilitates the manipulation of identities. But how does such manipulation relate to internal borders, and on what basis are local government units in South Sudan established?

The Turco-Egyptian authorities created the Sudanese state in the early nineteenth century by amalgamating different kingdoms, sultanates and 'tribal' communities (O'Fahey and Spaulding, 1974). Later, the British colonial authorities further restructured the territory to suit their interests, establishing provinces that were each divided into local government districts. When it gained independence in 1956, Sudan was divided into eight provinces, three of which (Upper Nile, Bahr el Ghazal and Equatoria) are in present-day South Sudan. These three provinces were divided into 21 districts (Hamid, 2002).

As part of their indirect rule strategy, the British colonial authorities often forcefully relocated communities.[2] In Equatoria province, resettlement was done to eradicate sleeping sickness (Bloss, 1960). This resettlement was followed by the appointment of chiefs and the establishment of borders delineating the jurisdictions of the newly appointed chiefs.[3] Borders between chieftainships were often arbitrarily created and frequently marked by landmarks such as rivers, mountains and big trees, though in most cases they were marked by main roads, leaving parts of those territories lacking roads without borders.[4] After gaining independence, Sudan generally maintained the territorial administration developed by the colonial authorities. Occasionally, however, governments renamed these provinces and districts, altered the administrative status of units or redrew borders (Hamid, 2002).

In 1992, the Sudanese government replaced the eight provinces with 26 states, 16 in the north and 10 in the south (Hamid, 2002). In the parts of the country under its control, the Sudan People's Liberation Movement (SPLM) established a three-level local government structure which consisted of counties, *payams* and *bomas* (Leonardi, 2013). Importantly, both the government and the SPLM used the territorial divisions implemented by the colonial authorities, either by merging colonial districts to create states or by including chieftaincies in the local government structure in the SPLM's 'liberated' areas. Reflecting colonial practices, ethnicity became a prominent aspect of the restructuring of these units.

When the interim period (2005–2011) began, the Southern Sudan government inherited 10 of the 26 states created by Khartoum in 1992, which it combined with the governance structures implemented by the SPLM in 1994. At independence, the Transitional Constitution of 2011 formally recognised the existing ten-state structure, which consisted of 86 counties divided into *payams* and *bomas*. Kiir's 2015 decree increasing the number of states to 28 and, later, to 32 has not yet been enshrined in the constitution. Adminstering the 86 counties and the unclear boundaries between them was one of the biggest challenges the government faced during the interim period, especially because these years marked a sharp rise in investor interest in land acquisitions. The increased value of land exacerbated conflicts throughout the territory (Deng, 2011).

Although current conflicts over land, administration and political power are the result of contemporary circumstances, some find their roots in Sudan's colonial history. First, a number of communities in the settlements created by the colonial authorities continue to claim ownership of the land they were relocated from, but at the same time attempt to consolidate control over their 'new land'. This often results in contested landownership claims based on indigenity, majority status or forced resettlement (Justin and van Leeuwen, 2016). Second, the lack of clearly marked borders between chieftaincies that were upgraded to local government territories has triggered border disputes. Lastly, the rationale behind the establishment of the county–*payam*–*boma* administrative system is unclear, resulting in different interpretations of how it should be implemented.

Some contend that boundaries between these units should be established along ethnic lines and that autochthony should be the basis of ownership claims in those territories, but others argue that majority group status ought to be the basis of such claims.[5] Within the normative framework of 'the land belongs to the community' (Badiey, 2014; Hirblinger, 2015), defining what constitutes a community becomes a source of conflict between local groups, who frequently have the support of their political élites. The apparent lack of institutional capacity to mitigate or resolve land and boundary conflicts throughout the country means that conflicts arising from such disputes can take violent turns, sometimes along ethnic lines (Schomerus, 2008).

Changes to the administrative and political systems within these territories also have an impact on the local power balance and contribute to increased tensions and violence (Pendle, 2014; Schomerus and de Vries, 2014).

Old borders and new stakes in Central Equatoria State

The ongoing civil war in South Sudan broke out in December 2013 as the result of a power struggle between President Salva Kiir and former vice-president Riek Machar. The conflict quickly took hold in the three states of Greater Upper Nile (Unity, Upper Nile and Jonglei) and flared sporadically in some parts of Greater Bahr el Ghazal. As the war continued, parts of Greater Equatoria were drawn into the violence and began to witness local rebellions or attacks by groups allied to the SPLM-in-Opposition (SPLM-IO) (de Vries, 2014). Particularly since the establishment of the 28 states, conflicts have erupted in what used to be Central Equatoria State and Western Equatoria State (ICG, 2016). Historically, Central Equatoria State comprised the Yei and Juba Districts, which were established by colonial authorities. After the CPA, what used to be Yei River District was divided into the four counties of Morobo, Yei, Kajokeji and Lainya, while Juba was split into the two counties of Juba and Terekeka (Transitional Constitution of Central Equatoria State, 2011). As a result of Kiir's creation of the 28 states, Central Equatoria State was re-divided into the three states of Terekeka State, Juba (renamed Jubek) State and Yei River State (Mayom, 2015). The new states reflected 'majority' ethnic groups or those considered autochthonous to those areas (Radio Tamazug, 2015).

The tendency to establish local government units on the basis of ethnicity began during the interim period. For instance, when appointing local executive power-holders, attempts to appoint 'outsiders' were often opposed by local élites. In 2012, for example, the governor of Central Equatoria State appointed a commissioner to Lainya County who came from neighbouring Terekeka County. The appointment generated a lot of resistance because the appointee was not 'native' to Lainya.[6] A year earlier, the same governor had appointed a commissioner to Yei River County from the Adiyo community, a minority group in the county. That appointment also drew criticism, with local leaders and chiefs taking issue as the appointee was not from the Kakwa majority group.[7] In the absence of local elections, the state governor succeeded in pushing through the two appointments, however, relations between the commissioners and their respective constituencies were tense.[8]

To further illustrate the complexities of identity, autochthony status and majority status in relation to political and economic interests, three case studies from Central Equatoria State will now be explored: an ownership claim in Mangalla Payam in Terekeka County, the disputed geopolitical status of Wonduruba Payam in Lainya County, and a border dispute between Yei and Lainya Counties.

The economic prospects of Mangalla Payam

Mangalla is a *payam* in Terekeka County. It is located some 70 kilometres north of Juba town along the White Nile. Although the Mundari are the majority ethnic group in Terekeka County, they are the minority in Mangalla. The Bari, on the other hand, are the majority in Mangalla as well as in neighbouring Juba County. According to local narratives, the Bari were the first settlers in this area, but had always coexisted peacefully alongside the Mundari,[9] even after the division of Juba District into Juba and Terekeka Counties in 2005. The question of landownership had never been an issue between the two communities. In 2009, however, investors began to express an interest in leasing land in the *payam*. This resulted in issues of landownership and the Juba–Terekeka county border becoming points of contention between the Bari and Mundari.

As David Deng (2011) notes, the interim period saw an unprecedented rush by both foreign and domestic investors to acquire large tracts of land in many rural areas in Southern Sudan, which brought the question of landownership and administrative borders in many rural areas to the forefront. For example, in 2007 the Madhvani Group, an Indian-owned Ugandan conglomerate, expressed a desire to lease a piece of land in Mangalla for agricultural and industrial purposes. It eventually signed two memoranda of understanding with the government: the first for a land lease and the second to build a sugar cane processing facility (Deng, 2011). According to the Land Act (2009), land-leasing negotiations in rural areas should involve consultations with local communities, who are presumed to be the landowners, and payment of adequate compensation (before the start of any activities) to those who will be affected by the investment in question. In addition, the Investment Promotion Act (2009) states that local communities should be given priority in terms of employment and the delivery of any services associated with the investment project. Determining whether the Mundari or the Bari are 'the community' of Mangalla thus became a fiercely contested issue.

The Bari claim to landownership was based on the fact that they are autochthonous to the area and also the majority group in the area. The Mundari, on the other hand, argue that Mangalla is in Terekeka County, where they form the majority.[10] Mundari and Bari chiefs, elders and intellectuals who did not live in Mangalla backed the claims made by their respective ethnic communities, thus taking the dispute beyond the borders of the *payam*.[11] Other conflicts between individuals from the Mundari and Bari were then framed as Mundari–Bari conflicts in an attempt to mobilise others to join these confrontations and provoke violent clashes. In January 2015, for example, a dispute between two families in Kworojik-Luri, Juba, quickly escalated and was framed as an 'ethnic conflict' between Bari and Mundari groups. The confrontation resulted in the death of 11 individuals and injury to about two dozen others (CECE-USA, 2015).

As a result, the investors suspended their activities and waited for the landownership question to be resolved.[12] The state governor proposed dividing the *payam* into Mangalla North and Mangalla South. This would have seen Mangalla North remain part of Terekeka County under the authority of Mundari chiefs and Mangalla South become part of Juba County under the authority of Bari chiefs. This proposal was rejected by representatives of both groups as it would have compromised their land rights: the Bari would have lost their ancestral land rights, whereas the Mundari would have lost part of 'their county' (Terekeka County) had Mangalla South become part of Juba County, which was considered a 'Bari county'.[13] Within the 28-states system, the two counties have been upgraded to states, based on the same contested borders, thus raising the conflict to a state-level dispute.

Shifting around Wonduruba's electoral constituency

The *payam* of Wonduruba provides us with another illustration of contestation between identity and territory. Unlike the Mangalla case, which was about landownership, the Wonduruba case concerns the *payam*'s political status as an electoral constituency. Wonduruba is located in Lainya County and is inhabited by the Nyangwara people. In Lainya County the Nyangwara are a minority group, and the Pojulu are the majority group. The 2010 national elections were the immediate trigger of the conflict in Wonduruba as Southern Sudan counties, *payams* and *bomas* formed the basis of the political constituencies for the elections.[14]

While campaigning for the election, an influential SPLM candidate from Wonduruba called for Wonduruba to be included in the political constituency of Juba County rather than of Lainya County, where the *payam* is administratively located. This demand was unique because it required inclusion of an administrative unit of one county in the political constituency of another county. This move resulted in a debate within the *payam* and put the administrations of Juba County and Lainya County at odds with each other.

This demand not only divided Nyangwara clans within the *payam*, it caused a split in local politics in Lainya County. At the county level, proponents of this move foresaw it resulting in an SPLM victory and thus vigorously supported it. Political élites at the national level shared this assessment. Those opposed to it argued that the change could potentially result in the permanent annexation of Wonduruba by Juba County.[15] As with many contentious issues in South Sudan, rather than solving this specific case politically through debate and the weighing up of arguments, a rush to violence was the preferred option.

The conflict resulted in 'unknown gunmen' attempting to assassinate the SPLM member who had proposed the constituency change.[16] To address the issue, the Central Equatoria State authorities suggested that they govern the *payam* until it was decided whether Wonduruba would remain part of Lainya County or become part of Juba County. During the 2010 elections, Wonduruba was an independent constituency without links to either county. The Central Equatoria State government continues to oversee the *payam*'s administration. With the recent division of Central Equatoria State into three states, Lainya County will become part of Yei River State, which will again bring the unresolved issue of Wonduruba back into the spotlight as it is unclear whether Wonduruba will be part of Yei River State or of Jubek State.

The border contests between Yei River and Lainya counties: the choice between cultural and administrative borders

The disputed border between Lainya and Yei River Counties illustrates the country's colonial legacy. Following a local land dispute, debate arose regarding the choice of administrative or 'traditional' borders. During the colonial era, the administration had designated the River Koya, located some 16 kilometres from Yei town towards Lainya County headquarters, as the border between two chieftaincies established by the colonial powers.

In 2005, the Southern Sudanese government chose this river to serve as the administrative border between Yei River and Lainya Counties.

In 2007, two neighbouring families, one from the *payam* of Mukaya in Lainya County and the other from the *boma* of Gimunu in Yei River County, had a dispute over the boundaries between their farms around this border location. Local attempts to resolve this disagreement failed, prompting two chiefs from Mukaya and Gimunu to become involved. However, sharp differences in opinion between the chiefs on how to resolve the dispute changed the focus of the discussions. Instead of focusing on resolving a local quarrel between two families, this issue turned into a dispute about defining the border between the neighbouring communities of Mukaya (primarily Pojulu ethnic group) and Gimunu (primarily Kakwa ethnic group).[17] For the Mukaya chief, the area in question falls within Lainya County. The Gimunu chief, on the other hand, believed the dispute occurred within his village, which falls within Yei River County. The discussion about the border issue became so complex that local government authorities and Central Equatoria State officials had to intervene.[18] The existing legal framework for conflict resolution stipulates that chiefs and other traditional leaders knowledgeable on landownership and traditional ways of resolving local disputes should mediate land conflicts in rural areas (Land Act, 2009; Local Government Act, 2009). This conflict, however, turned into a border dispute between two counties, with the chiefs becoming part of the problem rather than functioning as problem solvers. As in the case of Mangalla, representatives from the two counties framed their narratives in a way that supported claims made by their respective communities.[19]

The main argument presented by those from Lainya County was that the existing border divided two chieftaincies headed by Pojulu chiefs. Following the adoption of the county–*payam*–*boma* system, they asserted that it would be better to move the border between the counties to where it would divide the Pojulu community of Lainya County from the Kakwa of Yei River County. Accordingly, they believed the border should be moved to the Yei River, some three kilometres from Yei town. This proposal was rejected by those representing Yei River County.[20] They argued that moving the current border towards Yei would displace people from Yei River County living around the border area and include them in Lainya County against their will. Among the Lainya people, there is disagreement on whether the border should be changed or not. Certain Pojulu chiefs and elders (those who refer to themselves as 'Eastern Kakwa') are particularly opposed to this proposal because it could have negative implications for their 'other identity' as 'Kakwa'.[21] A committee appointed to resolve this issue presented its findings to the governor and to the two commissioners of Yei and Lainya counties, and suggested that the border should remain at its current location. Despite this advice, the commissioner of Lainya County publicly stated that adopting the committee's guidance might contribute to 'bloodshed' between the Pojulu and the Kakwa.[22] As in Mangalla and Wonduruba, the border dispute between the two counties remains unresolved. It is yet to be seen whether the recent merger of these counties to form Yei River State could help to settle this border dispute.

Linking (territorial) borders, identity and local government

As the three case studies show, the territorial borders established by the British colonial authorities in Sudan continue to form the basis of internal borders in South Sudan, although they have been subjected to multiple administrative and political changes by various post-colonial governments. Kiir's decisions to increase the number of states to 28 and later to 32, are the most recent administrative shifts, leading to the establishment of new counties, *payams* and *bomas*. The colonial authorities and the South Sudanese government exhibit considerable similarity in their approach towards establishing administrative units on the basis of ethnic majorities. This contributes to the growing exclusion of those who are perceived locally as 'outsiders' or minority groups. The contestations around the appointment of commissioners to Lainya and Yei Counties in 2011 and 2012, respectively, are illustrative of this. However, the literature and local narratives suggest that changes in governance structures were less violent during the colonial era than they are today. This raises questions about the relationship between local conflicts and national politics and its link to access to land and resources.

The three case studies reveal a number of intertwined factors that contribute to the increasing incidence of local conflicts in rural South Sudan. Most of these conflicts are sentimentalised as identity-related land conflicts or border disputes between communities. However, as the case studies show, competition over natural resources and economic and political power struggles are among the immediate causes of the conflict. Tensions are further exacerbated by weak institutional capacity to mitigate or resolve conflicts at the local and national level. Two aspects deserve further consideration, namely linking resource conflicts to identity and using identity as a political tool.

Linking resource conflicts to identity

The marginalisation of rural communities by various post-colonial governments in Sudan was a central factor in the protracted civil war between the south and the north (Deng, 1995). The interim period offered opportunities to develop policies that addressed the injustices of the past. In reality, attempts to address these injustices turned out to be counterproductive: they not only failed to address marginalisation, but also increased local conflicts. On the basis of the Local Government Act (2009), the government placed rural areas under the authority of chiefs, thus making chiefs local government officials. The Land Act (2009) gave more land rights to rural communities, including the right to decide how to use their land. With the lack of clarity about what constitutes a community, the policy gap in the two pieces of legislation made it easy for élites to manipulate local people on the basis of identity for personal economic, political or socio-cultural gains. From 2005, SPLM élites became deeply involved in leasing land that was traditionally owned by rural communities (Deng, 2011). With the government resorting to the creation of local administrative units along identity lines, the manipulation of these identities by élites became even more prominent.

In Mangalla, for example, the main question was how to share the spoils of investments in the area. The lack of clarity on what defines a community prompted intellectuals, chiefs, elders and other traditional leaders to 'construct' identities for the benefit of their own communities, at the cost of 'others'. Similar dynamics could be observed in the conflict in Wonduruba and the border dispute between Yei and Lainya Counties. In Wonduruba, attempts by a national political figure to win elections in the area shifted the discussion from a political debate to a question of identity, first within the *payam* and then between the two neighbouring counties of Juba (Bari) and Lainya (Pojulu). Likewise, the land dispute that started between two neighbouring families from Mukaya and Gimunu grew into a border conflict between the two counties of Lainya (Pojulu) and Yei (Kakwa).

The use of identity as a mobilisation strategy to exclude 'others' as a result of competition over resources is not uncommon in Africa. In Ivory Coast, for example, Alfred Babo et al. (2013) note that indigenity is used as a means to establish control over land and to distinguish between those entitled to land and those who are not. In Uganda, the Buganda people continue to call for federalism with the hope that it will limit landownership within the Buganda kingdom to the Buganda (Apter, 1961). In Ethiopia, 'ethnic federalism' was introduced as a strategy to distribute resources equally among the different 'nationalities' in the country (Abbink, 2011). Though it is too early to tell what impact the decision to increase the number of states in South Sudan will have on the relationships between identity, resources and local conflicts, emerging evidence suggests it is likely to contribute to more conflict and instability.

Identity as a political tool

Like the mobilisation of identities around resources, the use of identity as a political tool was also evident in the case studies discussed, particularly in the case of Wonduruba. Identity manipulation for political gain has a long history in Sudan (Deng, 1995; Jok, 2011). During the 1983–2005 civil war, for instance, the SPLM leadership appointed chiefs to head ethnic groups or clans in areas it controlled and used them to conscript soldiers and secure food for its fighting forces (Johnson, 1998; Leonardi, 2011). After independence, SPLM retained most of the chiefs it appointed during wartime, incorporating them into the government payroll and making them upwardly accountable to local government officials, who are predominantly from the SPLM. In this regard, chiefs became government agents rather than advocates for rural communities.

Chiefs continue to play a crucial role in local and national politics, often under instruction from the government. Towards the end of the interim period, chiefs vigorously mobilised their communities to vote for Southern Sudan's independence, which made a significant contribution to shaping the outcome of the referendum in favour of an independent state.[23] At the same time, as demonstrated by the Wonduruba case, some chiefs became more critical of the SPLM, especially those who were not given local government positions.[24] In the Wonduruba case, the division among the chiefs regarding whether Wonduruba should become a political constituency of Juba County or remain part of Lainya County resulted in splits within their respective constituencies. Ultimately, those divisions expanded beyond the identity question and went on to become a political issue in the county and the state.

The case studies show that the question of identity remains central to the establishment of local government structures in South Sudan. Often, the number of *payams* or *bomas* are reflective of the number of ethnic groups or clans in the area. But the fact that identities can also be constructed, reconstructed and even negotiated, as argued by Johan de Smedt (2011), means that using ethnic identity as the sole criterion for the establishment of local government structures is not a viable option. As noted elsewhere, distinctions can be made between members of the same ethnic group. In Burundi, for example, in addition to the general Tutsi–Hutu divide, distinctions are also made between early settlers and later comers and between stayers and those who fled the war (Voors and Bulte, 2014). Prior to the establishment of the county–*payam–boma* system, districts formed the basic local government structure. This meant that the borders between the Bari and the Mundari (both in Juba District) or between the Kakwa and Pojulu (both in Yei District) were of no political relevance. As Brian Smith (1979) and Joseph Ayee (2013) argue, the establishment of local governments is vital to the processes of state-building, yet it remains a complicated process, particularly in relation to the creation of borders. With the current trend of placing greater emphasis on ethnicity in the establishment of local government, local administrative units in South Sudan have become a source of contestation.

Conclusion

Since the signing of the CPA in 2005, there has been ongoing turmoil, including bitterly contested politics and armed rebellion. Protracted political differences within the ruling party escalated in December 2013 into a nationwide rebellion that quickly turned into another civil war. The causes of those contests are multifaceted but often intertwined, with those starting at the higher political order trickling down to cause tensions at societal level. Moreover, local conflicts have escalated into wider conflicts that have had serious implications at various political levels. The establishment of strong and legitimate local government institutions could potentially mitigate and resolve local conflicts, as well as be an effective way to minimise wider conflicts. However, the current tendency to employ ethnic identity as a strategy to establish local government structures makes it challenging to achieve this.

Drawing on case studies from Central Equatoria State in South Sudan, this chapter has focused on understanding the relationships between local administration, borders and conflicts. It shows, first, that past governance strategies resulted in the emergence of strong linkages between ethnic identities and territory in South Sudan, and that disputes over territories or borders often occur along ethnic lines. This, in some cases, has contributed to violent conflicts between communities with no history of ethnic conflict. Second, this chapter demonstrates that ethnic identities are not the immediate cause of many of these conflicts; rather, ethnicity is often manipulated by élites as a mobilisation strategy to achieve individual or group objectives. The increase in political, economic and socio-cultural stakes in land and territory reinforced this process. The lack of a clear legal and administrative framework contributes enormously to élites' use of manipulation and negotiation at various levels. The proliferation of states is likely to further deepen this persisting confusion, which will in all likelihood also result in new conflict over territory, borders and identities.

Notes

1   This chapter was first published as 'Governing unclear lines: Local boundaries as a (re)source of conflict in South Sudan' by Peter Hakim Justin and Lotje de Vries in the *Journal of Borderlands Studies* (2017). Copyright © Association for Borderland Studies. It is reprinted with permission of Taylor & Francis Ltd, http://www.tandfonline.com on behalf of Association for Borderlands Studies.

2   Author interviews, head chief, Tore, 20 May 2011, and head chief, Lasu, 31 January 2012.

3   Author interview, elder, Asole Boma, 3 May 2012.

4   Author interview, executive chief, Longamere, 12 May 2012.

5   Author interviews, executive director, Yei River County, 27 November 2012, and chairman of Pojulu community, Yei, 27 November 2012.

6   Author interview, SPLA officer, Lainya, 6 March 2013.

7   Author interview, Commissioner's office, Yei, 25 March 2013.

8   Author interview, Reconcile International, Yei, 20 March 2013.

9   Author interviews, head chief, Mangalla, 10 October 2012, and CES parliament, Juba, 10 October 2012.

10 Author interview, CES governor's office, Juba, 10 April 2014.

11 Author interviews, South Sudan's Human Rights Commission, 10 April 2013, and CES Ministry of Agriculture and Forestry, 10 April 2013.

12 Author interview, CES governor's office, 7 March 2013.

13 Author interview, CES Ministry of Agriculture and Forestry, Juba, 7 February 2015.

14 Author interview, CES governor's office, Juba, 7 March 2013.

15 Author interview, Centre for Peace and Development Studies at the University of Juba, 29 November 2011.

16 Author interview, paramount chief, Lainya, 30 October 2012.

17 Author interview, head chief, Mukaya, Yei, 9 September 2012.

18 Author interviews, Pojulu community, Yei, 31 October 31, 2012; Kakwa Community Association, 16 November 2012; and executive chief, Gimunu, 9 November 2012.

19 Author interview, paramount chief, Lainya, 6 February 2015.

20 Author interviews, Kakwa Community Association, Yei, 16 November 2012 and Pojulu community, Yei, 16 November 2012.

21 Author interview, executive director, Yei River County, 27 November 2012.
22 Author interview, CES governor's office, Juba, 10 April 2013 and 7 February 2015.
23 Author interview, University of Juba, 12 January 2012.
24 Author interviews, head chief, Tore, 25 May 2012 and executive chief, Longamere, 16 November 2012.

References

Abbink, Jon (2011), 'Ethnic-based federalism and ethnicity in Ethiopia: Reassessing the experiment after 20 years', *Journal of Eastern African Studies* 5, no. 4: 596–618.

Apter, David E. (1961), *The Political Kingdom in Uganda: A Study in Bureaucratic Nationalism* (London: Routledge).

Asiwaju, Anthony I. (2012), 'The African Union Border Programme in European comparative perspective', in Thomas M. Wilson and Hastings Donnan (eds), *A Companion to Border Studies* (Chichester, UK: Wiley Blackwell).

AUBP (2014), *Delimitation and Demarcation of Boundaries in Africa: General Issues and Case Studies* (Addis Ababa: African Union Commission).

Ayee, Joseph R.A. (2013), 'The political economy of the creation of districts in Ghana', *Journal of Asian and African Studies* 48, no. 5: 623–45.

Babo, Alfred, Christian Lund and Catherine Boone (2013), 'The crisis of public policies in Côte d'Ivoire: Land law and the nationality trap in Tabou's rural communities', *Africa* 83, no. 1: 100–19.

Badiey, Naseem (2014), *The State of Post-Conflict Reconstruction: Land, Urban Development and State-Building in Juba, Southern Sudan* (Woodbridge, UK: James Currey).

Berry, Sara, Christian Lund and Catherine Boone (2013), 'Questions of ownership: Proprietorship and control in a changing rural terrain; A case study from Ghana', *Africa* 83, no. 1: 36–56.

Bloss, J. F. E. (1960), 'The history of sleeping sickness in the Sudan', *Proceedings of the Royal Society of Medicine* 53: 421–6.

Central Equatoria Council of Elders in the United States of America (CECE-USA) (2015), 'Memorandum on the recent clashes between Mundari and Bari tribes in Kworijik-Luri 18–19 January 2015', *South Sudan Nation*, 15 February, http://www.southsudannation.com/memorandum-on-the-recent-clashes-between-mundari-and-bari-tribes-in-kworijik-luri-jan-18th-19th-2015.

Copnall, James (2014), *A Poisonous Thorn in Our Hearts: Sudan and South Sudan's Bitter and Incomplete Divorce* (London: Hurst).

Cormack, Zoe (2016), 'Borders are galaxies: Interpreting contestations over local administrative boundaries in South Sudan', *Africa* 86, no. 3: 504–27.

Craze, Joshua (2013), 'Unclear lines: State and non-state actors in Abyei', in Mareike Schomerus, Lotje de Vries and Christopher Vaughan (eds), *The Borderlands of South Sudan: Authority and Identity in Contemporary and Historical Perspectives* (New York, NY: Palgrave Macmillan).

Deng, David K. (2011), 'Land belongs to the community: Demystifying the "global land grab" in Southern Sudan', *Land Deal Politics Initiative*, http://www.future-agricultures.org/wp-content/uploads/pdf-archive/David%20K%20Deng%20Final.pdf.

Deng, Francis M. (1995), *War of Visions: Conflict of Identities in the Sudan* (Washington, DC: The Brookings Institution).

de Smedt, Johan V. A. (2011), 'The Nubis of Kibera: A social history of the Nubians and Kibera slums', PhD diss., Leiden University.

de Vries, Lotje (2014), 'Un mode de gouvernement mis en échec: dynamiques de conflit au Soudan du Sud, au-delà de la crise politique et humanitaire', *Politique africaine* 3: 159–75.

Englebert, Pierre (2009), *Africa: Unity, Sovereignty and Sorrow* (Boulder, CO: Lynne Riener).

Hamid, Gamal M. (2002), *Localizing the Local: Reflections on the Experience of Local Authorities in Sudan* (Riyadh: Arab Urban Development Institute (AUDI)).

Herbst, Jeffrey (2000), *States and Power in Africa: Comparative Lessons in Authority and Control* (Princeton, NJ: Princeton University Press).

Hirblinger, Andreas T. (2015), 'Land, political subjectivity and conflict in post-CPA Southern Sudan', *Journal of Eastern African Studies* 9, no. 4: 704–22.

International Crisis Group (ICG) (2016), *South Sudan's South: Conflict in the Equatorias; International Crisis Group Report No. 236 / Africa*, https://www.crisisgroup.org/africa/horn-africa/south-sudan/south-sudan-s-south-conflict-equatorias.

Investment Promotion Act of 2009.

Johnson, Douglas H. (1998), 'The Sudan People's Liberation Army and the problem of factionalism', in Christopher Clapham (ed.), *African Guerrillas* (Oxford: James Currey).

— (2012), 'The Heglig oil dispute between Sudan and South Sudan', *Journal of Eastern African Studies* 6, no. 3: 561–9.

— (2014), 'Federalism in the history of South Sudanese political thought', Public Lecture, Centre for Peace and Development Studies, Juba University.

Jok, Jok Madut (2011), *Diversity, Unity, and Nation Building in South Sudan* (Washington, DC: US Institute of Peace).

Justin, Peter H. and Mathijs van Leeuwen (2016), 'The politics of displacement-related land conflict in Yei River County, South Sudan', *The Journal of Modern African Studies* 54, no. 3: 419–42.

Land Act of 2009.

Lentz, Carola (2000), 'Colonial constructions and African initiatives: The history of ethnicity in Northwestern Ghana', *Ethnos* 65, no. 1: 107–36.

— (2013), *Land, Mobility and Belonging in West Africa* (Bloomington, IN: Indiana University Press).

Lentz, Carola, Paul Nugent and Kenneth King (eds) (2000), *Ethnicity in Ghana: The Limits of Invention* (Basingstoke, UK: St. Martin's).

Leonardi, Cherry (2011), 'Paying "buckets of blood" for the land: Moral debates over economy, war and state in Southern Sudan', *The Journal of Modern African Studies* 49, no. 2: 215–40.

— (2013), *Dealing with Government in South Sudan: Histories of Chiefship, Community and State* (Woodbridge, UK: Boydell and Brewer).

Leonardi, Cherry and Martina Santschi (2016), *Land Governance and Boundary Disputes in South Sudan and Northern Uganda* (Nairobi: Rift Valley Institute).

Local Government Act of 2009.

Lund, Christian and Catherine Boone (2013), 'Introduction: Land politics in Africa – constituting authority over territory, property and persons', *Africa* 83, no. 1: 1–13.

Mamdani, Mahmood (1996), *Citizen and Subject: Contemporary Africa and the Legacy of Late Colonialism* (Princeton, NJ: Princeton University Press).

— (2001), 'Beyond settler and native as political identities: Overcoming the political legacy of colonialism', *Comparative Studies in Society and History* 43, no. 4: 651–64.

Mayom, Jok P. (2015, October 4), 'President Kiir creates 28 states of South Sudan', *Gurtong*, http://gurtong.net/ECM/Editorial/tabid/124/ctl/ArticleView/mid/519/articleId/17532/President-Kiir-Creates-28-States-In-South-Sudan.aspx.

Natsios, Andrew (2015), 'South Sudan – Sudan', in Emmanuel Brunet–Jailly (ed.), *Border Disputes: A Global Encyclopedia* (Santa Barbara, CA: ABC-CLIO).

O'Fahey, R. S. and J. L. Spaulding (1974), *Kingdoms of the Sudan* (London: Methuen and Co.).

Pendle, Naomi (2014), 'Interrupting the balance: Reconsidering the complexities of conflict in South Sudan', *Disasters* 38, no. 2: 227–48.

Radio Tamazug (2015), 'Ethnic balance with 42% increased Dinka-land if 28 states approved', *South Sudan Nation,* http://www.southsudannation.com/ethnic-balance-with-42-increased-dinka-land-if-28-states-approved.

Schomerus, Marieke (2008), *Violent Legacies: Insecurity in Sudan's Central and Eastern Equatoria* (Geneva: Small Arms Survey).

Schomerus, Marieke and Lovise Aalen (eds) (2016), *Considering the State: Perspectives on South Sudan's Subdivision and the Federalism Debate* (London: Overseas Development Institute).

Schomerus, Marieke and Lotje de Vries (2014), 'Improvising border security: "A situation of security pluralism" along South Sudan's borders with the Democratic Republic of Congo', *Security Dialogue* 45, no. 3: 279–94.

Schomerus, Marieke, Lotje de Vries and Christopher Vaughan (2013), 'Introduction: Negotiating borders, defining South Sudan', in Christopher Vaughan, Marieke Schomerus and Lotje de Vries (eds), *The Borderlands of South Sudan: Authority and Identity in Contemporary and Historical Perspectives* (New York, NY: Palgrave Macmillan).

Smith, Brian C. (1979), 'The measurement of decentralisation', *International Review of Administrative Sciences* 45, no. 3: 214–22.

Sudan Tribune (2015), 'South Sudan president expands states to 28 as opposition accuses him of deal violation', 3 October, http://sudantribune.com/spip.php?article56581.

Transitional Constitution of Central Equatoria State of 2011.

Voors, Maarten J. and Erwin H. Bulte (2014), 'Conflict and the evolution of institutions: Unbundling institutions at the local level in Burundi', *Journal of Peace Research* 51, no. 4: 455–69.

Acknowledgements

This chapter is an output of the research programme 'Grounding Land Governance', which is funded by NWO–WOTRO Science for Global Development, The Netherlands. The authors also acknowledge support from the DFG-funded Collaborative Research Centre SFB700 (C10). For more information on NWO–WOTRO see https://www.nwo.nl/en/about-nwo/organisation/nwo-domains/wotro.

CHAPTER 3

Constructive Management of Diversity

A Strategy for Conflict Resolution and Nation-Building

Francis M. Deng and Daniel J. M. Deng

Introduction

African states were carved out of diverse racial, ethnic and cultural entities, which gave them a pluralistic configuration. African countries are largely composites of distinct ethnic units, many of which likely described themselves as nations in their own right at the time of colonisation (Ndulo and Kent, 1996). The tendency of colonial powers to treat certain groups and regions preferentially in social and economic development led to considerable disparities among ethnic groups in the shaping and sharing of power, national wealth, social services and development opportunities. This unequal treatment also effectively sowed the seeds for future conflict between different ethnic groups.

At independence, African governments frequently adopted the constitutional models and governance structures prescribed by their colonisers. Disparities in the distribution of power and representation were generally not addressed, and national unity was often emphasised to the detriment of ethnic minorities, who sought to be distinctively recognised and to participate in constitutional and governing frameworks. In a number of African countries, the tension between the colonially anointed governing élite and other ethnic groups subject to their rule culminated in internal armed conflicts, demands for democracy and, in some cases, calls for self-determination – to choose their own form of government or even to secede.

Modelling their post-independence constitutions on those of European colonial powers meant that many African constitutions did not provide mechanisms for managing diversity, as these provisions were less necessary in Europe's more homogenous societies. For an African constitution to effectively mitigate and manage conflicts, it is important that the constitution reflects the fundamental cultural values and norms of *all* of a nation's peoples and builds on a national worldview as the starting point for constitutionalism. For the most part, African governments, including that of South Sudan, have not yet achieved this standard of constitutionalism.

Constitutionalism as a normative framework for governing

Constitutionalism is the basis of a normative framework for governance, and is more than the constitutional document itself. Yash Ghai (1972) defines a constitution as the embodiment of all the political, economic, social, cultural, religious and historical forces conditioning the perception of a people, and powerful enough to be accepted as a guide for future action. Muna Ndulo and Robert Kent (1996) observe that, though a constitution should represent the basic structure of an organised society, in post-colonial Africa a constitution has become a single document outlining the exercise of political power. However, as the former Chief Justice of South Africa, Ismail Mohamed, once observed:

> The constitution of a nation is not simply a statute which mechani-
> cally defines the structures of government and the relations between
> the government and the governed, it is a 'mirror of the national
> soul', the identification of the ideals and aspirations of a nation,
> the articulation of the values binding its people and disciplining its
> government. (Hatchard, 2001: 210)

It is widely agreed that a constitution should reflect the spirit of the nation, and that people should see themselves and their aspirations represented by the text (Deng, 2010). The best constitutions are those owned by their people. This is why it is so important that the system of governance as provided for in the constitution should reflect the cultural values, norms and patterns of behaviour of a country's people.

Constitutionalism as a process of good governance

Gilbert Khadiagala has questioned whether African states will transcend the troubling legacy of constitutions without constitutionalism (Deng, 2010). Just as some form of a legal system exists in every society, big or small, to ensure peace, justice, security and order, so constitutionalism is a phenom-enon that characterises every community. Constitutionalism is essentially a mechanism of governance by which people, individuals and groups exercise power through institutions, use resources and achieve certain outcomes.

Constitutionalism is governed by fundamental concepts that set the rules for participating in the shaping and sharing of values. It should be seen as a living process that is constantly evolving with the participation of its people to promote their ownership of governing frameworks. While constitution-alism has conventionally been understood to constrain the use and abuse of power by the state, to promote fundamental rights and freedoms, and maintain the rule of law, it is increasingly being viewed as emphasising the promotion of human dignity.

In describing new trends in constitutionalism, Julius Ihonvbere (2002) notes that political discourses are no longer élite-driven. Whereas once they were an instrument for domination and violence, they are now also a weapon for liberation and include many important issues such as human rights, gender equality and social justice. He cites growing international support for civil society, increased sophistication of civil society in using human rights instruments, and coalition-building among non-state actors worldwide as encouraging popular participation and dialogue, and increasing focus on civic education in the constitutional process (Ihonvbere, 2002). Ihonvbere considers this participatory dimension as critical to the legitimacy and effectiveness of constitutions in the future.

Nevertheless, in most African states the overwhelming majority of the people never see a copy of their constitution, and studying and understanding the constitution remains an élite advantage. The success of future African constitutionalism will depend largely on leaders' ability to adopt bottom-up (rather than top-down) forms of decision-making and participatory models. Governments will need to ensure that citizens feel a sense of ownership and are both participants in and beneficiaries of the process. There are growing demands for this form of constitutionalism both from citizens wishing to improve government accountability and from the broader international com-munity, with possibilities for adapting through feedback, debate and dialogue.

The colonial roots of African constitutions

A cursory look at the way independence constitutions were drafted affirms the heavy influence of colonial powers in the process. Some constitutions were written by constituent assemblies, but they ultimately had to be approved by colonial powers before independence was granted. As Merwin Young notes, both colonial administrators and public opinion in the imperial metropolitan countries 'demanded that departure, if it had to come, should be honourable. Inevitably, honour was measured by the closeness of the apparent approximation of metropolitan institutions' (Young, 1994: 210). Proximity between the institutions of imperial powers and newly independent countries was particularly true of those countries that joined the Commonwealth. As Julius Go observes:

> The constitutions of Ghana, Kenya, Nigeria, and Tanganyika had to be signed by the British monarch with the same stroke that granted independence. The local political élites who took part in constitution-making or lent their support to the new constitutions appeared themselves eager to draw upon metropolitan models. (Go, 2002: 561–62)

Ben Nwabueze (1973) called this the hidden impulse of a foreign constituent power working through small groups of converts to western constitutionalism.

Focusing on constitutionalism in West Africa, Victor LeVine (1986) argued that post-independence constitutions failed not so much because they were imported, but because new African leaders lacked the will to implement them or used them for their own political ambitions. To the extent that these constitutions expressed the ideals of democracy, fundamental rights and civil liberties grounded in European political culture, it is true that African leaders did not live up to their precepts. To the extent that their principles failed to address the unique needs of the African situation, they were perhaps not fully implementable.

LeVine explained the similarity between post-independence constitutions in francophone African countries and those of the former colonial power on the basis that some African leaders had become so 'French' that they were unable to replace the French model with something more authentic to the local reality. Herein lies the paradox of African independence: instead of devising a system that would be oriented to African normative principles and institutions of governance, colonial bonds continued to dominate, with the colonial state embodying the preferred model of national leadership post-independence.

In hindsight, we can see that the adoption of colonial constitutional models was not always optional and that African leaders may have accepted these constitutional models as an imperative under the circumstances (Ghai, 1972). A movement towards more 'homegrown' constitutions was seen in many African countries after independence, with governments amending their constitutions for various reasons. In some cases, constitutional changes may have been an attempt to create distance from colonial influence, whereas in other instances it was to consolidate a ruler's power.

Far from recognising the diversities of the African states and their legitimising cultural characteristics, imported western-oriented constitutions fostered a homogenising, centralised unitary state that was intolerant of differing political and cultural aspirations. There was little African cultural flavour in constitutionalism, the administration of justice, or governance.

Constitutional adaptations to the African context

The experience of Africa's first independent nations shows the turbulence of the ideological tensions and conflicts involved in developing a constitutionalism tailored to these newly independent countries. In succession, Sudan, Ghana, Tanzania, Zambia and others stumbled in the early years of independence. In 1956, Sudan adopted a liberal Westminster model constitution at independence, but within three years it fell under military dictatorship and, later, one-party rule, socialism and Islamic fundamentalism. Similarly, while Ghana established regionalism at independence, Nkrumah soon consolidated power in the centre and created a one-party state.

In Tanzania, Nyerere denounced modelling constitutionalism on that of other countries, ostensibly in favour of constitutionalism and institutions designed to serve the needs of Tanzanians. He tried to pursue the principles of an African governance system inspired by the ideals of indigenous cultural values. He believed in African socialism and pursued a policy of *ujamaa* (socialism and self-reliance). Similarly, Zambia gained independence under a Westminster model constitution but soon became a one-party state. The one-party system created profound and pervasive restrictions on Zambians' political and civil rights, and politicians retained power at all cost to preserve their access to state resources (Ndulo and Kent, 1996).

These examples demonstrate the conflict between efforts to authenticate African systems of constitutionalism and governance, and attempts by post-independence leaders to disguise their efforts to bolster their personal power and ambitions as resistance to colonial ideological, political and economic concepts. The challenge for Africa now is to bridge that gap, with a focus on how to constructively and effectively manage identity conflicts, the utilisation of natural resources and the distribution of economic rents by the state.

Dynamics of identification

It is not diversity of identities that generates conflicts, but a failure to effectively *manage* diversity. Common bases of identity include race, ethnicity, culture, language and religion. Territory is often a complementary or affirmative factor. How a group identifies itself (subjectively) and how others identify the group (objectively) may differ. Identity is complex and there is often much myth behind labels, with frequent overlapping of identities and labels.

Two discrepancies might arise in the identity debate. The first concerns differences between subjective and objective identification. The second has to do with the degree to which individual or group identities are represented in the collective national identity framework. To the extent that identity issues impinge on the interests of other citizens, identity enters the public domain and ceases to be purely personal or exclusive to the group.

Several themes need to be highlighted regarding identity as a factor in conflict. First, identity is a subjective concept; it is what people perceive themselves to be that principally establishes who they are. Second, an important element of such subjective identification is, rightly or wrongly, genetically related, and in many instances this associates identity with ethnicity or race. Third, recognising identity as subjective does not mean that it cannot be challenged by objective facts or criteria, and it's possible for one's personal identification to differ from what others may view one to be. To the extent that this discrepancy has public policy implications, it ceases to be a private matter. Fourth, as a matter of policy, if one or more exclusive identities conflict with the requirements of national unity in a framework of diverse identities, then one of three options is generally pursued: (i) remove the divisive elements and redefine the national identity framework, (ii) design a system of coexistence among diverse groups through constitutional arrangements that accommodate at least the more significant diversities (perhaps through greater local autonomy or self-governance) or (iii) allow the diverse elements to go their separate ways and break away from the existing nation-state.

As David Lake and Donald Rothchild observe, 'competition for resources typically lies at the heart of ethnic conflict. Property rights, jobs, scholarships, educational admissions, language rights, government contracts, and development allocations all confer benefits on individuals and groups' (Lake and Rothchild, 1996: 44). Incompatibilities can relate either to tangible issues, such as the distribution of power, wealth and other assets, or to intangible issues, including how a nation is defined and what role various entities within that nation play. It is not how individuals and groups perceive themselves that is relevant, but how the *state* recognises those self-perceptions in its common framework, and what status is given to the groups concerned.

To avoid repeating the mistakes of the past, it is necessary to understand the historical roots of diversity and disparity challenges. Ethnic relations in African countries can be viewed contextually and historically with special reference to three phases: i) the pre-colonial period, ii) the colonial period and iii) the post-independence period. Each period has shaped the distribution of power, wealth, social services and development opportunities.

During the African pre-colonial period, the European concept of the state did not exist. Neighbours inevitably interacted with one another, most often co-operatively, and also came into conflict, but over time developed mechanisms to mitigate, manage and resolve conflict. That separate identities and intercommunal relations persisted in pre-colonial Africa evidences indigenous groups' mutual interest in peaceful, or at least functional, coexistence. A variety of societies operated during this pre-colonial era, ranging from acephalous (stateless) societies to centralised kingdoms, but the fundamental principles of consensual decision-making were widely shared, as documented in the literature of African jurisprudential and governance systems (Deng, 1971; Elias, 1956).

Under colonialism, centralised systems were favoured, shifting power and resources away from local arrangements. Colonial governments often favoured certain groups and regions over others, which led to a stratification of power and socio-economic opportunities that had not existed in pre-colonial times. This generated tensions that were contained by an emphasis on law and order, and resort to the colonial administration's relative neutrality as an outsider to internal identity dynamics. With independence, certain groups and regions (often those that had been favoured under colonialism and that had received power, resources, public services and development opportunities) became associated with the central government, leading to greater disparity. Since the process was geared towards the centre, it empowered those who shared characteristics with the holders of national power, while marginalising and alienating those who did not. The local balance of power that had sustained mutuality of interest in coexistence was disrupted, as identity groups struggled for control of the central power.

At their worst, identity conflicts can be zero-sum and, in some cases, they can become genocidal contests for national identity. What is at stake is the quality and level of participation of different groups in the political, civil, economic, social and cultural life of the country. If some groups can capture the machinery of state, they can use the identity of the state to justify their dominance over other national groups. Moreover, this is in part a practical expression of the indigenous social configuration of kinship expressing itself through constituency-responsive government, leading to a reasonable counter-demand to work against tribalism.

The larger the gap between the attributes considered representative of the national identity and the characteristics of a subordinated group, the more subordinated groups will feel threatened and the greater their resentment and animosity towards the dominant group. Depending on the degree of disparity, the resulting discrimination may trigger a separatist contest for the redefining and restructuring of the national framework to make it more accommodating of the groups that are excluded or grossly discriminated against. Since this would imply a major change in the status quo, there is often resistance from the dominant group.

National unity and self-determination

Preserving national unity is generally preferred. It may be in the interests of unity for countries to promote self-determination – not in order to encourage secession, but to create conditions that make unity attractive to potential secessionists. National integration should be cautiously promoted, with short-term efforts undertaken to strengthen governance through a constitutional system based on coexistence within a broader national framework of unity and diversity that accommodates all groups. With this goal in mind, whether the resulting constitutional system is labelled 'autonomy', 'federalism' or 'confederalism' is less important than effective distribution of powers and catering to the needs and rights of all peoples, regardless of their racial, ethnic, religious or cultural differences.

At present, in virtually all African countries confronted with national identity crises, demands for self-determination by ethno-regional groups run against the official objective of preserving national unity. Such calls for self-determination are therefore generally suppressed. Despite increasing global concern about minority rights, there is very little that the international community can do to protect minority rights in practice, due to the application of the principle of territorial integrity and preservation of colonial borders, as determined by the Organisation of African Unity (OAU), reaffirmed by the African Union (AU) and endorsed by the UN.

While the legal and political debates on the nature, scope and application of self-determination generate some of the most critical discussions on nation-building, even adversaries would agree that self-determination is a powerful force for change. In the name of self-determination, countries have emerged or broken apart, and colonised peoples have freed themselves from the shackles of foreign domination. The struggle for self-determination is today largely between ethnic minorities and governments and has embroiled countries in decades of civil war, causing mass atrocities and humanitarian disasters, and aggravating poverty. These civil wars have crippled not only nations, but entire regions.

As African communities and their respective nation-states exert efforts to manage identity conflicts, embrace democratic principles, promote human rights and strive for equitable economic development, self-determination contests generate paradoxes. At times, self-determination debates may indicate progress, while at other times they appear to hamper progress. The crucial issue is whether self-determination can serve as an incentive for equitable unification, or if it rather acts as a negative force for disintegration. Both outcomes are real possibilities, as experience shows.

Therefore, a delicate balance must be struck between the rights of states to protect their sovereignty, territorial integrity and national unity on the one hand, and the exercise of self-determination on the other (Hannum, 2002). It is becoming clear that neither of these principles of international law is absolute. Indeed, it is in this tension that one can find the root of so many sovereignty-based conflicts in Africa. Perceived as a threat to state sovereignty and territorial integrity, self-determination movements are rarely met with approval. However, if it's recognised that self-determination can be applied internally to maintain national unity, positive outcomes could be achieved.

Debate has grown around the scope and application of self-determination to distinct people, typically racial, ethnic and linguistic minorities living within states that have already achieved independence. Confusion arises because of the lack of consensus around how to define 'self-determination' and who can exercise it. Most scholars (for example Cassese, 1995; Kuol, 1996; Michalska, 1990; Partsch, 1982; Kiwanuka, 1988) believe that international law does not yet affirm that minority populations have a separate right permitting them to demand secession, independence or sovereignty over their natural resources. These populations may, however, exercise a right to self-determination together with the whole population of a country, and they may demand equal participation and access to governance in their country. Minority populations also have recourse to redress their oppression or discrimination and are afforded a number of protections under international law. Some scholars, such as Joseph von Komlossy (2000), see the guarantee and effective enjoyment of these rights as one way to implement and exercise 'internal' self-determination. Other forms include autonomy, federalism and other power-sharing arrangements.

Simon Chesterman et al. (2000) go further to describe minority rights, internal power-sharing, territorial autonomy and self-administration as the basis for a new, more modem interpretation of the right to self-determination in a post-colonial world. Abdullahi An-Na'im (1993) and S. James Anaya (1996) articulate a broader interpretation and application of self-determination, a position which has been increasingly debated as governments consider its application to indigenous peoples living within existing independent states. For example, many indigenous peoples, particularly in the context of international forums such as the UN and the Organisation of American States, have argued that the International Covenant on Civil and Political Rights (ICCPR) and the International Covenant on Economic, Social and Cultural Rights (ICESCR) affirms their *distinct* right to self-determination. That is, they assert that their right to self-determination includes not only a right to equal participation in the governance of the larger nation-state but also a right to increased self-governance and autonomy over their territories, and even permanent sovereignty over their natural resources within their country.

Much of the debate around self-determination is fed by differing legal, political and cultural perspectives that inform the inquiry into who might constitute a 'people'. These perspectives similarly permeate the related discussions about what constitutes 'peoplehood', or the 'self' in 'self-determination'. As discussed by R. S. Bhulla:

> The kind of 'self' that legitimately invokes the right to self-determination is a preliminary question before the right can be applied. This self, which is an indigenous self, is distinct from other selves. It is this distinctness which is a starting point in granting the right of self-determination. (Bhulla, 1990: 98)

Nonetheless, a legal, or even political or moral, right to secession by groups within an independent state is generally not desired by the international community. It is preferred that self-determination for distinct groups should be exercised within the existing national framework of the state where they reside. In practice, the distinct group in question might demand full democratic participation in the governance of the state in which it lives, and full protection of its minority rights to preserve and transmit its culture, language, group identities, traditional religions, family, social organisations, and so on. In cases where minority rights cannot be fully accommodated through the national governing framework of the state, minority groups may demand greater control over their destinies through different forms of self-governance, local autonomy and self-administration.

Demands for self-determination include the right of minority groups to be governed by their own institutions, to develop the natural resources within their territories, and to determine their economic destiny. Importantly, all of these forms of self-determination are carried out within the territorial unit of the state, and therefore still maintain territorial integrity. Consequently, the implementation of these remedies and the exercise of these forms of governance are often considered tantamount to the realisation of 'internal self-determination'.

While considering the tensions between the sometimes competing principles of self-determination and territorial integrity, some argue that where the government of an independent state discharges its responsibilities towards its citizens through democracy and respect for fundamental human rights and civil liberties, the sovereignty and territorial integrity of the nation should be respected. Conversely, if the government systematically and grossly fails to protect the fundamental freedoms and human rights of a distinct group within the country's borders, its territorial integrity and sovereignty will be violable to some extent, and the group in question may be entitled to secede and form an independent state.

Indeed, groups are unlikely to opt for the difficult and costly struggle for secession, or the prospects of political and economic uncertainties of independent statehood, if their rights are recognised and respected within an existing state. Rather than fragmentation, people tend to prefer a representative government concerned with their needs and accommodating them in a democratic framework.

That said, Africa has a legitimate fear that the open exercise of the right to self-determination by various groups within national borders could lead to the disintegration of many African states. Indeed, it was to forestall a pervasive threat to national unity that the OAU resolved in 1964 that colonial borders be maintained under the *uti possidetis* principle. This territorial integrity principle became one of the OAU's sacrosanct principles and has been widely recognised and reinforced. The AU and the wider international community still maintain that political stability and the territorial integrity of states are important values that must be safeguarded. Granting the right of self-determination to all ethnic groups and minorities with grievances, however valid, could

> bring about a major disruption of international relations, a serious threat to peace and the fragmentation of States into a myriad of entities that would often be unable to survive. One should therefore tread cautiously in this area and appreciate the concern of states for their stability and integrity. (Cassese, 1995: 328)

Given the choice between repressing the right to self-determination and risking violence, and addressing legitimate demands for recognition and equality in shaping and sharing power within a national framework, pragmatism would suggest the latter as the more prudent course of action. Although this seems obvious, the practical response to it in Africa is not so clear-cut.

An-Na'im notes the irony here, which is that the 'independent nation-state, once perceived as the essential prerequisite for the achievement of the peoples' right to self-determination, is now seen by many people(s) as a major obstacle to the realisation of that right' (An-Na'im, 1993: 106). He asserts that unity cannot be pursued at all costs, that it can only be secured by managing diversity within the nation and thereby securing the support of the people. It follows that unity can be best achieved when a national framework is put in place that allows each distinct community to preserve its identity while also participating, without discrimination, in the economic development and the national distribution of power. In other words, unity needs to be consensual and the national framework must address the genuine concerns of the constituent groups to reconcile conflicting visions for the nation, and to foster mutual interest in national identity.

The dilemma of the two Sudans

The Comprehensive Peace Agreement (CPA) of 2005 between the Government of Sudan and the Sudan People's Liberation Movement and Sudan People's Liberation Army (SPLM/A), which granted southern Sudan the right of self-determination and put it on a path that led to the creation of independent South Sudan, was an anomaly in Africa, but one that was quite enthusiastically accepted on the continent and internationally. Yet, it has generated tensions and even conflict within South Sudan and between Sudan and South Sudan.

The dilemma of the two Sudans is that, despite their partition through Southern Sudan's secession, the two countries remain bound together by internal conflicts that spill over their borders. The identity conflicts that characterised Sudan since its independence in 1956 linger on after the CPA and partition of the country. The Sudanese government has long been accused of committing mass atrocities and even genocide, for which President Omar al-Bashir and several senior government officials have been indicted by the International Criminal Court (ICC). Since the resumption of civil war in South Sudan in December 2013, the South Sudanese government is alleged to have committed similar crimes, prompting calls for sanctions against the perpetrators. There is a clear need for a better approach to preventing atrocities through constructive management of diversity.

As noted above, it is not merely identity differences that cause genocidal conflicts, but how these differences are managed, especially regarding how people are differentiated and how they are politically, economically and socially stratified. In acutely divided nations, some groups are marginalised, discriminated against, excluded, de-humanised, and denied the dignity and rights that normally accrue from citizenship. These extremely disadvantaged groups may react by engaging in conflict as a result of not having constructive, peaceful alternatives for pursuing equitable belonging in the nation. Resistance generates counter-reactions that can result in genocide or mass atrocities, depending on the balance of power.

It is somewhat counter-intuitive that more powerful groups feel an existential threat from weaker antagonists, which then motivates them to react with a genocidal onslaught. Unless the perpetrators are defeated militarily, it usually takes the involvement of a third party to mediate, to ensure both equity and face-saving. Of course, the irony of this is that the subjectivity with which people define themselves, as opposed to the objective realities of their identities, often means that what divides parties in conflict has more to do with myth than reality. The sides in a conflict are often not as different from one another as they think they are. In the medium to long term, public policy strategies should expose and correct these distorted perceptions.

One of the authors, Francis Deng, has been to Bosnia at the peak of the Balkan conflict, to Central Asia amidst civil wars, and to a number of African countries undergoing internal conflicts. Often, when you look at the people in conflict, it is not easy to tell who belongs to which side of the divide. Years ago, he met many people in Burundi, some of whom looked typically Tutsi, in the way we are told Tutsis look, some of whom looked Hutu, and many whom he could not differentiate as either Tutsi or Hutu. He asked the Minister of Foreign Affairs whether it was always possible to tell a Tutsi from a Hutu. His response was, 'Yes, but with a margin of error of 35 per cent.' That margin of error is common in many parts of the world torn apart by internal conflicts.

A Sudanese scholar who heard the story of this experience commented that in Sudan, especially in regions like Darfur, Southern Kordofan and Blue Nile, the margin of error would be even larger. The Missiriya, who are in conflict with the Dinka, have among them children of Dinka mothers and grandmothers who, when the Missiriya and the Dinka fight, are often at the front line to prove their questionable Arab identity. And, of course, the Dinka and the Nuer, who are the predominant parties to the current conflict, are virtually one people, ethnically and culturally.

If we take the challenge posed by identity conflicts as one of how to manage diversity constructively, to promote inclusivity, equality, a sense of belonging on an equal footing, pride in being a citizen who enjoys the dignity and rights associated with citizenship, then it follows that this is an objective which no self-respecting government can question, far less oppose. This provides a positive basis of engagement with other governments, the AU and the UN.

Diversity is a global phenomenon, and hardly any country can claim to be fully homogeneous. Even Somalia, recognised as one of the most homogeneous countries in the world, has been torn apart by clan differences and conflicting views on Islam. Not all countries characterised by diversity experience genocidal identity conflicts, and countries manage diversity with varying degrees of success. Sadly, Sudan is one of the countries that has failed dismally in constructively managing diversity.

Since independence in 1956, Sudan has intermittently been at war with itself. The CPA offered the people of Sudan and South Sudan the first opportunity to resolve the chronic crisis of national identity. Unfortunately, the implementation of the CPA has been at best ambivalent and half-hearted, and in some cases antagonistic. The legacy of the north–south conflict and the ongoing tensions in the implementation of the CPA have undoubtedly contributed to the crisis South Sudan is now experiencing.

South Sudan has struggled to build a system that can constructively manage diversity, adhere to the principles of democracy and good governance, respect fundamental rights and civil liberties, promote equitable socio-economic development and encourage gender equality. These are essential elements of the Vision of the New Sudan, which the SPLM/A under its late leader, John Garang, had championed since its inception. The challenge is to achieve these principles in practice.

Conclusion

The concept of 'unity in diversity' is predicated on the assumption that a successful nation is one that can manage its diversity in a manner that builds on its richness and does not alienate any group. Constitutional processes, substantive provisions and public institutions (both traditional and modern) that are deliberately modelled to encourage cultural liberty are more likely to assist in creating a national commonality essential to nation-building. When groups are excluded or discriminated against, identity conflicts result. What makes such conflicts particularly resistant to resolution is that identity is rooted in complex and multidimensional psychological, historical and cultural factors that are intangible and often difficult to define.

Social scientists, mediators and facilitators in such conflicts tend to focus on tangible interests that are more amenable to negotiation, such as representation, wealth-sharing and power-sharing, than on questions of identity. Although these interests feature very strongly in identity-based conflicts, they overshadow the deeper elements at stake, and any peace agreement that focuses exclusively on those interests is unlikely to survive in the long term. Identity issues are often unaddressed in peace agreements as, while deeply felt, they are highly intractable. It is frequently what is not said, rather than what is said, that causes division.

For constitutionalism to succeed, stakeholders must address these deeper identity conflicts. To ignore them is to deny certain groups the full exercise of their right to self-determination, which can endanger the peace, security and stability of the country. One way of reconciling discrepancies between subjectivity and objectivity of identification, and between exclusivity and inclusivity in the national identity framework, is to recognise groups that are self-defining, while at the same time foster an inclusive sense of nationhood that builds on shared objective factors. This would allow for a gradual process of equitable integration, as opposed to asymmetrical assimilation.

The crisis of national identity and the persistent failure to manage diversity constructively since independence raises several contextual challenges for both Sudan and South Sudan. First, South Sudan should correct the mistakes of the past by adopting a national identity framework that promotes inclusivity, equality and dignity for all ethnic groups, without discrimination. Second, Sudan should address the genuine grievances of its marginalised regions to ensure regional autonomy similar to the one Southern Sudan enjoyed during the CPA interim period, without the option of secession, but with equitable participation at the centre. Third, South Sudan must endeavour to make effective use of its indigenous cultural values and institutional structures as the essence of genuine self-determination. These indigenous principles can be used to develop norms and operational measures for conflict prevention, management and resolution. They can also be used to reinforce international human rights standards, to promote equitable socio-economic development, and reform gender relations towards mutual respect and equality between the sexes.

In conclusion, the South Sudanese must ask and answer some tough questions about what has gone wrong in South Sudan, how it can be corrected, and what is needed to ensure that is does not recur. South Sudan needs optimism – not blind faith, but an enlightened approach guided by prudent and well-informed strategy and action.

References

Abubakar, Dauda (2001), 'Ethnic identity, democratisation and the future of the African state', *African Issues* 29, no. 1/2: 31–6.

An-Na'im, Abdullahi A. (1993), 'The national question: Secession and constitutionalism; The mediation of competing claims to self-determination', in Douglas Greenberg et al. (eds), *Constitutionalism and Democracy: Transitions in the Contemporary World* (New York, NY: Oxford University Press).

Anaya, S. James (1996), *Indigenous Peoples in International Law* (Oxford: Oxford University Press).

Baregu, Mwesiga (1997), 'Nyerere', in John Middleton (ed.), *Encyclopedia of Africa: South of the Sahara* (New York, NY: C. Scribner's Sons).

Bhulla, R. S. (1990), 'The right of self-determination in international law', in William Twining (ed.), *Issues of Self-Determination* (Aberdeen: Aberdeen University Press.

Cassese, Antonio (1995), *Self-Determination of Peoples: A Legal Appraisal* (Cambridge: Cambridge University Press).

Chesterman, Simon, Tom Farer and Timothy D. Sisk (2000), *Competing Claims: Self-Determination and Security in the United Nations*, Research Report, International Peace Academy.

DeGeorge, R. T. (2001), 'The myth and the right of collective self-determination', in William Twining (ed.), *Issues of Self-Determination* (Aberdeen: Aberdeen University Press).

Deng, Francis M. (1971), *Tradition and Modernisation: A Challenge for Law Among the Dinka of the Sudan* (Yale, CT: Yale University Press).

— (2010), *Sudan on the Brink: Self-Determination and National Unity* (New York, NY: Fordham University Press and the Center for International Health and Cooperation).

Elias, Taslim O. (1956), *The Nature of African Customary Law* (Manchester: Manchester University Press).

Ghai, Yash (1972), 'Constitutions and the political order in East Africa', *International and Comparative Law Quarterly* 21, no. 3: 403–34.

Go, Julian (2002), 'Modeling the state: Post-colonial constitutions in Asia and Africa', *Southeast Asian Studies* 39, no. 4: 558–83.

Hannum, Hurst (2002), 'A principled response to ethnic self-determination claims', in Guðmundur S. Alfreðsson, Maria Stavropoulou (eds), *Justice Pending: Indigenous Peoples and Other Good Causes* (The Hague: Martinus Nijhoff Publishers).

Hatchard, John (2001), 'Some lessons on constitution-making from Zimbabwe', *Journal of African Law* 45, no. 2: 210–16.

Ihonvbere, Julius O. (2002), 'Military disengagement from politics and constitutionalism in Africa: Challenges and opportunities', in Ricardo Renè Laremont (ed.), *The Causes of War and the Consequences of Peacekeeping in Africa* (Portsmouth, NH: Heinemann).

Khadiagala, Gilbert (2009), 'Botswana: Bridging tradition and modernisation', in Francis M. Deng (ed.), *Self-Determination and National Unity: The Crisis of Divided Nations in Africa* (n.p.: Africa Research and Publications).

Kiwanuka, Richard N. (1988), 'The meaning of "people" in the African Charter on Human and Peoples' Rights', *The American Journal of International Law* 82, no. 1: 80–101.

Komlossy, Joseph von (2000), 'Self-determination in relation to the principle: National integrity of a state', in Y. N. Kly and D. Kly (eds), *In Pursuit of the Right to Self-Determination: Collected Papers and Proceedings of the First International Conference on the Right to Self-Determination and the United Nations* (Geneva: Clarity Press).

Kuol, M. A. (1996), 'Self-determination after independence: The case of modern Sudan', LLM diss., University of Essex.

Lake, David A. and Donald S. Rothchild (1996), 'Containing fear: The origins and management of ethnic conflict', *International Security* 21, no. 2: 41–75.

LeVine, Victor T. (1986), 'The state of formerly French West Africa', in Peter Duignan and Robert H. Jackson (eds), *Politics and Government in African States, 1960–1985* (London: Croom Helm).

Michalska, Anna (1990), 'The rights of peoples to self-determination in international law', in William Twining, *Issues of Self-Determination* (Aberdeen: Aberdeen University Press).

Ndulo, Muna (2010), 'Ethnic diversity: A challenge to African democratic governance', in Francis M. Deng, *Sudan on the Brink: Self-Determination and National Unity* (New York, NY: Fordham University Press and the Center for International Health and Cooperation).

Ndulo, Muna and Robert B. Kent (1996), 'Constitutionalism in Zambia: Past, present and future', *Journal of African Law* 40, no. 2: 256–78.

Nwabueze, Ben O. (1973), *Constitutionalism in the Emergent States* (London: C. Hurst).

Partsch, Karl J. (1982), 'Fundamental Principles of Human Rights', in Karel Vasak and Philip Alston (eds), *The International Dimensions of Human Rights* (Westport, CT: Greenwood Press).

Shivji, Issa (2001), 'The right of peoples to self-determination, an African perspective' in William Twining (ed.), *Issues of Self-Determination* (Aberdeen: Aberdeen University Press).

Young, Merwin C. (1994), *The African Colonial State in Comparative Perspective* (New Haven, CT: Yale University Press).

CHAPTER 4

How Electoral Systems and Systems of Government Can Contribute to Peace and Managing Diversity

Sarah Logan

Introduction

In December 2013, less than three years after South Sudan gained independence, civil war broke out between forces loyal to President Salva Kiir and opposition rebels affiliated with former vice-president Riek Machar. While violence was initially limited to the capital, Juba, it has since become widespread across much of the country. The toll exacted by the strife is staggering: tens of thousands have died in the conflict or as a result of the conflict, and over one third of South Sudan's population has been displaced, fleeing to refugee camps in neighbouring countries or to the protection of civilian camps within South Sudan (Reuters, 2018).

Repeated attempts to reach a lasting peace settlement have failed. The Intergovernmental Authority on Development (IGAD), Eastern Africa's eight-country trade bloc, has facilitated multiple rounds of peace talks, which have been held in member states. Little implementation was seen of the August 2015 Agreement on the Resolution of the Conflict in the Republic of South Sudan (ARCSS); similarly, the Agreement on the Cessation of Hostilities, Protection of Civilians and Humanitarian Access reached in December 2017 has not yet yielded any change (Reuters, 2018). While fighting continues and a ceasefire remains elusive, the humanitarian situation in South Sudan gets increasingly urgent and desperate.

In this dire context, it is vital to assess what led to the current conflict and why it is proving so intractable, so that lessons can be learned to mitigate the risk of conflict recurring in South Sudan in the future.

This chapter explores several governance features that may have left South Sudan particularly vulnerable to leadership crises and ethnic-based conflict. In the context of the country's notable ethnic diversity and division and a need for power-sharing and group autonomy, this chapter will consider, first, South Sudan's electoral system and, second, its system of government. It will argue that, while the mixed electoral system used appears appropriate for the country's context, adopting a presidential system was ill-advised and rendered South Sudan more prone to ethnic division, poor leadership and regime collapse. It will then look at the repudiation of promised federalism under the 2011 Transitional Constitution of the Republic of South Sudan (TCSS), and how this reversal of approach aggravated the country's susceptibility to ethnic conflict. Finally, it will discuss how weak institutions, partly as a result of undeveloped separation of powers, have been unable to constrain individual leaders in South Sudan. This chapter will attempt to provide recommendations on how some key changes to the country's governance arrangements could ensure a more peaceful and democratic future for South Sudan.

Governing diverse and divided societies

South Sudan is a particularly diverse and divided society, with an estimated 64 ethnic groups living in relatively geographically concentrated areas. These groups have a history of being fragmented, although a degree of unity and common purpose existed while southern leaders lobbied Khartoum to establish a federal system and, later, during the fight for independence after it became apparent that Khartoum would not accede to southern demands for federalism. A number of other African countries, notably Angola and Mozambique, experienced similar post-independence collapse into civil war after they failed to unite their plural societies into nation-states with a shared identity (Naanen, 1995). More recently, Angola and Mozambique have begun to successfully build stronger, more united, national identities.

Two factors are considered essential for establishing and maintaining peace and democracy in diverse and divided societies: power-sharing and group autonomy. Power-sharing entails representation of all significant groups in political decision-making, and group autonomy necessitates that all significant groups have the authority to manage their internal affairs (Lijphart, 2004). Both elements are vital for inclusiveness of participation and interests, and for diversity to be accommodated through empowering groups to determine their own norms and laws regarding issues crucial to groups' well-being within the state without requiring negotiation with the national majority (Poirier, 2008).

Importantly, autonomy can be territorial or non-territorial, or a combination of both, with institutions established on regional and local levels as well as at the national level (Poirier, 2008). In practice, to avoid isolation and a lack of national unity, a balance is needed between self-rule and joint rule, through representative participation in national level consultations and institutions, including quotas in the civil service, police, army and judiciary (Poirier, 2008).

A range of electoral systems and systems of government exist, and their suitability varies depending on the context. For South Sudan, with its ethnic diversity and division, the extent to which each system promotes power-sharing and group autonomy should be of utmost importance when determining which systems to adopt.

Which electoral system should be used? The politics of ethnic majority

Electing the national legislative assembly

Electoral systems vary in a number of dimensions, including district size, ballot structures, number of seats in the national assembly, open or closed lists and, most importantly, electoral formula (Norris, 1997). The three broad categories of legislative electoral systems are majoritarian, proportional representation and intermediate systems. Where a society is diverse and divided, electing a broadly representative legislature is critical for ensuring that all groups are adequately represented and all voices are heard. Which system is adopted has a considerable impact. Indeed, studies have found that the type of electoral system used appears more important than the system of government in preventing and resolving ethnic conflict (Saideman et al., 2002).

In majoritarian systems, a single member constituency-based approach is used and the winner must secure a simple majority of votes to win. Some systems require the winner to achieve an absolute majority, i.e. more than 50 per cent of the vote, even if this necessitates a second run-off ballot between the two candidates who secured the highest share of votes in the first round (Norris, 1997). The purpose of majoritarian systems is to, somewhat artificially, create an effective working parliamentary majority for government. A notable drawback is that this 'winner takes all' approach encourages the formation of a two-party system and undermines broad representation by excluding minority parties from government (Norris, 1997). It also raises the stakes of securing the presidency, as winners and losers are defined as such for the duration of the term in office (Linz, 1990). Given that majoritarian systems exclude some significant groups and raise tensions and the risk of inter-group conflict, it is unsurprising that there is clear scholarly consensus against using majoritarian systems in divided societies (Lijphart, 2004).

Proportional representation is able to achieve a broadly representative legislature with a high degree of proportionality and minority representation, while also treating all groups equally by not using special protection measures (Lijphart, 2004). Under this system, the composition of parliament should resemble that of the country at large, and the inclusion of more political parties in the legislature encourages conciliatory cooperation and coalition-building (Norris, 1997). Proportional representation has been found to reduce ethnic violence in divided societies by lowering the stakes of the 'winner takes all' system, allowing ethnic groups access to decision-makers, and providing a mechanism by which policies potentially harmful to minorities may be blocked (Saideman et al., 2002).

Either an open- or closed-list system can be used with proportional representation: with open lists, voters list the parties in order of preference, whereas with closed lists voters select only one party on the ballot. The closed-list system is easier to understand and operate, and can promote the formation of stronger and more cohesive political parties (Lijphart, 2004).

However, a notable criticism of proportional representation with a closed list concerns accountability. Since candidates are chosen from party lists determined by their political parties, they may be more accountable to and more likely to serve their political parties than the people, particularly in poorer countries, where being included on the party list likely means the difference between political candidates living in poverty or escaping poverty (Friedman, 2015). Further, without a constituency-based structure, elected representatives' responsiveness and accountability to clearly identified constituencies and sets of voters may be weak, as has been seen in South Africa.

These concerns may be overcome in several ways, such as using multi-member districts that are not too large. Limiting district size facilitates closer connections between voters and elected representatives (Lijphart, 2004), and the multi-member arrangement allows for a degree of proportionality while maintaining a constituency base.

Intermediate systems, either semi-proportional or mixed, may be another option. There is notable variation with these systems, but they generally offer a degree of proportionality and minority representation, although less so than pure proportional representation systems. Complications may arise in semi-proportional systems in determining which minority groups should benefit from the special protection measures, such as representation quotas, that may be used in these systems. Mixed systems may allow for a combination of majoritarian and proportional representation, as in Germany where the legislative assembly is elected partially using a majoritarian, constituency-based system, and then 'topped up' using candidates drawn from party lists to achieve overall proportional representation.

South Sudan uses a similar mixed system. Both the lower and upper legislative houses are elected using a mixed system: 60 per cent of seats are appointed using a majoritarian, constituency-based system, and the remaining 40 per cent are allocated on a proportional representation basis from national- and state-level party lists (TCSS, Art. 60(2)). This arrangement appears suited for South Sudan's context as it offers a degree of proportionality while still retaining the accountability of a constituency-based system.

It is unclear, however, how effectively this system has worked in practice to strengthen accountability or to align the composition of the legislative assembly with that of the country at large. It is vital that an assessment of this is undertaken and any obstacles undermining the functioning of the system be addressed. Further, the estimated ideal size of a lower legislative house is thought to be the cubed root of the population size which, using a population estimate of 12.23 million for South Sudan, should be around 230 seats. However, South Sudan's lower house has some 400 seats, thereby considerably exceeding the recommended number of seats and posing a notable additional cost to the public wage bill.

The case for a House of Nationalities

Along similar lines to Ethiopia's House of Federation, as outlined in this book by John Young in his chapter on Ethiopia's ethnic federalism, a number of commentators have called for the establishment of a House of Nationalities in South Sudan. It is envisioned that the House of Nationalities would comprise a representative from each of South Sudan's 64 or so ethnic groups, with geographically divided ethnic communities having a representative for each distinct section, bringing the anticipated number of members to around 90 (House of Nationalities, n.d.). Importantly, this arrangement would ensure equal representation between all ethnic groups, regardless of their size, thereby serving as a balance to majority dominance and giving all ethnic groups an equal stake (Mou Run, 2011). Equal representation of ethnic groups would differ from Ethiopia's House of Federation, which has one member representing each ethnic group plus an additional member for each one million people of each ethnic group – a system that favours greater representation for larger ethnic groups.

Similar to Ethiopia's House of Federation, the House of Nationalities would enable all ethnic groups to meet in mutual respect and dignity, and would act primarily as a mechanism to resolve inter-ethnic disputes, giving consideration to customary law (House of Nationalities, n.d.). In this way, the House of Nationalities could contribute tangibly to promoting respect for all different ethnic groups, to building a South Sudanese identity vital for strengthening South Sudan's nation-building, and achieving sustainable peace in the country (House of Nationalities, n.d.).

The House of Nationalities could serve as an upper house of the national legislature (as with Ethiopia's House of Federation) if it is determined that its mandate include certain legislative tasks, such as approval of laws or policies affecting the communities or on matters such as communal land or customary law. Members could either be voted in directly or appointed by regional or state councils (as in Ethiopia).

South Sudan already has a bicameral parliament, with the National Legislative Assembly serving as the lower house and the Council of States serving as the upper house of the National Legislature. There are 50 members of the Council of States, 30 of which are former Southern Sudanese representatives in Sudan's Council of States plus 20 representatives appointed by the president (TCSS, Art. 58). The Council of States is tasked with, among other things, overseeing national reconstruction; development and equitable service delivery in the states; monitoring the repatriation, relief, resettlement, rehabilitation and reintegration of returnees and internally displaced persons; and legislating for the promotion of a culture of peace, reconciliation and communal harmony among all the people of the states (TCSS, Art. 59).

Under the existing arrangement, membership of the Council of States does not reflect the ethnic composition of South Sudan, with most ethnic groups not represented, nor are members elected by the people or by their elected representatives in regional or state councils. Importantly, the Council of States does not have a specific mandate to mediate inter-ethnic conflict or disputes between different ethnic groups, which is a glaring lost opportunity for a conflict resolution mechanism that could strengthen inter-ethnic cooperation and nation-building in South Sudan.

The benefits of a parliamentary system

The two major systems of government are parliamentary and presidential, with a range of hybrid versions that combine aspects of the two. There is general consensus that, in diverse and divided societies, a parliamentary system lends itself to greater power-sharing in the executive, vital for ensuring that a plurality of voices and interests are represented. The vast majority of democracies are based on parliamentary rather than presidential systems, with the United States being the only example of a long-running presidential democracy (Linz, 1990).

Power and accountability

Under parliamentary systems, parliament is supreme as the only directly and democratically elected institution, tasked with appointing the executive and holding the executive to account. Parliamentary systems have a prime minister as head of government, who tends to be the leader of the party or coalition with a majority in parliament, and who is appointed by parliament rather than by direct vote. A constitutional monarch or ceremonial president with limited political power may serve as head of state (Lijphart, 2004). Where a presidential position is used, it is vital that his/her appointment is made by parliament rather than by direct vote, to ensure accountability to parliament and to prevent the creation of a competing pole of political power that may undermine parliament or the prime minister. A preferable arrangement, used in South Africa, has the head of government also serving as head of state, with this position being appointed by and accountable to parliament (Lijphart, 2004).

In parliamentary systems, the prime minister and a collegial cabinet together form the executive, and they serve as long as they have the confidence of parliament. In this way, power is intrinsically linked to accountability. The prime minister and cabinet members are equally accountable to parliament, an arrangement that encourages debate and independent voices within the executive (Linz, 1990). This multi-member executive, with little hierarchical divide between the prime minister and other cabinet members, enables greater collective decision-making and guards against the excesses of individual members.

Presidential systems differ in these respects. First, presidential systems have a one-person executive in the form of the president, who directs the composition of government and has a degree of law-making authority (Carey, 2005). The president's discretionary appointments include cabinet ministers, central bankers, senior military figures and high court judges (Siaroff, 2003). Additionally, the president may play a central role in foreign policy and/or have broad emergency or decree powers which may be valid for an unlimited time, although in most presidential systems decrees must be submitted to parliament for conversion into law after a period of time (Siaroff, 2003).

This arrangement gives the president more extensive authority than the powers rendered to a prime minister under a parliamentary system. The hierarchical divide between the president and cabinet members does not encourage debate or independent views as cabinet members know they can be fired at the president's whim (Linz, 1990). Second, a president is generally directly elected by voters which, while giving voters a say in who leads the executive, often results in presidents believing they have a direct mandate to rule with relatively unconstrained powers (Fakir, 2014). This is so even where a president wins by only a slender margin (Linz, 1990). The president is not accountable to parliament, and parliament can do little to restrain a president's excesses.

The dangers of a powerful and unrestrained president have been particularly apparent in South Sudan, where the powers concentrated in the presidency under the TCSS are greater than those normally vested in presidential systems. Indeed, the presidential powers in South Sudan more closely resemble those common under autocracies than democracies (Cope, 2014). The result is an unreasonable amount of authority being placed in an individual office and, more specifically, in an individual person. The risks of this arrangement are substantial, especially considering that the president is not accountable to parliament or subject to legislative confidence in South Sudan.

Term limits and removal from office

How long a prime minister or president can serve, and how they can be removed from office, are crucial aspects of these systems. Fixed term limits are a unique feature of presidential systems. While they serve to enforce

change in executive leadership, they also entrench short-term policy horizons, breaking policy processes into discontinuous periods based on terms,
and posing an obstacle to more long-term planning (Linz, 1990). This policy
discontinuity can be particularly harmful to the implementation of development policies in developing countries. Given that a prime minister serves
in his/her capacity as representative of his/her political party and is subject
to legislative confidence, allowing for relatively easy recall from office, term
limits are not used in parliamentary systems.

In parliamentary systems, the prime minister and/or the cabinet can be
removed by parliament by a vote of no confidence using a simple majority,
a feature that serves as a vital check on executive power. A government can
also be forced to resign or to call an election, or a vote of no confidence can
be passed in a certain policy. This facility allows for a degree of government
responsiveness to changing circumstances (Linz, 1990). These parliamentary
checks on executive power under parliamentarianism have proven attractive to
countries undergoing significant political changes (Radon and Logan, 2014).

As the president is not subject to legislative confidence in presidential
systems, the legislature cannot similarly remove the president by a vote of
no confidence. Instead, impeachment proceedings must be instituted, which
are comparable to indictment for a crime and only possible in instances of
gross misconduct or serious legal violations by the president.

In South Sudan, a hybrid arrangement has been adopted, with the lower
legislative house being able to pass a vote of no confidence to recall the
vice-president and/or any cabinet minister (TCSS, Art. 57(i)). However, the
president is not similarly bound by legislative confidence, thereby requiring
impeachment to remove him/her from office.

The recognised grounds for impeachment in South Sudan are high
treason, gross violation of the constitution or gross misconduct in relation
to national affairs, and a resolution must be passed by two-thirds of the
national assembly charging the president on one or more of these grounds
(TCSS, Art. 103(2)). A panel comprised of three Supreme Court justices must
then be established by the president of the Supreme Court to consider the
charges against the president. If the panel convicts the president, they must
notify the national assembly and the president is deemed to have forfeited
office (TCSS, Art. 103(5)). Grounds of mental infirmity or physical incapacity
may also suffice, with a report submitted by a medical board to be used as
evidence (TCSS, Art. 103(6)). It is apparent from the above that impeachment of the president in South Sudan is a difficult outcome to achieve,
requiring a two-thirds majority of the national assembly rather than a simple

majority, as well as a sufficiently independent judiciary to stand against the executive.

As votes of no confidence under parliamentary systems are relatively easy to secure, this feature has sometimes been criticised for promoting cabinet instability. However, cabinet reshuffles are also relatively common under presidential systems. Further, given the durability of parliamentary governments, cabinet reshuffles often trigger only superficial volatility that doesn't threaten regime stability (Linz, 1990). In contrast, presidential systems have been seen to be more prone to regime crisis, authoritarian collapse or democratic breakdown than parliamentarianism (Carey, 2005).

Given the features of presidential systems outlined above, it is unsurprising perhaps that presidential systems tend to be more common among newer democracies and countries with histories of political and constitutional instability (Carey, 2005). Indeed, since the end of the Second World War, two-thirds of developing countries that established parliamentary governments have made the transition to democracy successfully, whereas no developing country implementing a presidential system transitioned to democracy without experiencing coups or other regime crises or constitutional collapses (Linz, 1990).

By favouring a system where the president has notably greater executive powers than is generally the case in presidential systems, not subjecting the president to legislative confidence, and stipulating an impeachment process with little chance of successfully removing a president, South Sudan established a system vulnerable to political crisis. Specifically, it monopolised executive power in the president and situated the president beyond reach of parliamentary removal or impeachment, heightening the stakes of securing the presidency and encouraging political wrangling.

The advantages of federalism: managing diversity

As outlined in more detail elsewhere in this book, federalism is considered to be an effective way to promote autonomy in divided societies with geographically concentrated communal groups, as in the case of South Sudan (Lijphart, 2004). Studies have found that more concentrated groups are more likely to engage in conflict, including separatist efforts (Ayres and Saideman, 2000). Federalism, however, has also been seen to reduce interethnic conflict by giving groups greater control over outcomes (Saideman et al., 2002).

In a display of commitment to federalism, the 2005 Interim Constitution of South Sudan (ICSS) had installed three levels of government in Southern Sudan: national, state and local government, with some degree of executive, legislative and judicial authority at all three levels.[1] It was thought that such a system would serve the diverse people of South Sudan and help address the chronic lack of development in the southern states. Additionally, by distributing power relatively evenly among government actors with competing interests, it made it more difficult for any single government actor to gain a strangle-hold on power (Cope, 2014).

Despite federalism having been a key motivator behind South Sudan's drive for independence, the South Sudanese government abrogated their promise of federalism after independence, instead centralising the system under the TCSS. This move away from federalism further aggravated the vulnerabilities created by a powerful and relatively unconstrained presidency.

Backtracking on promises of federalism was problematic for two key reasons. First, it betrayed the people of South Sudan, who had fought a brutal struggle for independence so that they could establish for themselves the federal system of government that Khartoum had rejected. Instead, South Sudan's own post-independence government imposed a system on them comparable to that enforced by Khartoum. Second, South Sudan's considerable ethnic diversity and varying social and economic development challenges across the country meant that federalism (and decentralisation) was a more suitable system for South Sudan to adopt.

Reneging on promises of federalism

South Sudan's post-independence government may have been motivated by several factors when centralising government into a unitary structure and consolidating authority in the presidency. First, after having achieved independence from the north through secession, South Sudanese leaders must naturally have feared the possibility of further fragmentation in the south if federalism was adopted. After all, Southern Sudan had used its chance of limited self-rule to push for secession and full independence – what was to stop any of the southern states from doing the same, especially those states with the oil wealth that South Sudan so desperately needed? Despite undoubtedly recognising the need for federalism, the South Sudanese government may have seen a strong centralised government as the only way to keep the country together and South Sudan's oil firmly under central government control.

Second, in post-independent countries where the ruling classes have no personal wealth, as in South Sudan, there has often been a tendency for leaders to use state resources for personal gain (Campbell, 2014). Holding political office in South Sudan has become synonymous with having easy access to state resources and using public authority for factional and personal advantage (de Waal, 2014). Controlling state resources in as few hands as possible would enable the lucky few to secure maximum benefit for themselves, likely motivating élites to support greater centralisation. Self-enrichment is, at least partly, also attributable to a failure to construct a system of appropriate recognition and compensation for those who fought for independence and who were denied educational and commercial opportunities during the war.

The move away from federalism was reflected in the TCSS with the South Sudanese national government inheriting, en masse, all of the powers previously held by the Sudanese national government. Without any concurrent devolution of additional powers to states or local governments, the powers of sub-national governments diminished significantly relative to the national government. The accumulation of authority in the central executive appears to have been done consciously, notwithstanding the known dangers of highly centralised systems. This arrangement set South Sudan up to suffer many of the hazards often associated with strong centralised governments in Africa and elsewhere, namely abuse of power, high levels of corruption, regional inequalities and oppression of minorities and other vulnerable groups (Kimenyi, 2012).

The about-turn on federalism undoubtedly marginalised and angered minority groups, who had stood to participate more in the country's governance under federalism than a centralised government. Broken trust in the post-independence government led to allegiances reverting from national interests back to ethnic lines. Disenfranchised groups became more likely to resort to violence to increase their political and economic participation and to minimise further marginalisation (Kimenyi, 2012). The result was simmering instability in the country.

The case for federalism in South Sudan

In order to fully consider the diversity of interests among South Sudan's peoples and to address the varying development challenges facing different parts of the country, sub-national governments with a degree of autonomy are vital. A federal system that empowers state governments to enact their own laws and policies on issues of state importance (to the extent that they do not conflict with national codes) is preferable to decentralisation, where sub-national governments merely implement laws and policies adopted at the national level. Both federalism and decentralisation are thought to bring government closer to the people, empowering state and local governments to be more responsive to community needs and enabling them to better deliver basic services. Local governance also facilitates greater public participation and government accountability (Kimenyi, 2012).

There are, however, drawbacks of both federalism and decentralisation. Larger sub-national governments with greater powers and responsibilities may create a more expensive administration and demand greater human resource capacity than may be available in some developing countries, particularly in more rural and undeveloped areas. A deficit of qualified personnel at sub-national government levels may in fact be detrimental as inexperienced officials may be more likely to, for example, make poor decisions. Additionally, as noted in the chapter by Joseph Siegle and Patrick O'Mahony, pursuing decentralisation (or federalism for that matter) can in fact increase the risk of conflict and secessionism in instances where regional actors are armed and not fully controlled by the central government, local revenue sources are highly inequitable (such as in natural resource rich countries), politics are ethnic-based, or there is a history of ethnic conflict. They also note that the greater local legitimacy and responsiveness offered by decentralisation is unlikely to materialise in non-democratic settings.

Many consider that the risks posed by federalism and decentralisation could be outweighed by the importance of allowing limited local self-rule. Consequently, a number of countries are currently moving towards a more decentralised system of governance. However, as Siegle and O'Mahony suggest, it is important that a comprehensive risk assessment be undertaken to examine possible impacts of decentralisation (or federalism) on ethnic divisions and political polarisation before a decision to adopt such a system is made.

Weak institutions unable to restrain individual leaders

South Sudan's national government is composed of the common three branches of state: the executive, the legislature and the judiciary. Ideally, these branches should function independently of each other and, through a system of separation of powers, act as checks and balances on one another.

Separation of powers safeguards against authoritarianism by dividing government functions and powers between the distinct branches of government, ensuring that no one branch acts beyond its mandate or exercises the core functions of another branch (NCSL, n.d.). In this way, checks and balances constrain the excesses of each branch. In South Sudan, while a degree of separation of powers is entrenched in the TCSS, the principle is yet to fully take root or be effectively implemented in practice.

The ruling Sudan People's Liberation Movement (SPLM) heavily dominates the national legislative assembly. For a party to be eligible for the seats appointed by proportional representation, they need to secure a minimum of 4 per cent of the overall vote. This threshold is relatively high, making it difficult for opposition parties to gain many of the proportional representation seats. However, it is arguable that a 4 per cent threshold is important to encourage inter-ethnic cooperation, as a lower threshold would allow ethnic-based politics to dominate. In any event, the SPLM's domination of the national legislative assembly means that it lacks the strength and political independence to constrain the executive.

As far as laws and policies regarding the communities or customary law, communal land or culture are concerned, the Council of States should act as a check on the executive. However, in practice, it is not sufficiently independent to play this role, particularly given that the 20 non-legacy members are appointed by the president. If a more dynamic and representative upper house were established, along the lines of the House of Nationalities outlined above, members would likely be empowered to act more in the interests of their various ethnic groups rather than in the interests of the executive.

Similarly, although entrenched in the constitution as being independent of the executive and legislature, the country's judiciary is new and fragile and does not operate independently of the executive in practice. On several occasions, South Sudanese executive and military members have been reported to have unduly interfered in and influenced the exercise of judicial functions (ICJ, 2013). Executive and military meddling in judicial matters in South Sudan negates the judiciary's constitutional independence and prevents it from functioning as the check on the executive that it is intended to be.

It is apparent that much work is still needed in South Sudan to achieve proper separation of powers, both in the constitution and in practice. It is only through establishing an effective separation of powers and systems that facilitate representation and independence that institutions in the country will have the constitutional mandate to develop and become strong enough to counter-balance individual politicians and military leaders.

The way forward

Assess the mixed electoral system and slim down the size of the national legislative assembly

The mixed legislative electoral system currently used, where 60 per cent of seats in the lower house are appointed on a majoritarian, constituency basis, and the remaining 40 per cent of seats are appointed on a proportional representation basis from national and state-level party lists, appears appropriate for South Sudan's diverse and divided context. However, it is vital that an assessment be undertaken to see to what extent the system is, in practice, achieving the proportionality of representation and accountability it promises. There is also a need to reduce the size of the lower house, as best practice suggests that the ideal number of seats in the lower house be the cubed root of the population size. In South Sudan's case, assuming a population of about 12.23 million, this suggests the lower house should have about 230 seats, which is notably smaller than the current size of 400, which is cumbersome and expensive.

Replace the Council of States with a House of Nationalities

The Council of States should be replaced with a House of Nationalities, which would ensure the equal representation of all ethnic groups in South Sudan, regardless of size, creating a platform where all ethnic groups can meet in mutual respect and dignity, thereby promoting nation-building. In addition to playing a legislative role as far as laws and policies concerning the communities, communal land, customary law or culture are concerned, the House of Nationalities should be tasked with resolving inter-ethnic conflict and mediating disputes between the ethnic groups, a vital contribution to achieving sustainable peace in South Sudan.

Shifts towards federalism and parliamentarianism

Where possible, governance arrangements embodied in the national constitution should be modified to promote systems that ensure power-sharing and group autonomy across ethnic groups in order to reduce inter-ethnic tensions and the government's susceptibility to authoritarian collapse. A shift away from the current centralised, presidential system and towards parliamentarianism with a degree of sub-national autonomy is imperative. Notably, the president should be made subject to legislative confidence in the same way as the vice-president and cabinet. It is vital that a comprehensive risk assessment be carried out before decentralisation or federalism is adopted, to ensure that such a system would be overall advantageous to South Sudan and not merely aggravate ethnic divisions and political polarisation.

Development and capacity building

Conflict is more likely when a country's level of development is low and when the economy is in decline (Saideman et al., 2002). The issue of underdevelopment and lack of access to basic services needs urgent attention, and is a continuing trigger for instability and conflict in the country (Yasin, 2008). There is an immediate need to deal with the country's dire humanitarian emergency, in addition to its broader social and economic development needs.

Much investment in building the country's human resources, primarily through improved education, will be necessary, in order to grow and diversify the country's economy and reduce its reliance on oil. To achieve sustainable economic growth, South Sudan needs to look beyond exporting oil; rather, local manufacturing and services industries need to be developed so that employment opportunities may be created. Investing in capacity building for civil servants is also needed to raise adequate human capacity to effectively implement a federal system of government, and to ensure that all branches of government may develop the strength and independence necessary for a separation of powers to operate in practice.

Fiscal federalism

To achieve and maintain peace, it is necessary for South Sudan to adopt a system of fiscal federalism that can fairly and effectively serve the country, both while oil revenues remain dominant and after oil revenues decline. Resource transfers to states will be crucial to provide the resources needed to fulfil their functions under a federal government. These transfers should be rule-based and not subject to negotiation, so that fair redistribution among regions can be achieved (Yasin, 2008). The dangers of fiscal federalism in oil-dependent contexts need to be considered, including the unpredictable and exhaustible nature of oil revenues that complicates multi-year budgeting (Yasin, 2008).

Notes

1   Under the ICSS, the 'national' government was the Sudanese national government in Khartoum, since Southern Sudan was still part of Sudan during 2005–2011.

References

Ayres, R. William and Stephen Saideman (2000), 'Is separatism as contagious as the common cold or as cancer? Testing international and domestic explanations', *Nationalism and Ethnic Politics* 6, no. 3: 81–113.

Campbell, Horace G. (2014), 'The political struggle in South Sudan', *Counterpunch*, 10 January, http://www.counterpunch.org/2014/01/10/the-political-struggle-in-south-sudan.

Carey, John M. (2005), 'Presidential versus parliamentary government', in Claude Menard and Mary M. Shirley (eds), *Handbook of New Institutional Economics* (Dordrecht, Netherlands: Springer).

Cope, Kevin (2014), 'South Sudan's constitutional bait-and-switch', *Jurist*, 14 February, http://jurist.org/forum/2014/02/kevin-cope-south-sudan.php.

de Waal, Alex (2014), 'When kleptocracy becomes insolvent: Brute causes of the civil war in South Sudan', *African Affairs* 113, no. 452: 347–69.

Fakir, Ebrahim (2014), 'The electoral system: Is there vice or virtue in reform?', *Daily Maverick*, 22 May, https://www.dailymaverick.co.za/opinionista/2014-05-22-the-electoral-system-is-there-vice-or-virtue-in-reform/#.WmHcuVSFjBK.

Friedman, Steven (2015), *The System's Not to Blame? Electoral Systems, Power and Accountability*, report commissioned by the Council for the Advancement of the South African Constitution (CASAC).

House of Nationalities (n.d.), *A Space for Preserving the Diversity and the Unity of the South Of Sudan*, http://www.houseofnationalities.org/1_what_is_hon.asp.

ICJ (2013), *South Sudan: An Independent Judiciary in an Independent State?* (Geneva: International Commission of Jurists).

Interim Constitution of Southern Sudan of 2005.

Kimenyi, Mwangi S. (2012), *Making Federalism Work in South Sudan* (Washington, DC: The Brookings Institution, Africa Growth Initiative).

Lijphart, Arend (2004), 'Constitutional design for divided societies', *Journal of Democracy* 15, no. 2: 96–109.

Linz, Juan Jose (1990), 'The perils of presidentialism', *Journal of Democracy* 1, no. 1: 51–69.

Mou Run, R. (2011), 'Why House of Nationalities is necessary in South Sudan: Why the Constitutional Review Commission should enshrine the House of Nationalities into our nascent polity', *Gurtong*, 14 February, http://www.gurtong.net/ECM/Editorial/tabid/124/ctl/ArticleView/mid/519/articleId/4871/Why-House-Of-Nationalities-Is-Necessary-in-South-Sudan.aspx.

Naanen, Ben (1995), 'Oil-producing minorities and the restructuring of Nigerian federalism: The case of the Ogoni people', *The Journal of Commonwealth and Comparative Politics* 33, no. 1: 46–78.

NCSL (n.d.), *National Conference of State Legislatures: Separation of powers; An Overview*, http://www.ncsl.org/research/about-state-legislatures/separation-of-powers-an-overview.aspx.

Norris, Pippa (1997), 'Choosing electoral systems: Proportional, majoritarian and mixed systems', *International Political Science Review* 18, no. 3: 297–312.

Poirier, Johanne (2008), 'Autonomy and diversity', in Ronald L. Watts and Rupak Chattopadhyay (eds), *Building on and Accommodating Diversities* (New Delhi: Viva Books).

Radon, Jenik and Sarah Logan (2014), 'South Sudan: Governance arrangements, war, and peace', *Journal of International Affairs* 68, no. 1: 149–67.

Reuters (2018), 'U.S., Britain and Norway warn South Sudan parties over ceasefire violations', 2 January, https://www.reuters.com/article/us-southsudan-unrest/u-s-britain-and-norway-warn-south-sudan-parties-over-ceasefire-violations-idUSKBN1ER0LM.

Saideman, Stephen M. et al. (2002), 'Democratisation, political institutions, and ethnic conflict: A pooled time-series analysis, 1985–98', *Comparative Political Studies* 35, no. 1: 103–29.

Siaroff, Alan (2003), 'Comparative presidencies: The inadequacy of the presidential, semi-presidential and parliamentary distinction', *European Journal of Political Research* 42, no. 3: 287–312.

Sudan Tribune (2011), 'Council of State delegates elect speaker, take oaths', 6 August, http://www.sudantribune.com/Council-of-State-delegates-elect,39755.

Transitional Constitution of the Republic of South Sudan of 2011.

Yasin, Amin S. (2008), *How Effective Is Fiscal Federalism in Conflict Resolution in Sudan?*, paper prepared for the African Economic Conference, Tunis.

CHAPTER 5

The Federalism-Decentralisation-Peace Nexus in South Sudan[1]

Luka Biong Deng Kuol

Introduction

South Sudan came into being on 9 July 2011 and later became the newest member of the UN and the African Union. Its recognition came out of the long political struggle of the southern Sudanese for freedom and justice and the commitment of the international community to the implementation of the 2005 Comprehensive Peace Agreement (CPA). The CPA had granted the people of Southern Sudan the right of self-determination and put them on a path to the 2011 independence referendum. The birth of this new state came with the optimism that South Sudan would be both a viable state and would contribute to promoting peace and stability in the region. Despite this optimism, some analysts painted a bleak picture of the world's newest country and described it as a failed state even before it was born. South Sudan found itself caught in four traps: the conflict trap, the natural resources trap, the land-locked country with bad neighbours trap, and prolonged bad governance trap (Collier, 2007). It had been at war since before Sudanese independence in 1956, it has abundant natural resources, it is a land-locked country in a tough neighbourhood, and it is a small country with poor governance and policies inherited from both Sudanese and colonial rule.

In December 2013, less than three years after South Sudan's creation in July 2011, civil war resumed, reinforcing the idea that a country that has experienced war is vulnerable to relapsing into war. The conflict started within the ruling Sudan People's Liberation Movement (SPLM) and quickly turned into a national crisis blamed on the country's ethnic diversity. The civil war has brought enormous human suffering to South Sudan, causing the greatest refugee crisis on earth. The UN Office for the Coordination of Humanitarian Affairs (UNOCHA) estimated that half of South Sudan's population had either fled the country or starved by the end of 2017. It's estimated that the cost to South Sudan of the conflict persisting for another five years is between US$22.3 billion and US$28 billion, with the human cost of conflict in terms of death, hunger and disease amounting to US$6 billion (Frontier Economics, 2015). South Sudan's neighbours and the international community are equally affected, as they could save up to US$53 billion and US$30 billion, respectively, during the same time period if the conflict is resolved soon (Frontier Economics, 2015).

This chapter examines the system of government and its evolution in Sudan and South Sudan, and the relationship between systems of government and violent conflict. The first section reviews the literature on the relationship between systems of government, conflict and diversity. The second section discusses the evolution of systems of government in Sudan and South Sudan. The third section assesses South Sudan's current system of government in the context of federalism, and the final section concludes with policy implications for post-conflict South Sudan.

Systems of government: Conflict, diversity and public goods

There are divergent views about the causes of civil war in the literature on conflict. Some believe that greed or grievance are determinants. The few researchers who have analysed pre-war situations tend to impute the causes of civil war to socio-economic and political grievances generated by unpopular policies and/or extractive institutions that serve the interests of élites. During civil war, economic agendas and greed dominate, sustaining the warring parties' activities through privatisation of violence, insurgency and counter-insurgency warfare. Another strand of thought attributes the cause of conflict to relative deprivation caused by bad governance and the grievance that this produces (Gurr, 1970). For example, David Keen (1998) argues that much of the violence in contemporary conflicts is initiated not by greed, but by the élite trying to deflect political threats by inciting violent conflict.

Quality of governance is considered a key determinant of conflict, and the *type* of government rather than the *system* of government is thought to be of greater importance. Types of government are concerned with power *sources* in terms of who rules and participates in government, and systems of government concern power *structures* in terms of how power is distributed within government. Whereas the type of government deals with the *policy* arrangements for power, the system of government concerns *constitutional* arrangements of power. Most civil war studies have focused on types of government rather than systems of government, but recently the debate about the relation between conflict and governance has become a discussion about systems of government. There is a wide spectrum of systems of government (unitary, federation, confederation, league and alliance) within a constitutional continuum, determined by the level of centralisation of state sovereignty (Hueglin and Fenna, 2015). The three most common systems of government are: (i) unitary, such as in the Netherlands, France and Spain, (ii) federation, such as in USA and Germany, and (iii) confederation, such as the European Union. Briefly, unitary systems are characterised by the allocation of powers to one centre, whereas federal systems allocate powers to a number of centres. Confederations render constitutional supremacy and sovereignty to member states, rather than retaining these at the centre, as in federalism.

Federalism

The advantages and disadvantages of federalism

When comparing unitary and federal systems' ability to safeguard the interests of minorities, manage diversity and overcome mistrust and conflict, there is a growing literature that favours federalism. Zahar (2014) argues that federal systems are better than majoritarian unitary structures in helping to address distrust as countries move from civil war to peace. In the past, federalism has been adopted either to mitigate foreign threats or domestic insurrection, as in the USA (Hamilton et al., 2005), or to avoid aggressive and pre-emptive wars among states, as in Europe (Smith 1995).

Some contend that federalism does not prevent or eliminate conflict, but that it provides an institutional framework within which diversity can be better *managed* and acceptable solutions for resolving conflict can be found (Gagnon, 1993). Some argue that if federalism is properly designed and implemented, it can make government more responsive and accountable to citizens, improve transparency, encourage civic engagement and foster political stability (Siegle and O'Mahony, 2006). Since it is able to bring government closer to the people than unitary systems can, it is also likely to have greater allocative efficiency and better match development resources to local needs (Elazar, 1987). Selassie (2003) argues that federalism is a compromise option, as it lies mid-way between the extremes of a state promoting complete assimilation and suppressing diversity on the one hand, and the disintegration of the state on the other. Federalism is more appealing than unitary systems as it offers a constitutional mechanism that embraces, tolerates, protects and promotes diversity (Fleiner et al., 2002). Federalism is also more likely to strengthen the state by reducing the risk of civil war resulting from repressive policies aimed at distinct ethnic groups or territories (Selassie, 2003).

Despite these salient features of federalism, however, there are serious concerns about the efficacy of federalism as a constitutional approach for managing diversity and preventing conflict. Some argue that federalism may weaken national unity and promote ethnic rivalry and hostility (Haysom, 2003). Others have shown that unitary and parliamentary forms of government are better at reducing corruption than federal and presidential systems (Gerring and Thacker, 2004). There is a belief that federalism is ineffective in promoting stable governments, as evidenced by the breakdown of federations in multi-ethnic states in the twentieth century, particularly in communist, post-communist and post-colonial countries (Craven, 1991). For example, Suberu (2001) argues that the federal system adopted in Nigeria has failed to deliver peace, unity and good governance.

Territorial and ethnic federalism

There are two approaches to federalism: territorial and ethnic federalism. Territorial federalism advocates drawing boundary lines according to geographical or administrative convenience, as in Australia, whereas ethnic federalism advocates drawing internal boundaries and tiers of state along ethnic lines, as in Ethiopia. Territorial federalism is based on strong integrationist and assimilationist dispositions of a state, while ethnic federalism is based on a recognition that ethnic groups can best manage their own affairs and protect and promote their distinctiveness by having their own territorial autonomy (Smith, 1995; Selassie, 2003). Will Kymlicka (1995) argues that ethnic federalism provides effective self-rule to ethnic groups by enabling a majority in a territory to undertake autonomous decision-making and preventing outvoting by the broader national population.

Territorial federalism is criticised for sometimes making minorities vulnerable to the dominant positions of majorities (Selassie, 2003). Where ethnic divisions in a state are sharp and there's strong support for secession, territorial federalism may exacerbate divisions and cause violence (Anderson and Stanfield, 2005). On the other hand, ethnic federalism may pose a threat to the territorial integrity of a state, and territorial conflicts may become community conflicts, as in Belgium (Murphy, 1995). Ethiopia has boldly adopted ethnic federalism and, despite some critics' view that this was a recipe for disintegration, the country has emerged as a relatively stable state and a regional economic and political power. Some claim that the successful implementation of ethnic federalism in Ethiopia is largely explained by the centralised structure of the ruling political party (Aalen, 2002) and that, notwithstanding the observed stability in the country, there has been a deepening of inter-ethnic and intra-ethnic divides (Aalen, 2011). Indeed, Alemente Selassie (2003) argues that ethnic federalism in Nigeria, which initially established federation boundaries along three major ethnic lines, led to hegemonic ethnocentrism and secessionism in the country. Eventually, ethnic federalism was abandoned and replaced with territorial federalism in 1967.

Ethnicity as a cause of civil war, and partition as a solution?

There are competing views about the role that ethnicity, religion, culture and the influence of colonial boundaries play in triggering civil war in Africa. There is growing empirical evidence that suggests a positive association between religious polarisation and ethnic diversity and the incidence of civil wars (Huntington, 1996). Huntington's model of cultural fragmentation sees cultural rather than ideological factors as being dominant, and that conflicts caused by cultural divisions will be more intractable than those triggered by political and economic differences.

Some see African conflicts as being caused by irreconcilable ethnic differences (Laremont, 2002). Nation-building in Africa has been made difficult by the fact that modern states are artificial geographic units created by colonial boundaries. Francis Deng and I. William Zartman (2002) argue that modern African states lack cultural roots, as they were constructed by colonial authorities without regard to indigenous values and institutions. In 1964, the Organisation of African Unity (OAU) made the critical decision to accept national borders between African countries as they existed at independence. In the immediate post-colonial period, African political leaders moved to consolidate their states in order to contain threats of disunity and fragmentation, and little attention was paid to the social causes of division within countries (Laremont, 2002). While African political leaders largely succeeded in preserving unity, diversity and disparities within states have remained sources of tension and conflict (Deng and Zartman, 2002), and unity was often attained at the expense of accommodating diversity.

The apparent difficulty in resolving ethnic conflicts led to the development of 'partition theory', which assesses the value of partition as a solution to ethnic civil war (Kaufmann, 1996). Donald Horowitz (1985), for example, argues that it is a mistake to seek accommodation among antagonists by attempting to preserve co-habitation in a heterogeneous state; rather, it is better for different groups to live apart in more than one homogeneous state. Sudan provides a good example of how mismanagement of diversity resulted in partition in 2011. The political history of Sudan is generally characterised by an Islamic assimilationist unitary system or military centralised unitary system, adopted by the ruling élite to exclude the large majority of indigenous people from political, social and cultural life on religious and ethnic grounds. Religious and cultural diversity was seen as a threat, and Mansur Khalid (1989) believes that it is the northern élite's intolerance of diversity that haunted and continues to haunt Sudan. Such a system kindles deep resentments that largely explain the recurrent civil wars in Sudan (Deng, 2005).

Ethnic, religious and cultural diversity should be seen as a virtue rather than a curse. Diversity is inevitable in any society, and it is the way societies *manage* diversity that determines the level of peaceful coexistence or conflict (Deng, 2005). On the one hand, there are examples of similar community groups who failed to coexist peacefully, as in Sudan (Keen, 2000). The partitioning of Sudan occurred not because of its intrinsic ethnic, religious and cultural diversity, but because of the ruling northern élite's attempts to impose an assimilationist, integrationist and centralised unitary system that favoured an Arab-Islamic national identity. On the other hand, there are also examples of community groups with different ethnicities and religions who have been able to live peacefully alongside each other for long periods.

Partition theory has, however, been challenged on the basis that it does not provide a convincing reason for partition as the only way to end civil wars. Nicholas Sambanis (2000) shows with empirical evidence that partition does not reduce the risk of war, but is instead positively associated with the recurrence of ethnic wars. Paul Collier (1998) refutes the belief that ethnic diversity increases the risk of civil war, arguing instead that above a certain per capita income, increased ethnic diversity in fact reduces the risk of violence. Indeed, Fessha (2008) argues that diversity is a global phenomenon that should not be addressed through the universal rights of individuals, but rather through federal institutional arrangements. While federalism does not by itself provide a solution for managing ethnic diversity, its design may determine the extent to which the state is able to embrace unity and diversity (Selassie, 2003).

Decentralisation

How decentralisation differs from federalism

While federalism devolves powers through a *constitutional arrangement*, decentralisation devolves powers through a *policy choice* that can occur in either federal or non-federal structured states. In a decentralised system, the central government decides which functions and responsibilities it will devolve to and withdraw from the sub-national level, whereas in a federal system devolved powers are guaranteed by the constitution and cannot be withdrawn by the national government (Elazar, 1987). Some argue that federalism's objective to manage diversity can also be achieved by decentralisation, or even that these systems are complementary or interchangeable.

Different systems of government (unitary, federation and confederation) cannot be made synonymous with the choice of either centralisation or decentralisation, as the two concepts are different. Unitary, federation and confederation systems can either be centralised or decentralised depending on the policy choice and the actual distribution and allocation of powers, leading to a variety of arrangements. For example, in the decentralised unitary states of the United Kingdom and Sweden, the administration of public policies adopted by the central government is left to local self-government. In the centralised unitary state of France, the administration of regional departments is kept under strict national supervision (Hueglin and Fenna, 2015). In the centralised federal states of Germany and Australia, the federal governments sets national policies and the states and local governments implement these policies, while in decentralised federal states in Canada and Switzerland, the sub-national levels set their own policies.

The advantages and disadvantages of decentralisation

Some studies have shown that decentralisation outperforms federalism in the delivery of public goods, and it is argued that decentralisation may directly reduce conflict and secessionist tendencies by bringing government closer to the people (Brancati, 2006). Raymond Fisman and Roberta Gatti (2002) also find that fiscal decentralisation is positively and significantly associated with low corruption levels. Although these findings have been criticised on the basis of the indicators used for federalism and decentralisation (Blume and Voigt, 2011), many studies have unambiguously shown that decentralisation delivers better public goods. Lorenz Blume and Stefan Voigt (2011) show that decentralised federalism is positively associated with growth, in terms of productivity, government efficiency and happiness.

There is now a growing focus on decentralisation as a policy choice, as opposed to federal constitutional arrangements, to ensure sustainable delivery of public goods, including peace and stability. Joseph Siegle and Patrick O'Mahony (2006) argue that the risk of inter-group strife in ethnically diverse societies can be reduced by decentralisation, as more space is created for different ethnic groups to freely manage their own affairs. If implemented well, decentralisation can contribute to poverty reduction in fragile and conflict-affected countries, and can mitigate conflict by offering a path to national unity, a political solution to civil war, an instrument for deflecting secessionist tendencies, and a mechanism for co-opting grassroots support for central policies (World Bank, 2011).

In contrast, some argue that decentralisation can intensify conflict rather than offset it (Braathen and Hellevik, 2008), or be merely a temporary arrangement in the transition to secession (Bird, 2003). Dawn Brancati (2006) finds that decentralisation may indirectly increase conflict and secessionism by encouraging the growth of regional parties that may reinforce ethnic and regional identities. As much power remains with the centre in a decentralised system, the exercise of power will largely depend on the majority principle, which will not necessarily ensure the autonomy of ethnic minorities to manage their own affairs (Selassie, 2003).

Evolution of systems of government in South Sudan

This section will explore the evolution of systems of government in South Sudan during the following periods: (i) the pre-colonial period, (ii) the colonial period, (iii) post-independence Sudan and (iv) post-independence South Sudan.

The pre-colonial period

South Sudan's history can be traced to the Palaeolithic era using archaeo-logical evidence (Omer, 2009). Current consensus and nationalist histori-ography identifies the most important civilisation as the Kingdom of Kush, which emerged around 1070 BC (Leclant, 2004). Kush established a strong monarchic and centralised system of government, with Nubian religion and language. It was ruled by 'god-kings' and had a hierarchical structure with the king at the top, followed by a small group of high-ranking and wealthy officials, and a much larger group of bureaucrats and others below (Kisangani, 2005). Diverse administrative agencies were spread throughout Kush for effective management, and administration of justice was entrusted to priests. After invading Egypt in the eighth century BC, the Kushite kings ruled Egypt as pharaohs for a century before they were weakened by internal rebellions that led to the invasion and capture of the Kushite capital by the Ethiopian kingdom of Axum.

Many South Sudanese associate their ancient history with Kush, believ-ing that they have been implicitly referred to in the book of Isaiah, which describes the people of Kush as tall, having smooth black skin, and living in a country criss-crossed with rivers. Some scholars argue, however, that the term 'Kush' in the Bible might refer instead to the Kassites of the Zagros Mountain region, in modern-day Iran (Goldenberg, 2005). Either way, there is no solid archaeological or historical evidence linking the Kush civilisation to contemporary traditional communities in South Sudan.

Traditional systems of government undoubtedly played an important role in maintaining peace, stability and the rule of law in the pre-colonial period. South Sudan, with about 64 major ethnic groups, is one of the more diverse countries in Africa. Its ethnic groups can be broadly categorised into Nilotic groups, Nilo-Hamitic groups and the south-western Sudanic groups, with each ethnic group having its own traditional institutions and systems of government. Before colonialism, communities in today's South Sudan witnessed considerable migration, accompanied by acrimonious processes of forming alliances or confederations between various communi-ties, before settling as distinct ethnic groups in their current territories. The socio-political systems and structures adopted by various ethnic groups in the pre-colonial period ranged between centralised political authority, such as the Shilluk (Chollo) and Azande, and non-centralised political author-ity, such as the Dinka and Nuer (Omer, 2009). The adoption of different systems of government by different ethnic groups was largely shaped by the ecological environment, internal power struggles, economic activities and external threats.

The socio-political organisation of the Nuer and Dinka was based on age-set and a lineage system that was comprised of clans, tribes and sub-divisions, with legal and socio-political rules managed by elders without a permanent centralised individual authority (Deng, 1971). The Nuer and Dinka were described by Edward E. Evans-Pritchard (1940) as acephalous states lacking legislative, judicial and executive organs. Yet, the organisation's persistence and its coherent form made it far from a chaotic system and more akin to an ordered anarchy. The Ngok Dinka of Abyei have uniquely departed from the typical characteristics of stateless Niolete leadership and instead adopted a centralised political structure similar to that of the Shilluk (Kuol, 2014).

The Shilluk and Azande provide good examples of well-established, centralised political authority. The Shilluk nation was headed by a king or *reth* with administrative, political, judicial and spiritual sovereign powers (Graeber, 2011). The centralised authority was necessitated by the Shilluk's territorial circumscription, sandy ridges, limited movement for food-crop cultivation and external threats from their neighbours (Southall, 1976). The Azande adopted rather a different centralised authority that was an intricate mix of feudalism and traditional, administrative and spiritual authority (Omer, 2009). The Azande kingdom emerged from conquest and assimilation of other ethnic groups and uniquely established an aristocracy, with aristocrats and commoners (Evans-Pritchard, 1958). The Azande consisted of more than one kingdom and it prospered through military expansion and the use of military institutions to assimilate conquered peoples (Evans-Pritchard, 1971).

The various systems of government adopted by different ethnic groups before colonialism were tailored to fit their context and environment. The traditional institutions adopted by various ethnic groups had managed not only to maintain tranquillity but also to nurture common identity around their distinct cultures and customs. These systems of government showed remarkable resilience, not only during the pre-colonial period but also when they came into contact with colonialists. The systems of traditional authorities in South Sudan generally survived the turmoil of the Turkiyya slave-raids, the Mahdiyya's chaos, the Anglo-Egyptians' early tolerance of slave-raids, and subsequent decades of misrule by the post-independence northern élite (Kuol, 2014).

The colonial period

The colonial period for which the system of government in South Sudan can be assessed includes the Turco-Egyptian regime (1821–1881) and the Mahdiyya regime (1881–1898), as well as the Anglo-Egyptian regime (1898–1956).

Turco-Egyptian and Mahdiyya regimes: military and assimilationist system

The Turco-Egyptian regime, which arrived in Sudan in 1821, imposed a militarised, centralised unitary system of government, as it was considered the most effective way to plunder the country for slaves and ivory. This new system of government had a profound impact on African ethnic groups and their traditional systems of government, and changed the local balance of power in favour of Arab ethnic groups. During this period, the Turco-Egyptian authorities and private traders undertook slave, ivory and cattle raids on a vast scale into what is today South Sudan, and established al-Zubayr Pasha's slave-trading empire in Bahr el Ghazal. These slave raids by the Turco-Egyptian regime and Arab nomads deeply affected the prevailing traditional systems in the southern Sudan region. Some ethnic communities resisted the raids by strengthening their traditional institutions. Others became submissive and succumbed.

For example, with the arrival of foreigners, the Shilluk encouraged trade, imposed systematic taxes, and asserted their control by creating a royal monopoly. Most foreigners who visited the Shilluk area recognised that they were dealing with a bona fide monarch with a rudimentary administration (Graeber, 2011). However, such stability changed drastically when the new regime replaced the ivory trade with the slave trade. By 1861, the Turco-Egyptian regime and Arab traders triggered conflict with devastating slave raids that weakened the Shilluk kingdom (Udal, 1998). This warfare was exacerbated by the chaos of Mahdiyya, which imposed an Islamic assimilationist centralised unitary system, and which decimated the Shilluk's herds and caused carnage that halved the Shilluk population (Graeber, 2011).

The Ngok Dinka of Abyei offer another example of resilience of traditional governance in the face of an imposing colonial regime. When the arrival of the Turco-Egyptian regime increased the power of their Arab neighbours, the Misseriyia, the Ngok achieved a degree of stability by adopting new defensive strategies including diplomacy, using age-sets as a 'standing army' and electing 'war chiefs' for each village. In a bid to protect their people from slave raids, the chief of the Ngok Dinka, together with other Dinka chiefs in Bahr el Ghazal, accepted a truce offer from the Mahdist leaders and forged a temporary alliance to remove the Turco-Egyptian regime (Johnson, 2008). This led to the collapse of the formal Egyptian administration in Bahr el Ghazal.

Similarly, the Azande demonstrated through their systems and institutions of government a remarkable resilience and capacity to cope with the Turco-Egyptian slave raids and the chaos of the Mahdiyya regime, and to adapt more generally to processes of cultural assimilation and political integration. Azande resilience helped them to retain and preserve their values, institutions and political system despite the slave raids and chaos of the Turco-Egyptian and Mahdiyya regimes (Evans-Pritchard, 1958).

Anglo-Egyptian rule: restoring native administration

The post-pacification period under Anglo-Egyptian rule (1930–1954) was the only time Sudan experienced peace after the arrival of the Turco-Egyptian regime. Arab slave raids continued after the defeat of the Mahdiyya regime in 1898, and many ethnic groups in southern Sudan resisted this oppression. This resistance later contributed to the adoption of various ordinances which culminated in the British 'Southern Policy' in 1930.

Administration of southern Sudan was not a priority for the Anglo-Egyptian regime. As early as 1921, and before the formulation of the Southern Policy, governance of southern Sudan was based on the concept of 'native administration' or indirect rule. Native administration saw the Anglo-Egyptian authorities govern using local customary structures and law, an approach believed to be an effective means of governing and legitimising authority (Johnson, 2011). As native administration was relatively successful in maintaining the rule of law, peace and stability, the British rule incorporated it into the Southern Policy of 1930. The main aspects of this policy were 'to build up a series of self-contained racial or tribal units with structures and organisation based, to whatever extent the requirements of equity and good governance permit, upon indigenous customs, traditional usage and beliefs' (Henderson 1965: 165).

This policy was instrumental in restoring and protecting the systems and institutions of traditional authorities in southern Sudan. For example, Anglo-Egyptian rule managed to revive and reinvent the royal institutions of the Shilluk kingdom after they had fallen into abeyance during the slave raids of the Turco-Egyptian regime and the chaos of the Mahdiyya period (Graeber, 2011).

Post-independence Sudan: military, centralised and assimilationist unitary system

The post-independence northern Sudanese élites who took over power from the British in 1956 adopted a centralised unitary system with the aim of establishing an Arab-Islamic state. They attempted to dismantle the Southern Policy, which was based on traditional systems of government, and to replace it with a policy of Arabisation and Islamisation. Well-established religious, cultural and educational norms in southern Sudan were eroded during the years of Arabisation (1954–55).

Post-Sudanese independence, a system of deconcentration of power was adopted, with power being transferred from the central government to local governments based in the nine provinces, including the three provinces of southern Sudan. Each province delegated powers to local government units, known as rural councils in rural areas and municipal or town councils in urban areas. When the communist regime took over in 1969, a more decentralised system was adopted, devolving authority from central government to local governments in the provinces and giving local authorities greater autonomy in policymaking and executive functions.

In 1972, the Addis Ababa Agreement granted southern Sudan regional autonomy. Consequently, the central government devolved authority through constitutional arrangements to the regional government of southern Sudan, which exercised legislative and executive authority, but not judicial authority. During this decentralised unitary period (1972–1981), Sudan and southern Sudan enjoyed relative peace and improved access to basic services. Decentralised local government continued in southern Sudan until 1981, when the southern Sudan regional government was dissolved and a new caretaker government was appointed to oversee the repeal of the Addis Ababa Agreement and redivision of the southern Sudan region into three regions (Bahr el Ghazal, Equatoria and Upper Nile).

After the Addis Ababa Agreement was abrogated and the second civil war erupted in 1983, both the Sudanese government and the SPLM governed southern Sudan until the conclusion of the CPA in 2005. During the early struggle years of the 1980s, the Sudan People's Liberation Army (SPLA) relied heavily on traditional authorities to govern SPLA-controlled areas. As more territory came under its control, the SPLM held the National Convention in 1994 and resolved to set up a civil administration with its structures based on a decentralised system of government (SPLM, 1994).

In 1996, the SPLM created the Civil Authority of the New Sudan (CANS), intended to be an effective, democratic, participatory and accountable civil authority (SPLM, 2014). CANS had an elaborate five-level government structure, implementation of which suffered from an absence of a legal framework, inadequate financial resources, lack of a motivated and skilled workforce, weak institutions and poor physical infrastructure. As such, the system of government during the liberation struggle remained largely militarised and depended entirely on traditional systems of government.

The Islamic federal system

The National Islamic Front (NIF) assumed power in 1989 and stepped up Islamisation efforts by enforcing Sharia law and using social and political means to create an Islamic state (ICG, 2002). An Islamic, assimilationist and autocratic unitary system was adopted and powers were vested in the state governor or *wali*. In practice, the *wali* delegated powers to local government councils. Local government systems disintegrated over time and service provision was poor.

In an effort to consolidate its authority and to appeal to the population, particularly the people of southern Sudan, the Islamic regime resolved to adopt an Islamic federal system (Kacuol, 2008). The Islamic regime issued a number of constitutional decrees related to the establishment and organisation of federal institutions and division of powers between the federal, state and local governments. However, lack of implementation indicated that federalism was mere political rhetoric, and the system of government remained largely an assimilationist and centralised unitary system. Meanwhile, the central government continued to employ violence to govern, especially in the peripheral areas, including southern Sudan, Darfur, Eastern Sudan, the Nuba mountains, Blue Nile, and Nubi in far northern Sudan.

CPA: the realisation of the federal system in Sudan

Although the federalism debate in Sudan started in 1954, serious discussions about the appropriate system of government for Sudan first took place during the Government of Sudan (GOS) and SPLM negotiations in Abuja (1991–1993) and the CPA (2005). During the first round of Abuja negotiations in 1992, an appropriate system of government to manage diversity (federalism, confederation and others) was an agenda item. The Abuja negotiations followed the 1991 split of the SPLM into SPLM (Torit) and SPLM (Nasir), and the factions participated in the Abuja negotiations as separate parties.

Prior to the 1992 negotiations, Nigeria, as the mediator, proposed federalism as the best way of resolving conflict in Sudan. GOS put forward its Islamic Federal Structure as its best mechanism of resolving the conflict (Wondu and Lesch, 2000). SPLM (Torit) wanted a weak federalism that favoured confederation, while SPLM (Nasir) sought independence for southern Sudan as the only way of resolving conflict in Sudan. The Nigerian mediators felt that the proposals did not reflect the 'true federalism' needed for managing diversity in Sudan (Wondu and Lesch, 2000).

Ahead of the second round of peace negotiations in Abuja in 1993, Nigeria presented a modified federalism proposal that spelt out exclusive, concurrent and residual powers for the three tiers of government. The Sudanese government's negotiating team refused to discuss confederation or to place it on the agenda, as it viewed this as 'separation in disguised form', but it accepted the Nigerian proposal as it considered this compatible with its proposed federalism (Wondu and Lesch, 2000). The SPLM tabled confederation, but was ready to discuss the Nigerian proposal on the understanding that federalism in Nigeria operates in a secular context. The SPLM criticised the GOS federalism proposal, viewing it as a 'unitary system' that failed to devolve powers along the lines of the Addis Ababa Agreement (Wondu and Lesch, 2000). The SPLM argued that Sudan would inevitably break up if GOS insisted on dominating other Sudanese with the Islamic-Arab unitary system of government (Wondu and Lesch, 2000). They felt that Sudan would be better off adopting a confederation system than continuing with the current unitary system that would make separation the most likely outcome. Given the divergent views of the warring parties, the second round of Abuja peace negotiations broke down and failed to produce a peace agreement.

After the failure of the Abuja peace negotiations, the Intergovernmental Authority on Development (IGAD) facilitated peace negotiations between GOS and SPLM in Kenya between May 2002 and December 2004. Unlike the Abuja peace negotiations, the IGAD-led mediation did not discuss the system of government but instead focused on tiers of government and their powers, principles of decentralisation, and the devolution of powers at all levels of government. Although the CPA did not explicitly mention federalism, the system of government agreed upon by the parties was a federal, decentralised system. The CPA provided for the establishment of 25 states and the Abyei Area Administration, with a number of local governments in each state. The exclusive, concurrent and residual powers of all levels of government except local government were detailed.

The system of government agreed in the CPA met the core elements of a typical federal system. Administrative federalism was established by creating four tiers of government, and political federalism was established by making each tier of government autonomous with its own legislature, executive and judiciary. Fiscal federalism was established by designating each tier of government with fiscal competence to collect and spend its own revenues. Each tier of government had clearly delineated exclusive, concurrent and residual powers, and the subsidiarity principle was adopted in allocating tasks to the tiers of government.

On the basis of the provisions of the CPA, the Interim National Constitution (2005) and the Interim Constitution of Southern Sudan (2005) (ICSS) were promulgated and adopted as legal guarantees for the implementation of the CPA. The system of government in Southern Sudan during the interim period of CPA (2005–2011) was a decentralised federal system; interestingly, territorial federalism was adopted at the level of the state and ethnic federalism was implicitly adopted at the level of local government.

Post-independence South Sudan: regression from the decentralised federal system

Decentralised federalism after the referendum on self-determination was guaranteed in ICSS. Specifically, ICSS made it clear that if the outcome of the self-determination referendum favoured secession, ICSS and its decentralised federal system would remain in force as the constitution of a sovereign and independent South Sudan (Article 208(7)).

Contrary to the provisions of ICSS, the Transitional Constitution of the Republic of South Sudan 2011 (TCSS) instead adopted a centralised, semi-federal system. While TCSS explicitly states that South Sudan shall be governed on the basis of a decentralised democratic system (Article 1(4)), many of its provisions clearly favour a centralised system of government and are inconsistent with a typical system of federalism. One glaring departure from the ICSS federal system is seen in Article 3(2) which states that the authority of the government is derived from the constitution and the law (rather than the will of the people), an approach inconsistent with a typical federal system.

Other departures from federalism in TCSS include the exceptional powers given to the president to remove an elected state governor and/ or dissolve the state legislature in the event of a crisis in the state that threatens national security (Article 101(r) and (s)). These provisions are exercised without due process and without clear guidelines as to how they should be objectively exercised. Empowered by this constitutional provision, President Kiir removed the governors of Lakes State and Unity State from their elected positions in what was seen to be a politically motivated move. Additionally, constitutional quality and political competence of tiers of government include that each tier of government should have its own judiciary and, while ICSS provided for the establishment of a state judiciary (in Article 171), TCSS does not. As such, the states of South Sudan do not exhibit constitutional quality of state or political competence.

In comparing the two constitutions, ICSS and TCSS, it is clear that South Sudan departed considerably from a decentralised federal system after independence. The current system of government in South Sudan is not only centralised, but exhibits features of an autocratic unitary system. It is a paradox that the people of southern Sudan, who overwhelmingly voted in favour of federalism at their first Pan-Southern Conference in Juba in 1954, have been unable to adopt a true federalism even after they gained independence in July 2011.

Conclusion

While the type of government is usually used to assess the quality of governance that contributes to the prevalence of conflict, this chapter shifts the debate to the nexus between systems of government and conflict. Although the literature is not conclusive on the choice between unitary and federal systems in managing diversity and conflict, there is a strong argument in favour of federalism. There is also growing evidence to suggest that decentralisation is more effective than either a federal or a unitary system in managing diversity and conflict.

The account of the evolution of systems of government in Sudan clearly shows the strong link between centralised and unitary systems of government and violent conflict. More recently, although southern Sudan adopted a federal decentralised system, there was regression towards centralisation after independence. Perhaps not surprisingly, peace did not last long, with war resuming in December 2013. Although many factors contributed to the resumption of civil war, the centralised and autocratic unitary system adopted by independent South Sudan was undoubtedly a factor.

In light of the above, one can conclude that the system of government does matter in managing diversity and conflict. South Sudan's own experience of federalism and decentralisation, as well as evidence from elsewhere, suggests that the country's best chance to achieve peace and unity may lie with a decentralised federal system. However, the success of such a system rests on a conducive democratic environment and the political will of a visionary and strategic political leadership.

Notes

1 Disclaimer: the views expressed in this paper are those of the author and are not an official policy or position of the National Defense University, the Department of Defense, the US Government, the Peace Research Institute Oslo or the University of Juba.

References

Aalen, Lovise (2002), *Ethnic federalism in a dominant party: The Ethiopian experience 1991–2000*, CMI Report R2002:2 (Bergen: Chr. Michelsen Institute).
— (2011), *The Politics of Ethnicity in Ethiopia: Actors, Power and Mobilisation Under Ethnic Federalism* (Leiden: Brill).
Addis Ababa Agreement of 1972.
Anderson, Liam and Gareth Stansfield (2005), 'The implications of elections for federalism in Iraq: Towards a five-region model', *The Journal of Federalism* 35, no. 3: 359–83.
Bird, Richard M. (2003), *Local and Regional Revenues: Realities and Prospects*, manuscript (Washington, DC: World Bank).
Blume, Lorenz and Stefan Voigt (2011), 'Federalism and decentralisation: A critical survey of frequently used indicators', *Constitutional Political Economy* 22, no. 3: 238–64.
Braathen, Einar and Siri B. Hellevik (2008), 'Decentralisation, peacemaking, and conflict management: From regionalism to municipalism', *Journal of Peace, Conflict and Development* no. 12: 1–23.
Brancati, Dawn (2006), 'Decentralisation: Fueling the fire or dampening the flames of ethnic conflict and secessionism', *International Organisation* 60, no. 3: 651–85.
Craven, Greg (1991), 'Of federalism, secession, Canada and Quebec', *Dalhousie Law Journal* 14: 231–62.
Collier, Paul (2007), *The Bottom Billion: Why the Poorest Countries Are Failing and What Can Be Done About It* (Oxford: Oxford University Press).
— (1998), 'The political economy of ethnicity', *CSAE Working Paper Series 1998–2008*, Centre for the Study of African Economies, University of Oxford.

Comprehensive Peace Agreement (2005).

Deng, Francis M. (1971), *Tradition and Modernisation: A Challenge for Law Among the Dinka of the Sudan* (New Haven, CT: Yale University Press).

Deng, Francis M. and I. William Zartman (2002), *A Strategic Vision for Africa: The Kampala Movement* (Washington, DC: Brookings Institution Press).

Deng, Luka B. (2005), 'The challenge of cultural, ethnic and religious diversity in peace building and constitution-making in post-conflict Sudan', *Journal of Civil Wars* 7, no. 3: 258–69.

Elazar, Daniel J. (1987), *Exploring Federalism* (Tuscaloosa, AL: University of Alabama Press).

Evans-Pritchard, Edward E. (1940), 'The Nuer of Southern Sudan', in Meyer Fortes and Edward E. Evans-Pritchard (eds), *African Political Systems* (Oxford: Oxford University Press.

— (1958), 'The ethnic composition of the Azande of Central Africa', *Anthropological Quarterly* 31, no. 4: 95–118.

— (1971), *The Azande: History and Political Institutions* (Oxford: Clarendon Press).

Fessha, Yonatan T. (2008), 'Institutional recognition and accommodation of ethnic diversity: Federalism in South Africa and Ethiopia', PhD diss., University of the Western Cape, South Africa.

Fisman, Raymond and Roberta Gatti (2002), 'Decentralisation and corruption: Evidence across countries', *Journal of Public Economics* 83, no. 3: 325–45.

Fleiner, Thomas et al. (2002), 'Federalism, decentralisation and conflict management in multi-cultural societies', in Raoul Blindenbacher and Arnold Koller (eds), *Federalism in a Changing World: Learning from Each Other* (Montreal: McGill-Queen's University Press).

Frontier Economics (2015), *South Sudan: The Cost of War*, in collaboration with the Centre for Conflict Resolution (CECORE) and the Centre for Peace and Development Studies (CPDS).

Gagnon, Alain (1993), 'The political uses of federalism', in Michael Burgess and Alain Gangnon (eds), *Comparative Federalism and Federation: Competing Traditions and Future Directions* (London: Harvester Wheatsheaf).

Gerring, John and Storm C. Thacker (2004), 'Political institutions and corruption: The role of unitarism and parliamentarism', *British Journal of Political Science* 34, no. 2: 295–330.

Goldenberg, David M. (2005), *The Curse of Ham: Race and Slavery in Early Judaism, Christianity and Islam* (Princeton, NJ: Princeton University Press).

Graeber, David (2011), *The Divine Kingship of Shilluk: On Violence, Utopia, and the Human Condition, or: Elements for an Archaeology of Sovereignty* (Edinburgh: Edinburgh University Press).

Gurr, Ted R. (1970), *Why Men Rebel* (Princeton, NJ: Princeton University Press).

Hamilton, Alexander, John Jay and James Madison (2005), 'Federal theory in *The Federalist*', in D. Karmis and W. Norman (eds), *Theories of Federalism* (New York, NY: Palgrave Macmillan: 105–33.

Haysom, Nicholas (2003), 'Constitution making and nation building', in Raoul Blindenbacher and Arnold Koller (eds), *Federalism in a Changing World: Learning from Each Other* (Montreal: McGill-Queen's University Press).

Henderson, Kenneth D. D. (1965), *Sudan Republic* (London: Benn).

Horowitz, Donald L. (1985), *Ethnic Groups in Conflict* (Berkeley, CA: University of California Press).

Hueglin, Thomas O. and Alan Fenna (eds) (2015), *Comparative Federalism: A Systematic Inquiry* (Orchard Park, NY: Broadview Press).

Huntington, Samuel P. (1996), *The Clash of Civilisations and the Remaking of World Order* (New York, NY: Simon and Schuster).

ICG (2002), *God, Oil and Country: Changing the Logic of War in Sudan* (Brussels: International Crisis Group Press).

Interim Constitution of Southern Sudan of 2005.

Johnson, Douglas H. (2008), 'Why Abyei matters: The breaking point of Sudan's Comprehensive Peace Agreement?', *African Affairs* 107, no. 426: 1–19.

— (2011), *The Root Causes of Sudan's Civil Wars: Peace or Truce*, revised edn, (Woodbridge, UK: James Currey).

Kacuol, Abednego A. (2008), *Implementation of Federalism in the Sudan* (Khartoum: Sudan Currency Printing Press).

Kaufmann, Chaim (1996), 'Possible and impossible solutions to ethnic civil wars', *International Security* 20, no. 4: 136–75.

Keen, David (1998), *The Economic Functions of Violence in Civil Wars* (Oxford: International Institute for Strategic Studies).

— (2000), 'Incentives and disincentives for violence', in Mats Berdal and David Malone (eds), *Greed and Grievances: Economic Agendas in Civil Wars* (Boulder, CO: Lynne Rienner Publishers).

Khalid, Mansur (1989), *The Government They Deserve: The Role of the Elites in Sudan's Political Evolution* (London: Kegan Paul International).

Kisangani, Emizet F. (2005), 'Development of African administration: Pre-colonial times and since', in Krishna K. Tammula (ed.), *Public Administration and Public Policy* (New York, NY: EOLSS and UNESCO), pp. 113–34.

Kuol, Luka B. D. (2014), 'Political violence and the emergence of the dispute over Abyei, Sudan, 1950–1983', in *Journal of Eastern African Studies* 8, no. 4: 1–17.

Kymlicka, Will (1995), *Multicultural Citizenship: A Liberal Theory of Minority Rights* (Oxford: Clarendon Press).

Laremont, Ricardo René (ed.) (2002), *The Causes of War and the Consequences of Peacekeeping in Africa* (Portsmouth, NH: Heinemann Educational Books).

Leclant, Jean (2004), *The Empire of Kush: Napata and Maroe* (London: UNESCO).

Murphy, Alexander (1995), 'Belgium's regional divergence: Along the road to federalism', in Graham Smith (ed.), *Federalism: The Multi-Ethnic Challenge* (London: Routledge).

Omer, Rabah A. (2009), 'The integration of traditional leaders in the democratisation process', PhD diss., Iowa State University.

Robertshaw, Peter (1987), 'Prehistory of upper Nile basin', *The Journal of African History* 28, no. 2: 177–89.

Sambanis, Nicholas (2000), 'Partition as a solution to ethnic war: An empirical critique of the theoretical literature', *World Politics* 52, no. 4: 437–83.

Selassie, Alemante G. (2003), 'Ethnic federalism: Its promise and pitfalls in Africa', in *Yale Journal of International Law* 28, no. 1: 51–107.

Siegle, Joseph and Patrick O'Mahony (2006), *Assessing the Merits of Decentralisation as a Conflict Mitigation Strategy* (Washington, D.C.: USAID).

Smith, Graham (1995), 'Mapping the federal condition: Ideology, political practice and social justice', in Graham Smith (ed.), *Federalism: The Multi-Ethnic Challenge* (London: Routledge).

Southall, Aidan (1976), 'Nuer and Dinka are people: Ecology, ethnicity and logical possibility', *Man* 11, no. 4: 463–91.

SPLM (1994), *The Resolutions of the SPLM National Convention* (Chukudom: Sudan People's Liberation Movement).

SPLM (2014), *The Manifesto* (Juba: Sudan People's Liberation Movement).

Suberu, Rotimi T. (ed.) (2001), *Federalism and Ethnic Conflict in Nigeria* (Washington, DC: United States Institute of Peace).

Transitional Constitution of the Republic of South Sudan of 2011.

Udal, John O. (1998), *The Nile in Darkness: Conquest and Exploration, 1504–1862* (Norwich, UK: Michael Russell).

UNECA (2007), *Relevance of African Traditional Institutions of Governance.*

Wondu, Steven and Ann Lesch (eds) (2000), *Battle for Peace in Sudan: An Analysis of the Abuja Conferences, 1992–1993* (Lanham, MD: University Press of America).

World Bank (1999), *World Development Report 1999/2000: Entering the 21ˢᵗ Century* (Oxford: Oxford University Press).

— (2011), *World Development Report 2011: Conflict, Security and Development* (Washington DC: World Bank).

Zahar, Marie-Joelle (2014), 'A problem of trust: Can federalism silence the guns?', in Grace Skogstad et al. (eds), *The Global Promise of Federalism* (Toronto: University of Toronto Press).

CHAPTER 6

Federalism in the History of South Sudanese Political Thought[1]

Douglas H. Johnson

Introduction

Building on the author's previous work on self-determination in South Sudanese political thought, this chapter looks at the history of federalism in South Sudan. Federalism has featured prominently in South Sudan's political history, and it has arisen again in political debate. This chapter is neutral on the suitability of federalism in South Sudan and does not consider the advantages and disadvantages of the idea. Rather, it explores how federalism has meant different things to different people at different times in South Sudan's history. Drawing on rich, informative accounts of conference discussions on federalism and governance throughout South Sudan's history, it discusses attitudes towards federalism and the ways it has been presented from before Sudan's independence in 1956 up to independent South Sudan today.

1947–1957: Self-determination, federalism and independence

The Juba Conference, 1947

The first time that the collective opinion of the southern Sudanese was canvassed concerning a national political issue was at the Juba Conference in 1947. Since 1930, British administrative policy in Sudan had kept open the possibility that the southern provinces might one day be transferred to the colonial authority in British East Africa. This remained a theoretical option only; it could not be done as long as Sudan remained an Egyptian colony, since Egypt was a partner in the condominium that ruled Sudan. Also, East African governments were unenthusiastic about the idea of the southern Sudanese provinces joining them.

In 1946, with Egypt attempting to reassert its sovereignty over the whole of Sudan and with northern nationalist groups articulating demands for self-government and self-determination within Sudan's geographical boundaries, a separate administrative future for southern Sudan was no longer even a theoretical possibility. The Sudanese government prepared a new policy linking the future of the 'south' inextricably with that of the 'north'. Some consultation with the educated leadership of the south, primarily junior administrative officials, teachers and chiefs, was deemed necessary, if only for form's sake. Following a preliminary survey of southern opinion, a conference was convened in Juba in June 1947 (Wawa, 2005).[2]

The conference was exploratory and could take no decisions by itself. Its main purpose was to find out if the nascent leadership of the southern, educated class was willing and able to take part as appointed members in the Legislative Assembly that was being established in Khartoum (Robertson, 1974). The first day of the conference ended with no agreement, but that night the southern delegates held a meeting with some 200 southern clerks and junior officials living in Juba. The meeting lasted until 2 a.m. Finally, Paulino Cyer Rehan, one of the Dinka chiefs at the conference, spoke: 'Gentlemen,' he said,

> we now have stayed too long. Why should we be afraid of the Northerners? [...] if anything happens, if the Northerners want to make injustice to us, well, we have young children, young men: they will take up the response and fight them; they are men like ourselves. (Dellagiacoma, 1990: 53)

In the end, the southern representatives agreed to participate in the Legislative Assembly, but at no point in the conference was any system of government discussed. Despite what many South Sudanese now believe (SSPD, 2014), there was no mention of federalism.

Southern representatives in the Legislative Assembly

Thirteen southerners were appointed to the Legislative Assembly, including Stanislaus Paysama and Paulino Cyer Rehan from Bahr el Ghazal, Buth

Diu and Edward Odhok Dodigo from Upper Nile, and Benjamin Lwoki and Andarea Gore from Equatoria. The southern members formed a bloc of opinion but were not yet a party. They initially had no agreed plan for a system of government.

When the Umma Party, an Islamic centrist party in Sudan, brought forward a self-government motion in 1950, southerners opposed it on the grounds that it did not enable the south to participate in self-government on an equal basis. The southern representatives proposed a special minister of 'southern affairs' in a future self-governing Sudan, but this was rejected by northern members. Only when northern legislators accepted a provision for the Governor-General to retain reserve powers over the southern provinces and the civil service did the southerners agree to continue to participate in the constitutional process. Southerners saw the Governor-General retaining reserve powers as an important safeguard against potential abuse of power by a future northern majority government. This provision was highly unpopular among northern parties.

The political landscape of Sudan abruptly changed with the All Parties Agreement of January 1953. Under this agreement, Egypt, supported by northern parties, stipulated its preconditions for agreeing to a new Anglo-Egyptian treaty that would establish the terms for self-government in Sudan and the exercise of self-determination. The Governor-General's reserve powers over the south and the civil service were to be removed, and self-determination for Sudan as a whole was to be a choice of either union with Egypt or complete independence.

The southern representatives had been excluded from these talks. Together with the northern parties' extra-parliamentary repudiation of the constitutional formula agreed with southern representatives in the Legislative Assembly, and the Egyptian government's attempt to further circumvent the south's parliamentary representatives, this led to two important developments. First, southern Sudan's first political party, the Liberal Party, was formed to contest the 1953 elections. Second, the idea of possible separate self-determination for the south was articulated, with the threat that the south would withdraw from the constitutional process and explore 'other alternatives to determine its own future'.[3]

Following the 1953 elections, the formation of the first all-Sudanese cabinet under the pro-Egyptian National Unionist Party (NUP) further hastened southern political thinking concerning federation and self-determination. Federation now emerged as the *condition* for southern participation in Sudan's self-determination as a single, independent country. One of the earliest statements of this came in a petition addressed to the British Governor-General. It was forwarded by Abdel Rahman Sule, a Muslim merchant from Juba and co-founder of the Liberal Party, who, shortly before the new cabinet was sworn in, claimed:

> No one in the South would like at the moment to see this Egyptian proposal carried out. We in the South are still undeveloped econom- ically, socially and politically. If the Egyptian proposal to deprive us of our safeguards vested in the Governor-General is accepted, we ask Your Excellency that there will be not any other way for us except to ask for federation with the North. Failing to federate, we shall ask as alternative for the appointment of a High Commissioner from the British Foreign Office to Administer the South under the Trusteeship of the United Nations till such time as we shall be able to decide our own future.[4]

Federation was therefore presented as the only viable option for a united Sudan, and self-determination for a separate southern Sudan was identified as the only acceptable alternative to federation.

The first pan-southern conference, 1954

The southern leaders who became prominent Liberal Party organisers and promoters of the new idea of federalism were Benjamin Lwoki (president of the Liberal Party), Abdel Rahman Sule (chairman of the Juba branch), Buth Diu (in the House of Representatives), and senators Paulo Logali Wani (from Equatoria) and Stanislaus Paysama (from Bahr el Ghazal). These leaders organised the first ever pan-southern conference, held in the Juba Cinema (now an Episcopal church) in October 1954, to debate the south's future in Sudan.

Some 250 delegates from all three southern provinces – Bahr el Ghazal, Equatoria and Upper Nile – attended the pan-southern conference, including traditional chiefs, representatives from the southern diaspora in Khartoum, and southern members of the ruling NUP. Deliberations were conducted in English but translated into five other languages: Bari, Zande, Lotuko, Dinka and Arabic. The conference debated two main questions: first, the political future of Sudan as a whole and, second, the political future of the south. It was intended that the southerners arrive at a common position on these two issues prior to the elections that were to decide these questions.

The idea of federalism was publicly debated by a pan-southern grouping for the first time at this conference (Wawa, 2005).[5]

Very quickly, the conference came out in favour of Sudan's independence and against union with Egypt. Participants then proceeded to debate the form of government that southerners would support in an independent Sudan. Attillion Attor, a Shilluk from Upper Nile Province, was the first to speak in favour of federation. He was supported by Yona Lumanga, a teacher from Yei. But not everyone was convinced. Awad Somit from Juba opposed federation and spoke in favour of the NUP government, and Necodemo Gore, also from Juba, objected to any discussion of Sudan's future as there were no northern representatives present.

Senator Stanislaus Paysama, the vice-president of the Liberal Party, explained what federation means, and he described different types of federations adopted by different countries. His explanation had to be translated into all the languages of the conference, which took over two hours. The conference minutes concluded that 'by then, the house was well informed with the meaning of Federation'.

A 'hot debate' then followed. Necodemo Gore raised the pertinent question: 'In case we receive Federation where shall we get our people to run it? How shall we Finance it?' Buth Diu responded with passion:

> May I draw your attention gentlemen, chiefs, of all tribes, elders, Citizens present in this house, I should like to know whether you in this house want to be SLAVES or it will be better for you to be poor and Free and happy? I should like to know whether you understand the meaning of 'FEDERATION' as explained to you. Federation does not mean SEPARATION but internal Law and order in the united Sudan, for you to be able to look after your own affairs. [...] My honourable gentleman NECODEMO GORE brought the question of management and finance of the Federation now under debate by Southerners. [...] With regard to the first part of your question the present Government must be bound to manage the federation of [the] South for fear of Separation, if they cannot we can manage to separate the country. This I am quite sure the Present Regime has in mind. To conclude my dearest friend Mr. NECODEMO GORE we are here for Freedom and not money.

Chief Abdalla of Torit-Katire in Equatoria Province then broadened the debate about federation to include peoples from northern provinces – the

Fur of Darfur, Fung of Blue Nile and Nuba of Kordofan – declaring, 'I and my people Strongly request Federation to safe [*sic*] my fellow Blacks in the North.' This call was repeated by Musa Beshir, a non-tribal delegate from Khartoum, who announced:

> I am deligate [*sic*] of 25,000 Southerners in the North this includes Nuba, Fur and Fung who carry the same idea of Federation. In this respect I am not representing tribe but I would prefer to say colour since the three communities referred to again and again. There are backward area[s] in the North far too Backward than the Southern Sudan. Therefore I am speaking here for the Blacks who favoured your demands for Federation. Federation must go ahead to meet our demands in all our backward area[s] namely Fur, Fung and Nuba Mountains.

A vote was then taken and federation was approved by 227 votes to zero, with seven abstentions from the NUP delegates.

The decision of the conference was conveyed to the foreign ministers of Britain and Egypt, the British Governor-General of Sudan, and Sudan's prime minister in a letter signed by Benjamin Lwoki, in which he declared that the only alternatives facing Sudan were:

> (1)   Either Autonomy in the South and Autonomy in the North under Federation, or if that is not acceptable to the Northerners.

> (2)   A devided [*sic*] Sudan each ruling itself independent of each other. [...] As the South went into Parliament on [its] own will so it can choose to walk out of [it] [...] We must determine to the future of the South in the way we think suits us or our aims. (Johnson, 1998; Wawa, 2005: 137–140)

There seems to have been no reply from any of the recipients of Benjamin Lwoki's letter.

There are several important points to highlight about the 1954 conference. First, federalism was presented as a way to maintain a united Sudan. Second, support for federalism was voiced by delegates from all three southern provinces, as well as from the southern diaspora living in the north. Third, the southern Sudanese looked beyond their own borders and embraced the other marginalised areas of Sudan – the Blue Nile, the Nuba

Mountains and Darfur – in their call for federalism. Fourth, while forms of federalism might have been discussed, there was no explicit proposal of what form a federal Sudan might take or what balance of powers between the federal government and federated states should be achieved. Federalism might have been an ideal, but at this point it remained only an idea without a blueprint. Finally, self-determination leading to independence was presented as a fail-safe alternative for the southern Sudanese, should they fail in their primary goal of achieving federation for all of Sudan.

Both Britain and Egypt were committed to a lengthy process of self-determination for Sudan. However, once the NUP formed the first Sudanese government, removing the possibility of Sudan becoming independent under the Umma Party, Britain and Egypt suddenly changed their policy from favouring union with Egypt to supporting full independence for Sudan. The August 1955 mutiny of southern soldiers and police in Torit and other towns of the south convinced the British government that the sooner it was released from its residual responsibility for Sudan the better. According to a letter from W. H. Luce to T. E. Bromley, Sudan's prime minister, Ismail al-Azhari, was advised that if the Sudanese parliament declared independence, Britain would recognise it, even though parliament had no mandate to make such a decision (Johnson, 1998).

Southern members of parliament initially opposed a Sudanese declaration of independence, believing it premature if made before a constitution for the new country could be agreed. As Britain was reluctant to recognise Sudanese independence without the full support of the south, for a while it looked as if southern opposition could halt the momentum towards independence. In the end, southern legislators agreed to vote for Sudanese independence on the basis of a vague undertaking from the northerners that parliament would 'consider' federalism in the future (Johnson, 1998).

True to its word, parliament did consider the federal option in 1957 – and quickly rejected it. The northern Sudanese equated federation with secession and did not view it as a way to maintain national unity (Beshir, 1968). Advocacy for even moderate federal demands by southerners was considered tantamount to subversion and was treated as such.

The push for federalism gains momentum

In the context of anti-federal sentiment in the north, the formation of the Federal Party in the south, with Ezboni Mundiri as president and Darius Bashir as secretary general, was a significant advance in developing specific proposals on the idea of a federal Sudan. The Federal Party studied models of federation from around the world and proposed a constitutional structure similar to that of the United States, with the legislative bodies of the federal government replicated in the northern and southern federal states.

Whereas earlier demands for federalism had been vague about structures, the Federal Party emphasised the fact that accepting the federal principle meant creating 'states on the one hand and a Central Government on the other'. It justified the creation of two federal states on the grounds of racial and territorial differences between the 'North' and the 'South'.[6] The Federal Party's four-page outline of a draft constitution defined the powers of the president, judiciary, federal parliament and state parliaments, and where federal and state parliaments would hold separate or concurrent powers.[7]

Between them, the Liberal and Federal parties returned a large pro-federal bloc of southerners to the Constituent Assembly in 1958. Prominent federalists came from all three provinces and included Senators Stanislaus Paysama and Paulo Logali Wani, and Representatives Joseph Oduho, Buth Diu and Fr. Saturnino Lohure (a Roman Catholic priest). Outside parliament, southern politicians made approaches to other regions, including Darfur and Eastern Sudan, which began to take an interest in a federal constitution. This lobbying for federation was one of the factors that precipitated an army coup to supposedly prevent the country from falling apart. The coup marked the end of the first parliamentary period and the beginning of the first military government under General Ibrahim Abboud.

In this first period of political discussion, the federal idea evolved from a theoretical ideal to a more practical blueprint of the structure of government. Southern Sudanese legislators supported federalism because of legislative disappointments arising from the northern majority voting against proposals that southerners regarded as essential to safeguard their interests. At an early stage, southerners sought political allies in the quest for a federal constitution among other Sudanese peoples in marginalised areas who shared their concerns. Throughout this period, federation within a united Sudan remained southern leaders' primary goal, and secession was only secondary.

Exile, self-determination and the revival of federalism

The Abboud regime put an end to parliamentary politics and any public discussion of federalism as a constitutional solution for Sudan. This drove several southern leaders into exile to organise armed opposition to Khartoum. With the outbreak of civil war in southern Sudan in the early 1960s, the idea of federation was driven underground and some southerners began to opt for the idea of total independence. Fr. Saturnino Lohure and Joseph Oduho, both staunch federalists in parliament, formed the exiled Sudan African National Union (SANU), whose stated goal was self-determination, a code word for independence.

The downfall of the Sudan military government in 1964 led to a renewal of open party politics and a commitment to a public forum on southern Sudan at a round table conference convened early in 1965. A new party, the Southern Front, identified itself with African nationalism and proclaimed freedom from Arab domination as its goal, though it left the ultimate form of that freedom undefined. Despite SANU originally standing for self-determination, the first public statements by its leader, William Deng, favoured nothing stronger than federation. There appeared little difference between the policies of SANU and the Southern Front (Beshir, 1968; Sudan Informazioni, 1965; Wawa, 2005).[8]

The Round Table Conference, 1965

Differences emerged at the Round Table Conference convened in Khartoum in March 1965. Aggrey Jaden, SANU's deputy, returned to the principle of self-determination as the only means of solving the 'Southern Problem', equating self-determination with independence. However, SANU's leader, William Deng, declared that complete unity of Sudan was out of the question, and the country could either '1) voluntarily break up into two or 2) federate'. The other southern parties, including the Liberals, did not go so far as to advocate separation, but proposed federation or regional autonomy in a variety of forms. In the end, SANU and the Southern Front proposed a joint plan that went beyond the original provisions of federation and towards something more resembling confederation, with northern and southern Sudan each having control of their own finances, foreign affairs and armed forces (Beshir, 1968; Sudan Informazioni, 1965; Wawa, 2005).

The outcome of the Round Table Conference was to be a disappointment to most southerners. SANU split into the William Deng ('inside') and Aggrey Jaden ('outside') factions. William Deng remained in Sudan and Aggrey Jaden returned to exile and the guerrilla movement. Southern parties participated in the Twelve Man Commission, which had been set up to follow through on the Round Table proposals. The Liberal Party re-emerged as an advocate of regional autonomy, something less than full federalism. The Southern Front adopted the principle of self-determination as a *process*, and was keen to set out the details of each of the options being proposed – independence, federation, regional autonomy and local government – for southern Sudanese to choose from (Wawa, 2005).[9]

SANU and the Southern Front again formed an alliance in the constitutional committee following the 1968 elections and sought to build a parliamentary alliance with other smaller regional parties. Together, they opposed draft constitution provisions that denied regional diversity and imposed Islam and Arabic as the state religion and language of Sudan. They withdrew their delegations when the northern majority voted against their amendments. This precipitated a constitutional crisis that eventually resulted in the military once again overthrowing the parliamentary government.

1969–83: The Nimeiri period

In May 1969, a second period of military government began, bringing with it an acceptance of the principle of regional autonomy for the south. However, the Nile Provisional Government (NPG), one of the main exile groups with a presence in southern areas not held by the government, rejected regional autonomy as soon as it was proposed in June 1969. The growing strength of the southern guerrilla movement and sudden internal weakening of the Khartoum military government shifted the sides' bargaining power, finally making negotiations possible. By this time, there was a strong southern desire for a mediated solution.

Not all southern Sudanese were happy with this turn of events. The NPG, whose leaders lived in political exile in Kinshasa, had been displaced by Joseph Lagu's Southern Sudan Liberation Movement (SSLM). In a meeting between envoys of the SSLM and the 'Kinshasa group', the exiles objected to the precondition stipulated by Khartoum that negotiations would proceed on the basis of a united Sudan. The SSLM had a completely different understanding of 'regional autonomy' from what the government was proposing, and were confident that they would get federation out of the negotiations.[10] The SSLM assumed that 'autonomy' meant federation, and their delegation, led by the veteran pro-federalist Ezboni Mundiri, went to the Addis Ababa peace negotiations armed with a proposal for a full federal structure.[11]

The first major disagreement between the two sides was over the very use of the term 'federal' to describe the role of the future central government.

Khartoum's delegation argued that the People's Local Government Act of 1971 provided all the decentralisation needed for the proposed Southern Regional Government to run effectively. Mundiri countered that 'the main question facing the conference was whether the Sudan Government delegation accepted "Federal System" as the only way of solving the problem of the Sudan'.[12] The SSLM delegation objected to the government's detailed restrictions on the powers of the regional governments. It proposed instead that the powers of the central government should first be clearly defined and all other powers then reserved for the regions, a formula adopted from the US constitution. The SSLM's goal was to have a southern region and a northern region, with the central government autonomous from either region and not synonymous with the north. Mansour Khalid, a member of the Khartoum government delegation, brought all discussion of federalism to an end, however, when he declared that 'they could not impose Regionalism on the North when they had not asked for it'.[13]

The SSLM was offered, and finally accepted, something that might be termed 'federation lite' in what became the Southern Regional Government. The Addis Ababa Agreement was accepted by both Nimeiri's Sudan government and Lagu's SSLM in 1972. Self-determination as a process was abandoned and the agreement was never subject to popular ratification, although it was retroactively incorporated into the 1973 Permanent Constitution. This was to be the agreement's undoing, for the constitution allotted powers to the president that he eventually used to override and then abolish the Southern Region.

The internal politics of the Southern Region during the Addis Ababa peace period (1972–83) was seriously divided. First, between 'insiders' and 'outsiders', those who had remained inside the political system in Sudan during the war and those who had gone to the bush or into exile. Second, between the former Southern Front and SANU parties. Third, between 'Nilotics' of Bahr el Ghazal and Upper Nile provinces, and 'Equatorians' of the southernmost province. Nimeiri took advantage of these divisions to periodically dissolve the regional government, require new elections and form new governments, something that would not have been possible in a true federal system that had limited the power of the federal government to intervene in the internal affairs of the states.

Nationally, Nimeiri followed a policy of decentralisation. In 1976, he divided all of Sudan's provinces into two. Regionalism was then introduced in the north in 1980, when the old northern provinces were reassembled as regions. The powers of these northern regional governments were considerably less than the powers conferred on the Southern Region by the Addis Ababa Agreement. Retired general Joseph Lagu and his mainly Equatorian supporters used the north's regionalisation to propose further regionalisation of the south in a process colloquially known by its proponents as *kokora*, the Bari word for 'divide' or 'division', and as 'redivision' by its opponents.

The redivision-debate was triggered by political power struggles in the Southern Region and the belief of many in the two Equatoria provinces that they were being excluded from power by the numerically larger Nilotic Dinka and Nuer peoples. The proposal to abolish the Southern Region and replace it with the three smaller regions of the restored Equatoria, Upper Nile and Bahr el Ghazal provinces gained considerable support among northern Sudanese who had long considered regional autonomy to be a threat to national unity. This question was hotly contested by the majority of southern Sudanese. Nimeiri opted for the solution that favoured the north and abolished the Southern Region by presidential decree in June 1983 (Wawa, 2005).

In practice, *kokora* meant the expulsion of non-Equatorians from government and civil service positions in the regional capital of Juba and elsewhere, and their reposting to their home regions. There had been no discussion among *kokora*'s proponents about retaining a pan-regional superstructure through which southerners could coordinate and protect their common interests. If Equatorians had hoped that their new region would assume all the powers of the old Southern Regional government, they were soon disappointed as all three southern regions were put on a par with the much weaker northern regions. If the Southern Region had been a form of 'federalism lite', the three new southern regions were 'federalism even liter'.

The second civil war and the position of the SPLM/A

As in the first war, the renewal of civil war in 1983 changed the political debate among southerners and between southerners and northerners. Focus shifted away from government structures for southern Sudan only, and towards government reform for the whole of Sudan.

The Sudan People's Liberation Movement (SPLM) and its armed wing, the Sudan People's Liberation Army (SPLA), became the main opposition force actively fighting the Khartoum government. The SPLM/A's manifesto was broadly Marxist in tone, but its analysis of the failure of the Addis Ababa Agreement was rooted in pre-1972 debates. Many of its features reached back to the early days of a federalist alliance between southern and regionalist parties in the 1958 and 1968 parliaments, including its structural analysis of the Southern Region's weaknesses, its repudiation of a 'southern problem' to be considered in isolation from the rest of the country, its replacement with what it termed the 'nationalities problem', and its proposal for a restructured, united Sudan. The SPLM/A's manifesto was silent, however, on what form of government a restructured, united Sudan might adopt.

In direct negotiations with various northern political groups between 1986 and 1988, the SPLM/A showed how far the debate had progressed since the Round Table Conference in 1965, redirecting it from proposed constitutional arrangements for the south alone to a broader debate about power in Sudan. Gone were calls for either federation or self-determination; instead, they were replaced by a consistent demand for a National Constitutional Convention (SPLM, 1983).

With Nimeiri's overthrow in April 1985, new southern Sudanese parties emerged, many with broad, national-sounding names that in reality represented only provincial or even smaller constituencies. Southern political leaders disagreed on their objectives. The most common proposal was a return to the provisions of the Addis Ababa Agreement and the resurrection of a single Southern Region as a means by which southerners themselves could resolve their differences. However, the SPLM/A maintained that a return to the pre-1983 constitutional structures was out of the question. In their analysis, the Addis Ababa Agreement had failed to address the fundamental inequalities in the country, leaving the Southern Region vulnerable to manipulation from the centre. As an agreement, its demise was proof of its weakness.[14]

Throughout the period of Sadiq al-Mahdi's government (1986–89), more and more southern Sudanese leaders began to publicly agree with the SPLM/A's analysis, whatever doubts they had about the SPLA and its leader, John Garang. They began to speak in terms of a 'nationalities question', 'the ruling clique' and 'uneven development' throughout Sudan. They also made direct reference to the south's first demand for federation in 1954 and stated that frustrations concerning this was one of the causes of continued civil war.[15]

By the beginning of 1989, there was broad agreement between parties within Sudan that negotiations with the SPLM/A should lead to a broad-based National Constitutional Conference. To prevent this from happening, the National Islamic Front (NIF) coup of 30 June 1989 overthrew Sadiq al-Mahdi's coalition government and ended the negotiations.

In the twenty-year period between 1969 and 1989, the idea of federalism had effectively been replaced nationally by policies of 'decentralisation' and 'regionalisation'. Under these policies, the central government largely retained its power, devolving only service provision responsibility to the regions who were still denied the resources to fulfil that responsibility.

1989–2005: Federation under the NIF

The NIF/military regime of Omar al-Bashir adopted the language of federalism to describe its own policy of decentralisation. In the south, this was part of a strategy to isolate the SPLM/A and manufacture an internal peace. The SPLM/A had wavered in its commitment to national restructuring and begun to place more emphasis on southern secession as a solution.

Within the government-held areas of Sudan, southerners explored what sort of peace was possible in the context of the new political developments at the centre. Peter Cirillo, an ex-Anyanya soldier, former governor of Equatoria and one-time energetic foe of the SPLM/A, addressed the September 1989 National Conference on Peace, convened by the new government in place of the proposed National Constitutional Conference. He showed surprising sympathy for the SPLM/A's analysis of the causes of war. However, his preferred solution – a federalism that fell short of reconstituting the former Southern Region – showed that he was still committed to the old regional politics. Other Equatorian leaders also adopted the language of 'nationalities' popularised by the SPLM/A. They argued for federalism as the logical extension of decentralisation, urging that the current consultation exercises should be no substitute for the aborted constitutional conference. They, too, began to call for separation in the absence of any agreement over federalism with the north (Wawa, 2005).[16]

Internal dissent within the SPLM/A eventually led to a split. Ostensibly aimed at resolving the SPLM/A's internal contradictions, the breakaway movement of the Nasir commanders had its own contradictions. Its stated objective was the independence of southern Sudan, but at its very inception it received military and political support from Khartoum, from the very government from which it claimed it wanted to secede (Nyaba, 1997). The SPLM/A had already been preparing a new position on self-determination, signalling a major shift of position, and in September 1991 declared its priority of options: 'The position of the SPLM/A on the system of Government shall be based on resolving the war through a united secular democratic Sudan, confederation, association of sovereign states or self-determination' (Garang, 1992: 284).

The two factions of the SPLA remained bitterly hostile to each other on the battlefield, but outside Sudan attempted to reconcile their positions. At peace talks in Abuja, Nigeria in 1992 and Washington, D.C. in 1993, the two sides tried to forge a national commitment with a more narrowly defined political solution for southern Sudan. They proclaimed support for self-determination not just for the South, but also for Abyei, the Nuba Mountains and Blue Nile, which were all outside the administrative boundaries of the southern provinces but were territories where the SPLA was active.[17]

With self-determination now the primary goal, federalism dropped out of the equation. Neither faction described what form an interim government would take should peace be reached with Khartoum, or if southern Sudan achieved independence. At the 1992 Abuja talks, the SPLM/A delegation was sceptical of the different terms being discussed between the Nasir faction and Khartoum. William Nyuon Bany, then still a member of the mainstream SPLM/A and the delegation's leader, declared:

> In the Sudan serious words like 'federalism', 'participatory democracy', 'grassroots democracy', 'people's congresses' are thrown about here and there without any concrete content. They have become [an] alibi for dictatorship. No system is federal merely because it claims to be federal. No system is democratic merely because the word 'democratic' has been tagged on to its name as one of its descriptive adjectives.[18]

In the meantime, the government in Khartoum proceeded to introduce its own form of federalism throughout Sudan. In 1994, a federal constitution created 23 new federal states, including ten in the South. The southern states were largely theoretical, because government forces did not control most of the territory in the proclaimed states. The process of creating states in the south was also somewhat arbitrary: originally nine states had been agreed, until the southern governor of Bahr el Ghazal Region insisted that his home area be made a state, too. Consequently, Warrap State was carved out of Northern Bahr el Ghazal State for no other reason than that one of the government's most important southern allies wanted it that way.

From this point on there were two separate strands of negotiation that eventually converged to produce the Comprehensive Peace Agreement (CPA), with its own contradictions. The SPLM/A negotiated with Khartoum and the northern opposition parties separately, reaching a series of agreements combining the principle of a secular state for Sudan with the right to self-determination through a referendum for the south. The Khartoum government reached an agreement with its southern allies, appearing to grant them the right to determine their constitutional future at some undetermined date. A Coordinating Council for southern Sudan's federal states was eventually created in place of a single regional government. By 1999, however, it was clear from the implementation of these agreements that the Khartoum government's version of federalism was highly centralised and that the Coordinating Council had little real authority.

There were two main points of disagreement between many exiled southern Sudanese and the SPLM/A leader, Garang. The first point of disagreement concerned the voting options for self-determination. Garang wanted to define the options in advance of a ceasefire and interim arrangements, and he put forward three options: regional, federal and confederal governments. Other political figures, such as Bona Malwal, suggested that the interim arrangements should be the alternative to independence. This group asserted that southerners should also be asked to decide if they wanted to remain in Sudan under the type of government that Khartoum was administering at the time of the referendum.

The second point of disagreement was over who would be given the right of self-determination. Garang appeared to insist on including the peoples of the Nuba Mountains, southern Blue Nile and other marginalised areas in the exercise of this right, together with the south. Bona Malwal again articulated opposition to this, insisting that a resolution for southern Sudan should not be delayed by attempts to accommodate other marginalised areas. Lam Akol, one of the former Nasir coup leaders who continued to lead his own movement based in the southern Shilluk territory, was quoted as declaring that the inclusion of the Nuba Mountains and Blue Nile in southern self-determination was 'preposterous paternalism' (Sudan Update, 1994).

This was the context in which the IGAD peace negotiations restarted in earnest in 2002. The outcome of those negotiations was that Khartoum's 'decentralised' federal system was retained as the formula for a united Sudan, rather than a more robust federal structure for the whole nation. The right to self-determination was narrowed to include only southern Sudanese peoples. The peoples of the Nuba Mountains and Blue Nile were effectively abandoned, leaving an unstable situation along most of southern Sudan's northern border.

2011 and after

In principle, the southern Sudanese rejected Khartoum's version of federation when they voted for independence. At independence, they inherited Khartoum's division of the south into ten states, with 'decentralisation' rather than federation. Debates over the balance of powers between the central and state governments began with the drafting of the transitional constitution, and substantive calls for a federal system were made as early as 2011.[19]

The SPLM-in-Opposition (SPLM-IO) has adopted federalism as its political platform, complicating the federation debate further. The initial reaction of the Juba government was to follow Khartoum's example and equate federalism with subversion and disloyalty.

If we are to learn anything from southern Sudan's political history, it is that federalism means many things. As the SPLM/A warned in Abuja in 1992, 'no system is federal merely because it claims to be federal'. Federalism has been used to describe what are, in practice, highly centralised systems of government, as well as more radical projects of devolution that remain untried. Until there is a full and open discussion of federalism, there will be no common understanding of what it might mean for South Sudan or, once understood, whether the majority of South Sudanese will want to adopt it.

Much of the current public debate on federalism has been conducted online, dominated by the diaspora. Few specifics have been considered; rather, discussions fall back on dictionary definitions or text-book outlines (Sebit, 2014; SSPD, 2014). Some federalism advocates use the same argument that earlier advocates used for federalism in Sudan, namely that it will promote unity, good governance and development. Others advocate federalism for more parochial reasons, seeing federalism mainly as a means for removing persons of other ethnic groups from their own states.

In Juba, there are some who now advocate a return to *kokora* as a federal solution. Some claim that the word is misunderstood and misrepresented (Lupai, 2013). However, factors sullying support for *kokora* include the way some Equatorians are reviving anti-Dinka (or anti-Jieng) propaganda in support of federalism (Kopling, 2014) and the tribalist manner in which *kokora* advocates applied it at the beginning of the last civil war. Those who lived through *kokora*, who were abruptly and brusquely told to leave jobs and return to home regions, have every reason to be suspicious of the advocates of the new *kokora*.

To be clear, *kokora* is not the same as federalism, and it did not create a federal state in Equatoria or elsewhere in southern Sudan. Rather, it weakened the powers of the regions while leaving the power of the central government in Khartoum untouched, or even enhanced. Those who want genuine federalism are best advised not to adopt *kokora* as their model.

Currently, the term 'ethnic federalism' has become a popular slogan, appearing to offer each community control of its own resources and affairs. Ethiopia is frequently presented as a model for ethnic federalism, yet Ethiopian federalism has, in practice, also been described as a means by which the ruling party has divided the opposition along ethnic lines, making it difficult for a united opposition to form and challenge its power.

The problem with Ethiopian federalism is not that it is insufficiently ethnic, but that it is insufficiently federal, and it is possible that its emphasis on ethnicity is the source of that weakness (Levine, 2008). Current proponents of ethnic federalism in South Sudan have proposed a number of federal states irrespective of current demography or economic viability. The SPLM-IO's proposal to create 21 states along the 1956 boundaries of the southern districts (SPLM-IO, 2014) threatened to take the Ethiopian example to the extreme, creating weak states unable to challenge or restrain the federal government. President Salva Kiir's unilateral decision in 2015 to increase the number of states to 28 (and, later, to 32) suffers from the same problem.

The focus of many South Sudanese has been on the creation of federal states, rather than on balancing power between the federal and state governments. It would be prudent to remember the point the Federal Party made back in 1957, namely that accepting the principle of federalism means creating *both* a central government *and* state governments. It does not mean creating state governments alone. Under federalism, there must be a central government; however, its powers need to be defined. It will have a presence wherever its capital is located, and it will also have a presence through various federal agencies in every state. The creation of a federal government goes hand in hand with the creation of federal states. Past regional experiments in Sudan failed because this was not appreciated, and the construction of decentralised states and regions was done primarily to protect the powers of the central government.

Is federalism alone a sufficient solution to South Sudan's political crisis? One sceptic has drawn attention to the difference between a political system and a system of governance, warning that 'federalism cannot solve the country's problem because it is a system of governance and not a political system. In other words, federalism will only thrive under a hospitable political system which appreciates its benefits and promotes its development' (Abeyi, 2014). Or, as another South Sudanese said to this author, 'with this mixed perception of federalism South Sudanese have, do they consider which would be easier: to remove one big tyrant or several petty tyrants?'

For the south, the idea of self-determination was originally connected with federalism, with secession only a possibility to be pursued if a federal system for the whole of Sudan were rejected. The suppression of open debate on federalism by a succession of Khartoum governments and their rejection of a true federal system elevated secession to become the south's primary goal. Federalism has once again emerged as central to the discussion of how South Sudanese wish to govern themselves and live together now that they have achieved independence. Self-determination means more than choosing independence, it also means choosing a form of self-government. The South Sudanese are yet to make that choice.

Notes

1   This is a revised and expanded version of the lecture delivered at the Centre for Peace and Development Studies, University of Juba, on 5 July 2014.
2   Letters from Siricio Iro, Hassan Fartak, P. A. Rehan, B. Madut Akol, Southern Staff Aweil, L. Bey and C. Mboro, government school teachers Tonj, Philibert Ucini and Patrisio Lojok, Juba Police Force to governor, Equatoria Province and deputy governor Bahr el Ghazal (April–June 1947), Sudan Archive, University of Durham 519/2/1–2, 5–12, 14–19. All documents in Wawa, 2005, documents 1–9: 23–44. I am indebted to Yosa Wawa for making available to me other documents not included in this publication.
3   This quote is from the Rumbek Emergency Committee to the governor general of Sudan, 25 November 1952, National Archives, Kew, UK (NA) Foreign Office (FO) 371/102737, no. 28.
4   Abdel Rahman Sule to the Governor-General, 20 May 1954, NA FO 371/108324, no. 127.
5   All quotations are from 'Minutes of Juba conference 18–21 October 1954', NA FO 371/108326, no. 193, found in Wawa, 2005: document 24: 115–137. Note that the spelling and punctuation of the original document have been retained.
6   E. M. Gwonza, 'Conclusion, Reasons for Adopting U.S. Constitution', South Sudan National Archive (SSNA) EP SCR 10.B.33.
7   E. M. Gwonza, 'Federation for the Republic of the Sudan', SSNA EP SCR 10.B.33.
8   The Constitution of the Southern Front, 1964, SSNA EP 10.A.1; letter from SANU to the prime minister of the Sudan, Sirr al-Khatim al-Khalifa, November 1964, published in Beshir, 1968, Appendix 10: 154–8; letter from William Deng to the prime minister of the Sudan, January 1965 (unpublished document collected by Yosa Wawa); 'A Memorandum of the Southern Front to the Council of Ministers', 9 December 1964, and

letter from the Southern Front to the prime minister of Sudan, concerning the killing of the Southern Sudanese in the south by security forces (Wawa, 2005: documents 37 and 38: 193–203).

9   Other sources for this point come from unpublished sources collected by Yosa Wawa, including Liberal Party, 'Proposal for the government of the southern region of Sudan', 10 August 1965, NRO South 1/44; Southern Front, 'Press release concerning the Southern Sudanese exclusion at the celebrations marking the first anniversary of the October Revolution', 12 October 1965.

10 A. C. Agolong, 'Summary of the Meeting between the Representative J. Lagu, Messers: Wol Wol and Mading de Garang and the Kinshasha [sic] Group', 20 August 1971 (unpublished document collected by Yosa Wawa).

11 South Sudan Liberation Movement, 'Revised (and Amended) Recommendations for a New Constitution for the Republic of the Sudan (Based on a Federation of two Regions)', SSNA Ministry of Southern Affairs, 1.A.1.

12 Minutes of Conference on the Southern Sudan held in Addis Ababa between Sudan Government and Southern Sudan Liberation Movement, 1972: 8–15.

13 Ibid.

14 Samuel Aru Bok, 'The Southern Sudan Political Association (SSPA) Stands for Respect and Application of the Provisions of the Sudan Transitional Constitution, Article 16(2) and the Southern Provinces Self-Government Act, 1972 regarding the Establishment of Reasonable Regional Government in the Southern Sudan', 15 December 1986 (unpublished document collected by Yosa Wawa); SPLM/SPLA, 'Press Statement on the Causes and Continuation of War in the Sudan after the overthrow of Dictator Nimeiri', 13 January 1987 (Wawa, 2005: document 70: 351–5).

15 The source for this information also includes the 'Position Paper by the African Parties, concerning war and peace in the Sudan', 26 September 1987 (unpublished document collected by Yosa Wawa).

16 The source for this information also includes: 'Elders, Religious Leaders and Intellectuals of the Equatoria Region, 'Position Paper on Peace in Sudan', September 1989, and 'Speech by the Chiefs of the Equatoria Region to the Visiting Political Committee from Khartoum to Juba', 11 September 1990 (unpublished documents collected by Yosa Wawa).

17 SPLM/A 'Joint Abuja Delegation declaration', 1 June 1992; text of Washington Declaration, SPLM/A Update 2/41, 24 October 1993, p. 2.

18 Bany, Opening Address to the Abuja Peace Talks (1992).

19 'Equatoria Conference 2011 Resolutions', 29 May 2011.

References

Abeyi, Jack L. W. (2014), 'South Sudan: Federalism and the prisoner's dilemma: Part one', *Gurtong*, http://www.gurtong.net/ECM/Editorial/tabid/124/ctl/ArticleView/mid/519/articleId/15364/South-Sudan-Federalism-and-Prisoners-Dilemma.aspx.

Addis Ababa Agreement of 1972.

Bany, William Nyuon (1992), Opening address to the Abuja Peace Talks, unpublished document collected by Yosa Wawa.

Beshir, Mohamed O. (1968), *The Southern Sudan: Background to Conflict* (London: Hurst).

Dellagiacoma, Fr. (ed.) (1990), *How a Slave Became a Minister: Autobiography of Sayyed Stanislaus Abdallahi Paysama* (Khartoum: no publisher).

Garang, John (1992), *The Call for Democracy in Sudan* (London: Kegan Paul International).

Johnson, Douglas H. (2013), 'New Sudan or South Sudan? The multiple meanings of self-determination in Sudan's Comprehensive Peace Agreement', *Civil Wars* 15, no. 2, 141–56.
— (ed.) (1998) *Sudan, 1951–56: British Documents on the End of Empire Project, Vol. 5, Part 2* (London: The Stationery Office).
Kopling, Peter (2014), 'Peaceful coexistence: How the Equatorians got it right!', *South Sudan Nation*, http://www.southsudannation.com/peaceful-coexistence-how-the-equatorians-got-it-right/.
Levine, Donald (2008), 'Review of *Ethnic Federalism: The Ethiopian Experience in Comparative Perspective* by David Turton', *The Journal of Modern African Studies* 46, no. 1: 167–8.
Lupai, Jacob K. (2013), 'Kokora: Often misunderstood, grossly misinterpreted and most feared', *South Sudan Nation*, 28 January, http://www.southsudannation.com/kokora-often-misunderstood-grossly-misinterpreted-and-most-feared/.
Nyaba, Peter Adwok (1997), *The Politics of Liberation in South Sudan: An Insider's View* (Kampala: Fountain Publishers).
People's Local Government Act of 1971.
Permanent Constitution of Sudan of 1973.
Robertson, James W. (1974), *Transition in Africa: From Direct Rule to Independence: A Memoir* (London: C. Hurst).
Sebit, Sindani (2014), 'Proposed federal system for future South Sudan: Let's serialize it', *Gurtong*, 24 June, http://www.gurtong.net/ECM/Editorial/tabid/124/ctl/ArticleView/mid/519/articleId/15377/Proposed-Federal-System-For-Future-South-Sudan-Lets-Serialize-It.aspx.
SSPD (2014), *Negotiating Peace Through Federalism: A Proposal for Good Governance in Post-Conflict South Sudan*, https://paanluelwel2011.files.wordpress.com/2014/07/negotiating-peace-through-federalism.pdf.
SPLM (1983), Manifesto.
SPLM-IO (2014), 'SPLM-in-Opposition proposes 21 states with Ramciel as national capital', *Gurtong*, 17 July, http://www.gurtong.net/ECM/Editorial/tabid/124/ctl/ArticleView/mid/519/articleId/15464/SPLM-In-Opposition-Proposes-21-States-With-Ramciel-As-National-Capital.aspx.
Sudan Informazioni (1965), *Round-Table Conference on the Southern Sudan, Khartoum, 16–25 1965*, Sudan Informazioni News Agency Documents.
Sudan Update (1994), 'SPLM/A (U) Mid-West Upper Nile Press Statement', *Sudan Update* 5, no. 19 (7 September): 2.
Transitional Constitution of the Republic of South Sudan of 2011.
Wawa, Yosa (2005), *Southern Sudanese Pursuits of Self-Determination: Documents in Political History* (Kisubi: Marianum Press).

CHAPTER 7

Ethiopian Ethnic Federalism

A Model for South Sudan?[1]

John Young

Introduction

There's a widely held belief that southern Sudanese representatives advocated for and were promised federalism at the 1947 Juba Conference. Despite this, the Arabo-Islamic élite, to whom the departing British handed over power, constructed a unitary state in Sudan. This laid the basis for the ethnic-based conflict that continues to the present. In response to the south's marginalisation in the 1960s, the South Sudan Liberation Army (SSLA) launched an insurgency demanding secession, but agreed to federal arrangements for southern Sudan under the Addis Ababa Agreement of 1972. When that agreement broke down, the Sudan Peoples' Liberation Army (SPLA) revolted and called for federalism under the banner of the New Sudan, and maintained this position until the eve of the independence referendum in 2011.

The virtual consensus on federalism broke down when the Sudan Peoples' Liberation Movement (SPLM) became the ruling party at independence and, in all but name, constructed a unitary state. Interest in federalism continued, however, and since civil war resumed in December 2013, it has increasingly come to the fore as a major demand of the breakaway Sudan Peoples' Liberation Movement-in-Opposition (SPLM-IO). The peace agreement reached in August 2015 stated that federalism was a wish of the South Sudanese and that agreement should be reached on the form it would take by the end of the 30-month transitional period (IGAD, 2015).

Afflicted by ethnic conflicts not dissimilar to South Sudan, the Tigray Peoples' Liberation Front (TPLF) in Ethiopia and the ethnic-based coalition it created, the Ethiopian Peoples' Revolutionary Democratic Front (EPRDF), established a federal system in which Ethiopia's ethnic groups were made part of the political process and granted the right to self-determination. This 'ethnic federalism' approach challenged African governments, who have generally attempted to overcome ethnic diversity by political or violent means to establish a nation-state. The Ethiopian model of federalism has not found much favour on the continent. Indeed, SPLM leaders from the time of John Garang, the first leader of the SPLM, through to Salva Kiir, the current president of the Government of the Republic of South Sudan (GRSS), and Riek Machar, leader of the SPLM-IO, have all rejected the Ethiopian model of ethnic federalism. However, African efforts to overcome ethnicity and construct a nation-state modelled on western nations have frequently not been successful. The resumption of civil war in South Sudan makes clear the need to address the problem of ethnic conflict and to consider alternatives to the present failed model of governance.

This chapter will briefly consider the theory surrounding ethnicity, and will then examine the ethnic-based conflict in Ethiopia that provided the background to the EPRDF's unique model of federalism. It will then outline the Ethiopian federal system and assess how the federal system works in practice. Lastly, the chapter will consider whether Ethiopia's system of federalism could or should be adopted in South Sudan. It must be stressed that, for purposes of analysis, it is not easy to separate ethnic federalism from EPRDF governance in Ethiopia.

Ethnicity: a theoretic interlude

Ethnicity was initially characterised by academics as 'primordial' and critical to human organisation and identity (Geertz, 1963), with some assuming ethnicity to be genetically based and necessary to ensure group preservation (Chapman, 1993). These theorists held that ethnic groups had clearly demarcated and largely unchanging boundaries which produced permanent identities. These hallmarks of an earlier generation of academic thinking have, however, now largely been rejected.

Present orthodoxy considers ethnic identities to be social constructs that emerge as a result of historical and political conditions. Instead of current ethnic identities and conflicts being due to age-old processes, they are likely to be the product of more recent social and political change and the interaction between groups. Ethnic boundaries are typically fluid and shifting, and this permits people to have multiple identities, any of which may come to the fore depending on circumstances. Colonialism was critical to identity formation, as older identities became meshed with newly adapted identities to meet the needs of changing conditions.

Ethnic identities in Africa and elsewhere may manifest themselves in cultural, social, economic and political guises, but it is the politicisation of ethnicity and its application in mobilising opposition to those holding state power that has gained the most attention. Ethnic conflict typically arises as a result of state actions related to issues of distribution and domination, often within the context of so-called nation-building (Fiseha, 2005). The focus is the state, because it provides access to scarce material and social resources under the control of ethnic monopolies. The humiliation that ethnic monopolies produce in some communities is a factor motivating people to revolt, and is frequently more difficult to address than material inequities. In the Horn of Africa, ethnic monopolies have been common: Ethiopia was ruled by an Amhara élite for hundreds of years before the EPRDF captured state power; in Sudan, an Arabo-Islamic élite in the riverine core was handed power by the departing British; in Djibouti, the Somalis have long dominated the Afar; and in Somalia, various clans have used state power to oppress other clans.

While colonialism favoured particular groups, national movements attempted to overcome these divisions to create mass movements in opposition to colonial power. The departure of the colonial authorities saw power transferred to national élites, setting the stage for another round of conflict that continues to take an explicitly ethnic form. In Ethiopia and Sudan, the language and religion of the dominant ethnic groups were forcefully identified with the 'nation-state' and became further obstacles to marginalised groups attempting to achieve assimilation, national integration and advancement. Ethiopia's many ethnic groups and multiple religious traditions do not conform to the ideal of the nation-state, and successive political regimes have failed to accommodate this diversity through appropriate institutions and policies (Fiseha, 2015). The same can be said for Sudan and, more recently, South Sudan.

The failure of states to accommodate ethnicity may lead ethnic groups to aspire to nationhood and a separate state. However, secession does not end ethnic-based conflicts, particularly if mechanisms are not developed to manage ethnic-based tensions, as seen from the experience of Eritrea and South Sudan. The threat that politicised ethnic groups pose to social stability arises from their exclusion from a system organised to allow favoured ethnic groups to monopolise power and maintain this status quo (Markakis, 1994).

It is therefore ethnically monopolised states, and not marginalised ethnic groups, that are the cause of power instability in the Horn.

Nonetheless, mainstream academia typically views ethnicity as dangerous because it leads to politicisation, undermines shared values, produces élites with sectional interests and weakens stability (Fleiner, 2000; Clapham, 2001; Horowitz, 1985). Other analysts go further and claim that ethnonationalist demands can make federalism impossible and even lead to civil war (Nordlinger, 1972; Elazer, 1987). Most academics probably agree that structuring regional boundaries to cut across ethno-linguistic and religious lines serves to undermine identities rather than reinforce them, thereby encouraging inter-ethnic alliances at the central state level (Lipset, 1983). This approach to dealing with conflict in ethnically divided states assumes, however, that ethnic élites are not territorially based, are not a product of intense mobilisation, and are loyal to the state (Liiphart, 1994). None of these conditions applied in Ethiopia, Sudan or South Sudan, and that made maintaining a unitary state highly problematic.

The genesis of Ethiopian ethnic federalism

The social structure of Amhara-Tigrayan society that formed the pre-revolutionary core of Ethiopia was the 'classic trinity of noble, priest, and peasant [and] the relationship to the only means of production, that is land' (Markakis, 1994: 83). The state extracted surpluses through a tithe on land, taxes on livestock and trade, and the provision of various services to the Church and nobles, while Muslims were denied access to land. The historical origins of this system lay in Tigray, but from at least the thirteenth century onwards power passed to the Amhara.

Land, hunger and the desire to fend off encroaching western imperialism stimulated the southern expansion of the Amhara which, in turn, laid the basis for ensuing ethnic conflicts (Markakis, 1994). The state assumed a central role in the production and distribution of material and social resources, as well as being the main source of employment for the western-educated intelligentsia. The result was that Ethiopia became a classic example of an 'ethnocratic state' (Mazrui, 1975). Although Amhara peasants belonged to the dominant group in cultural, religious, linguistic and psychological terms, they had no share of power, and their poverty was often as pervasive as that of the people in the colonised south. Thus, class distinctions and class conflict were always a feature of traditional Ethiopia.

While capital flowed to the south, with its abundance of fertile land and other resources, Tigray stagnated and resentment grew (Young, 1997). This resentment took on violent form in Eritrea where, under British tutelage after the expulsion of the Italian colonisers during the Second World War, a level of economic and political development was achieved that was unknown in the rest of the country. In 1961, the largely Muslim and lowland-based Eritrean Liberation Front (ELF) launched a rebellion calling for national self-determination. It was overtaken in the 1970s by the highland-based Marxist Eritrean Peoples' Liberation Front (EPLF). In the 1960s, a student movement emerged that could both analyse the country's problematic political dynamics and lead the opposition. Although the students largely adopted the class analysis of Marxism, they condemned Amhara ethnic chauvinism for the cultural oppression of other ethnic groups. The TPLF adopted an oppositional approach based on ethnicity at a tactical level, while still affirming class at a strategic level. Due to the limited development of an urban working class and the students' weak links to both the peasants and Eritrean revolutionaries, it fell to the military to overthrow the tottering regime of Haile Selassie. Similarly, Sudan had a rebellion in the periphery and a radical intelligentsia at the centre. In both the Ethiopian and Sudanese cases, the military failed to overcome the national revolts, which ultimately proved their undoing.

Lacking a coherent ideology, junior Derg officers looked to the students for direction and to carry out land reform which, virtually overnight, eliminated the feudal class. Businesses were nationalised and landlordism ended, and the small but growing bourgeoisie disappeared. In addition to raising the standard of living of peasants and granting Muslims the right to hold land, the Derg promoted local languages and cultures. It also established the Institute for the Study of Ethiopian Nationalities, which carried out important studies of Ethiopia's ethnic communities that the EPRDF later used to formulate its model of ethnic federalism. The regime treated the national question as a cultural phenomenon, rather than a political one that would have been amenable to power-sharing. As a result, the national question was not adequately addressed and a myriad of demands led to the Derg collapse amid depletion of resources and legitimacy.

In searching for a governance model free of ethnic domination, the TPLF drew on the student movement, which was strongly influenced by the Bolsheviks. Like the Ethiopian revolutionaries, the Bolsheviks were confronted with the practical problems of capturing power in a largely feudal empire with a small urban working class and many ethnic groups, and administering the country upon taking power. To win the support of ethnic minorities, Stalin attacked 'Greater Russian chauvinism', recognised the sovereignty and equality of the empire's nations, and mobilised marginalised nations around a commitment to national self-determination. Crucially, Stalin defined a nation as a stable community with a common language, single territory, coherent economy and common psychology (Stalin, 1913). The TPLF/EPRDF employed this model and drew on the early experience of the Soviet Union in their future organisation of the Ethiopian state.

Having accepted the need to unite Ethiopia's various ethnic communities against the Derg, the TPLF organised a democratic front which gave it a hegemonic position with a single organisation, programme, leadership and army, although the separate national components were given a measure of autonomy. The EPLF would not join because it was committed to secession, and the Oromo Liberation Front (OLF) was not prepared to accept the dominant position of the TPLF. In the absence of suitable coalition candidates, the TPLF established its own ethnic movements beginning with the Amhara under what later became the Amhara National Democratic Movement (ANDM). In 1989, the TPLP and ANDM came together as the EPRDF. Meanwhile, the TPLF began to construct the Oromo Peoples' Democratic Organisation (OPDO) from captured Derg soldiers and, in 1990, OPDO joined the EPRDF. A host of other armed ethnic-based groups joined or affiliated themselves with the EPRDF, both before and after the EPRDF defeated the Derg. A skeleton multi-ethnic coalition was thus in place when the EPRDF assumed power in 1991.

Ethiopian ethnic federalism

Many were convinced that the EPRDF would bring about the dissolution of the country, and the EPRDF's efforts to create ethnic-based groups and ignore pan-Ethiopian groups fed these fears. In the end, a national conference was convened in July 1991, with 27 organisations attending, 19 of which represented ethnic groups and only three of which were of a pan-Ethiopian persuasion. A Transitional Period Charter was adopted which laid down the legal framework for reconstituting the state and devolving power along ethno-regional lines (Tewfik, 2010). The EPRDF was essentially able to dominate the Transitional Government, pursuing its political programme and realising its plans to structure Ethiopia along ethnic lines. With power linked to ethnicity, there was a proliferation of ethnic-based organisations that could participate directly in the new political dispensation. Critics viewed the EPRDF's policies as a threat to the existence of Ethiopia as they attempted to ensure dominance of the EPRDF (Balcha, 2007; ICG, 2009). However, the EPRDF claimed that its policies were designed to both preserve the unity of the state and harness ethnic energies to promote development. Twenty-five years later that debate is still ongoing.

Putting flesh to its principles, the Transitional Government passed Proclamation No. 7/1992 to divide the country into ethnic blocs. A boundaries commission was established, and it created 14 regions using language as the critical variable in defining ethnic markers. Divisions within regions were left to local governments. Tigray, Amhara, Oromo, Somali and Afar regions had ethnic cores, but the other regions were formed by bringing different ethnic groups under one unit. Addis Ababa and Harar were given special status and not included in Oromia despite their Oromo majorities. The resulting configuration was far from clear and the regions were highly diverse with respect to size, population and resources. The lack of ethnic homogeneity in even the five regions with ethnic cores necessitated creation of special zones and *woredas* (districts) to accommodate minorities. The Southern Region was the most ethnically diverse, and 14 zones and five special *woredas* were established. The restructuring process was not always peaceful, as some groups grappled to have the status of region or *woreda* in order to gain recognition. However, without complementary power-sharing mechanisms or any other means of guaranteed representation in regional governments or institutions, Ethiopia's system provides insufficient protection of minority rights.

Under the 1995 Constitution, the EPRDF explicitly rejected the nation-state model that underpins western states and which had been transplanted to Africa, often with disastrous results. Instead, it represented an agreement not just between citizens, but between ethnic groups, and closely followed Stalin's idea that

> a nation, nationality or people is a group of people who have or share a large measure of common culture or similar customs, mutual intelligibility of language, belief in a common or related identities, a common psychological make-up, and who inhabit an identifiable, predominantly contiguous territory. (Constitution, Article 39)

In practice, the definition proved sufficiently vague (the distinction between nation, nationality and people was never made) that determining boundaries would largely be made politically and pragmatically. In keeping with devolving power to ethnic groups, the powers of the federal government were limited, and residual powers were reserved for the states (Constitution, Article 52). The constitution tasked the federal government with formulating and implementing policies and strategies for overall economic, social and development matters (Article 51/2), and the states were empowered to formulate and execute policies and strategies for the state (Article 52).

The most controversial element of the constitution is undoubtedly the provision granting the nations, nationalities and peoples of Ethiopia the right to secede from the federation (Article 39/1), a provision that fed fears of Ethiopian disintegration. Others doubted that the conditions under which this right could be exercised, namely gaining a two-thirds majority in the relevant state legislature, followed by a majority vote in a referendum, and agreement on the division of assets, could ever be realised in practice.

The constitution provided for a bicameral legislature at the centre, made up of the House of Peoples' Representatives and the House of Federation. The House of Peoples' Representatives is elected by direct universal suffrage for five years and has exclusive power to make laws. The House of Federation explicitly represents ethnic groups, and representatives are selected by the regional or state councils, with every recognised nationality having at least one representative and an additional representative for every million people. At last count there were 137 representatives of 69 regions. The House of Federation is tasked with resolving issues related to the country's ethnic groups, mediating disputes between them, and acting as a court of last resort through its Committee for States' Affairs, which deals with such disputes. In the early years of the newly structured state, the House of Federation handled many disputes as the system was worked out. It decides on the division of joint federal and regional tax sources and subsidies of the federal government to the regions. Notably, the House of Federation nominates a largely symbolic president for the country, who must then be approved by a two-thirds majority in both houses.

Language was considered the determining characteristic of ethnicity. The constitution grants equality to all of the country's languages, but makes Amharic the 'working language' of the federal government and gives the regions the right to determine their own working languages (Article 5). Language policy is usually controversial, but there was little dispute over recognising Amharic as the working language of the federal government since there was no realistic alternative. Meanwhile, allowing the regions to determine their own language practices served to mute this divisive issue at the national level. The major non-Amharic speaking groups began teaching in their indigenous languages for the early years of school, and many of the ethnic language groups in the Southern Region abandoned the Abyssinian Geez script in favour of the Latin alphabet. However, after initially encouraging the widest possible use of indigenous languages in support of the principle of diversity, the EPRDF began stressing unity and efficiency and discouraged administrative proliferation as the problems of isolation and lack of resources became increasingly evident. With no clear definition of ethnicity and every incentive for local politically ambitious groups to call for their own region, zone or *woreda*, the ruling party felt compelled to slow down or even stop a process that had logically followed from their own political programme.

Ethnic federalism does not sufficiently accommodate the fact that nationalities do not always coincide with established regional boundaries, and tends to undervalue shared histories of nationalities, their changing character, and their mobility. Also, a notable portion of the population in Ethiopia has a mixed or uncertain ethnic background (Clapham, 2001). Critics of Ethiopian ethnic federalism have argued that the system restricts labour and capital mobility (Tronvoll, 2000). However, the past decade of rapid economic growth may serve to discount arguments that Ethiopia's ethnic federalism impedes development.

Ethiopia's ethnic federalism in practice

Any assessment of Ethiopia's model of federalism is difficult because of the complexity of the system and the difficulty in separating ethnic federalism from EPRDF governance more generally. Since much of the criticism of the EPRDF's ethnic federalism proceeds from what many consider to be its authoritarianism, it is important to distinguish the EPRDF's approach to democracy from that of liberal democracy. Liberal democracy, as developed in the west, is associated with individual rights, the rule of law, regular multi-party elections and, more recently, endorsement of capitalism and rejection of economic democracy (Abrahamsen, 2001). In contrast, the EPRDF considers liberal democracy to be a product of a particular stage of economic and class development in the west and views it as inappropriate for poverty-stricken Ethiopia throwing off the last vestiges of feudalism. The EPRDF instead emphasises ethnic and class rights, economic justice and equality, and holds that these objectives can only be realised under the auspices of a vanguard party and democratic centralism. Called 'revolutionary democracy' by the EPRDF, it is focused on the peasantry being the large majority of the population and the political base of the EPRDF, and holds that development is its primary concern.

Critics accuse the EPRDF of being élitist and opaque, running roughshod over competing political organisations, having scant respect for elections, controlling parliament, having a fetish about control, opposing the emergence of an independent judiciary, viewing urban dwellers and middle-class Ethiopians as potential enemies, and assuming a proprietorial position over the peasantry (see, for example, Ottaway, 1995; Gudina, 2003; Aalen, 2006; Balcha, 2007). While cultural diversity is encouraged, political pluralism is not, and independent voices in civil society, the media and trade unions have been repressed by the EPRDF. Intolerance was manifest in the wake of the 2005 national elections in which almost 200 unarmed demonstrators were killed by security forces and thousands arrested, after which tight controls were applied to the media and political parties.

That said, most critics would acknowledge that the EPRDF is committed to local-level decision-making, self-sufficiency, land reform, women's rights, economic equality and justice, challenging social and traditional hierarchies, controlling its own foreign policy, and not leaving economic development solely up to a so-called impartial market. While the EPRDF's revolutionary democracy should undoubtedly be challenged, non-western notions of democracy should also be acknowledged, as should the increasingly constrictive form western democracy takes in the era of neo-liberalism, the war on terror and mass surveillance.

Two decades have passed since the constitution gave regions the right to secession, and no region has yet attempted to enact its provisions on self-determination. Either the constitution has served to overcome the reasons why regions might want to secede, or the conditions needed to realise self-determination are too difficult to achieve. Alternatively, it may be that the EPRDF is indeed committed to a united Ethiopia and will take measures, both fair and foul, to ensure that none of the country's ethnic groups leave. A close analysis of the past two decades suggests that all of these reasons likely explain why no constituent part of Ethiopia has attempted to secede. While ethnic groups may not be permitted to secede in practice, this does not entirely negate the significance of the constitutional right to self-determination, as it still acknowledges the legitimacy of these groups and would serve to politically empower them should there be widespread support for secession.

Another commonly expressed concern has been that ethnic federalism undermines national identity and loyalty. However, Ethiopian nationalism has been evident, including in response to Eritrea's attempts to capture disputed border territory in 1998, showing that loyalty to the overarching Ethiopian state and regions can coexist in a federation that endorses multiple centres of power and endeavours to balance both federal and national loyalties. Critics have also highlighted the lack of assertiveness of the regions under Ethiopia's system of federalism. However, given that Ethiopia's regions did not exist independently before federalism's introduction, they cannot be expected to have the same level of independent-mindedness as seen in federations formed out of pre-existing independent units, such as the United States.

In the past, conflicts between ethnic communities tended to be over resources, but now increasingly take the form of disputes between regional governments (Asnake, 2013). These disputes can be resolved through negotiation between unit administrations, with the possibility of House of Federation intervention. However, in the lowland states, with their large numbers of pastoralists, neither state boundaries nor regional authorities have gained sufficient legitimacy, necessitating that conflicts be resolved by traditional authorities. Unlike the pre-1991 period when inter-ethnic conflicts raged and ultimately brought down the government, disputes today do not typically threaten the stability of the central state.

Unlike other federal systems where regional and central authorities often disagree over power and access to resources, such disputes are not evident in Ethiopia because the ruling party maintains a high degree of unity and, when disagreements arise, they are resolved internally. This approach has the advantage of maintaining stability, but often at the cost of open debate on matters of public policy. Moreover, the dependence of the federation on an all-powerful party raises concerns that should the EPRDF disintegrate, as almost occurred in 2001 when a major dispute broke out among the TPLF leadership, the country could collapse in similar fashion to the Soviet Union when the Communist Party dissolved.

Claims that ethnic federalism has recentralised power rather than led to radical devolution are common and are true to some extent, for several reasons (World Bank, 2001; Gudina, 2003; Balcha, 2007; ICG, 2009). First, while some fiscal decentralisation has occurred under the EPRDF, it has not been dramatic. While the regions are responsible for delivering most social services, including health and education, only 20 per cent of revenue is collected by states, with 80 per cent of total revenue still being collected by the federal government. Second, under Meles Zinawi's leadership, collegial governance ended as he purged the TPLF and EPRDF and consolidated power in himself, becoming the uncontested chairman of both fronts, as well as prime minister and, unofficially, the ideological guide for both parties and the government. However, Hailemariam Desalegn, who succeeded Meles, neither attempted to acquire similar authority nor opted for a more pluralistic approach to decision-making.

Third, in response to anger in the wake of the 2005 national elections, the EPRDF gave further emphasis to the notion of the development state modelled after the South-East Asian experience. Building on its rejection of the neo-liberal model of development and resistance to opening up the political system, the EPRDF made rapidly rising living standards, particularly for the poor peasantry, its primary objective. The regime can claim considerable successes in this regard. However, these accomplishments have further empowered the central state, particularly in economic policy, undermining regional state powers. Some analysts assert that, ideologically at least, the centralisation of power under the developmental state is incompatible with the EPRDF's vision of a decentralised, ethnic-based federation (Fiseha, 2012; Clapham, 2013).

There are enormous differences across Ethiopia in terms of economic development, reflecting inequities in the distribution of resources and a legacy of the centre's oppression of the periphery. This has constrained some regions' capacity to develop and implement economic policies, and while there have been dramatic improvements in living standards, the peripheral states under the EPRDF have not overcome their legacy of oppression and under-development. Moreover, the lack of government reach in the borderlands has meant that ethnic and sectional conflicts are common and not easily contained. While local-level conflicts do not pose a threat to the state, limited government control over these areas attracts regime-threatening groups, including the OLF, Ogaden National Liberation Front and Al-Itihad al-Islamiya (an Islamist group in neighbouring Somalia).

The Ethiopian government must ensure that conflicts in neighbouring states, notably South Sudan and Somalia, do not spill across their shared borders. Consequently, security has been the EPRDF's priority in the western and eastern lowlands, and local élites' commitment to the federal system and the EPRDF has been actively nurtured. However, while increased education of indigenous government employees at the Civil Service University in Addis Ababa and training within the public sector have improved regional administration, the local élites in the lowlands have generally not lived up to expectations.

Living standards have generally been improved, through the central government providing infrastructure, roads and links to the centre, and building schools and health facilities. However, marginalised groups such as pastoralists and traditional farmers in the lowlands have had their meagre livelihoods threatened by the government leasing land to private (usually foreign) agro-industrial and energy companies, a trend that has exacerbated resource conflicts.

According to Assefa Fiseha, the EPRDF 'dictates the institutions of democracy, hence the party – not the people – is sovereign', although he acknowledges that 'multicultural federalism remains the only defensible option to hold Ethiopia together' (Fiseha, 2012: 26, 88). Party hegemony in the state is not unique to Ethiopia, or even Africa; nonetheless, Fiseha's point is valid: the achievements of the EPRDF's ethnic federalism are threatened by the effective party-state merger of the EPRDF, a weakness that set the Derg on the road to destruction. Horowitz (1994) contends that under an ethnic-based system of federalism, majority rule leads to domination by the leading ethnic group, while the holding of power by minority ethnic groups results in authoritarianism and centralised control.

Despite the many criticisms of the EPRDF's ethnic federalism, only a minority of Ethiopians want to turn their back on ethnic federalism, even though they do not approve of the way it operates under the EPRDF. In the past decade, which can roughly be associated with formal commitment to the Growth and Transformation Plan or the 'democratic developmental state', the level of economic development and poverty reduction has been impressive. Between 2000 and 2011, Ethiopia's annual per capita growth-rate averaged about 10 per cent (almost double the sub-Saharan African average) and life expectancy increased from 52 years to 63 years. At the same time, poverty dropped from 56 to 31 per cent of the population living below US\$1.25 a day (World Bank, 2015). There are equally impressive statistics that demonstrate rapid improvements in school attendance, vaccination take-up, and reducing maternal and infant mortality. Equally significantly, this growth can largely be attributed to the EPRDF's rejection of neo-liberalism, with central government instead playing a leading role in directing the economy.

At the same time, the importance of the central government in this process threatens to undermine the authority of the regional governments. Critics contend that the EPRDF's land policies and its federal system discourage movement from ethnic homelands to the cities, and that this will ultimately constrain development. Many governance challenges also persist, and the International Crisis Group (ICG) has expressed fears that the international community might be prepared to overlook the EPRDF's undemocratic practices as a result of its economic achievements (ICG, 2009). In the same vein, David Smith (2014) has stated that Ethiopia is 'the darling of the global development community and the scourge of the human rights lobby'.

While the EPRDF's goal to make Ethiopia a middle-income country by 2020 is ambitious, it is not unrealistic. Although the dangers of politicised ethnicity are not over, the rapidly growing economy has meant that the biggest threat to both the regime and its progressive orientation comes from the expanding urban middle class created by the EPRDF's own policies and their demands for freedom under a generally authoritarian regime. The EPRDF's challenge will be to gain the support of the urban poor, small businesses and workers, without undermining links to the peasantry upon which the survival of the regime depends. The peasantry will also become increasingly economically differentiated, with the wealthy likely coming to oppose the state-imposed constraints on land ownership. The appointment of Abiy Ahmed as prime minister in April 2018 and his promotion of wide-ranging reforms will hopefully serve to bring greater government accountability to Ethiopia, but at the time of writing he has not indicated that there will be any fundamental changes to the system of ethnic federalism.

Is Ethiopia's ethnic federalism a model for South Sudan?

The TPLF and SPLA were established at similar times, fought against regimes of a similar character, and both concluded that the central hegemonic state was the principal problem. They thus called for a radical decentralisation of state power. The SPLA condemned the monopolisation of power by the successive Arabo-Islamic governments it fought, and called for a transfer of power to the marginalised peoples of the periphery. However, after Garang died, the SPLA dropped its commitment to a united federal New Sudan and, upon achieving independence, it reproduced a centralised state not unlike the one it had fought. South Sudan suffers endemic ethnic-based conflicts that compare to those that continue to destabilise Sudan. Meanwhile, the EPRDF has developed a system of ethnic federalism which has not ended ethnic conflicts, but has largely channelled them along institutional lines where they can be contained and do not threaten state survival. By recognising the cultures of historically oppressed groups, giving written form to domestic languages and teaching their languages in schools, the Ethiopian federal system has given people dignity, fostered cultural pluralism and encouraged national unity.

The wholesale transplanting of the Ethiopian model of ethnic federalism to South Sudan is not feasible for several reasons. Ethiopian ethnic federalism is largely a product of a highland peasant society, whereas the majority of South Sudanese are agro-pastoralists. It was introduced in Ethiopia only after extensive studies of the country's ethnic communities had been undertaken, and knowledge of South Sudan's ethnic makeup remains limited. Moreover, it is inconceivable that the present dysfunctional state and divided South Sudanese leadership would have the capacity to implement and manage such a complex system of federalism, even if there was the political will. Mention has been made of the danger of an unequal federalism developing in Ethiopia because of historical under-development in the lowland regions, relative to the more developed highland regions. The regional inequities in resource distribution are equally great in South Sudan, and reaching agreement on distributing oil revenues is daunting. However, devolving power and responding to ethnic-based conflicts with appropriate systems of local governance are aspects that South Sudan should adopt from Ethiopia.

Another key lesson for South Sudan is the need for the central government to give political recognition to ethnic groups. This was an important element of South Sudan's struggle for independence that was not honoured post-independence. Indeed, most of the fighting during the later years of the war with Khartoum was between southern Sudanese, and the war did not in fact end with the signing of the CPA but with the Juba Declaration, an agreement between a Dinka-dominated SPLA and a Nuer-dominated South Sudan Defence Forces (SSDF) (Young, 2006).

Upon coming to power, government departments and their personnel in South Sudan were effectively divided along ethnic lines. Tensions between the centre and the peripheries that characterised Sudan were replicated in South Sudan and ethnic-based conflicts over resources proliferated. The SPLA did not follow the TPLF in building a popular base and a programme to resolve ethnic conflicts and marginalisation. Moreover, while the TPLF stressed self-sufficiency, the SPLA has always been beholden to outside powers – initially the Derg, then the US and now Uganda. Similarly, the SPLA never developed effective systems of administration in its liberated territories, and that lack of experience is reflected in the post-independence weakness of the South Sudanese government.

The outbreak of conflict in December 2013 took place within the context of a systemic breakdown of governance in the country, endemic theft of state resources by élites, widespread ethnic-based conflicts, and the inability of the SPLM élites to peacefully resolve their internal disputes. While the civil war began as an ethnic conflict between the Dinka and Nuer, it has increasingly taken the form of a coalition of ethnic groups opposed to the Dinka-dominated state of Salva Kiir.

Machar and the SPLM-IO leadership aspire to assume power, but are not committed to a fundamental transformation of the state, unlike the TPLF/EPRDF which was dedicated to overthrowing the entire edifice of ethnic-based rule. While the TPLF/EPRDF held that an Amhara élite was the cause of ethnic marginalisation and not the entire community, the SPLM-IO ignored class in its attack on a system of ethnic domination. As a result, SPLM-IO supporters are largely motivated by hatred of the Dinka, and the popularity of federalism in the rebel camp is due to the belief that it will create 'Dinka-free' local governments.

TPLF federalism took form in an environment in which western liberalism had no social basis in Ethiopia. Similarly, the only basis of liberalism in South Sudan is a civil society that was largely created by western aid agencies together with a handful of professionals, many of whom serve in the government bureaucracy and are so deeply embedded within the ruling party as to seriously compromise any commitment to liberalism. Moreover, the SPLM/A accepted a neo-liberal economy and rejected economic democracy despite the enormous inequities that afflict the country. In addition to an inappropriate economic model, the government adopted a range of governance institutions based on western experience, making it only a matter of time before they broke down. Ethiopian experience suggests the need to develop systems of governance that meet the unique needs of the people and to not be unduly influenced by western models that evolved under very different circumstances.

The EPRDF system of federalism is not without problems. One difficulty is that it assumes a largely primordial understanding of ethnicity in which ethnic groups are contained within clearly demarcated territories, despite experience showing the malleability of both ethnic identities and boundaries. This has proved problematic in pastoralist areas, where people and animals move across regional boundaries. South Sudan has a much larger pastoralist economy than Ethiopia and hosts many Sudanese pastoralists, making boundary demarcation even more complicated. Successive movements of internally displaced persons have further complicated boundary demarcation. While the EPRDF opted to utilise traditional leaders to resolve conflicts in pastoral areas, the SPLM has limited the role of traditional rulers in governance and conflict resolution, despite their legitimacy and the frequent lack of authority of the local government leadership. It is essential to incorporate traditional leadership into national governance in South Sudan.

Until Kiir's recent unilateral decision to increase the number of states from ten to 28, and later to 32, state boundaries in South Sudan had cut across ethnic communities, a practice favoured by liberal academics who, like African leaders, fear that embracing ethnicity poses a threat to achieving national unity. With very little consideration for the long-term implications, the Kiir government is creating a haphazard ethnic-based system, largely in response to local ethnic communities, patronage dispensation and the desire to undermine the SPLM-IO. It is doing this in a context of war and limited resources, and the 'states' created are in practice little more than districts under the complete control of the national government which appoints state governors. An ethnic-based system of federal states without a plan, without popular consultation, without resources, without clear demarcation of boundaries, and being pursued for narrow political reasons will not end well. Indeed, this approach, which began with the government's refutation of the peace agreement, will almost certainly encourage the further ethnicisation of politics in the country, potentially making the country ungovernable.

Conclusion

This chapter has examined Ethiopian ethnic federalism at a time when it is undergoing challenges and faith in South Sudan's system of governance has virtually disintegrated. Nonetheless, if South Sudan's civil war and the collapsed August 2015 peace agreement have produced anything positive, it is that there is now a consensus in favour of federalism, with public consultations being required to determine the form it should take (ARCSS, 2015). It must be stressed that federalism can only provide a *means* to resolve South Sudan's problems and should not be viewed as a short-cut to reforming the SPLM/A, containing corruption, sharing power, raising living standards, overcoming economic inequities, providing services, or the many other problems that bedevil the country. Crucially, no version of federalism can overcome the fundamental problem of a lack of capacity.

This chapter assessed Ethiopian federalism because it was designed to overcome ethnic conflicts and regional disparities – problems that have brought South Sudan to its present sorry impasse. While concluding that much can be learned from a study of Ethiopian ethnic federalism, the wholesale adoption of the system by South Sudan is impractical. Instead, the South Sudanese need to develop approaches to governance that confront the problem of politicised ethnicity, and should not rely on inappropriate western political and economic models, nor establish systems of governance because of the pressures of war.

South Sudan would benefit from Ethiopia's experience by establishing an institute of ethnic studies that could identify and analyse the country's ethnic groups and their traditional forms of governance, as a step towards formalising the role of traditional leaders and adopting elements of traditional governance systems. The South Sudanese would also be advised to encourage and give support to local cultures and foster the use of indigenous languages, which has been one of the most successful elements of Ethiopian ethnic federalism. It is striking that, although much of the SPLM/A mobilisation took the form of affirming an African identity in the face of an Arab-dominated state, it has taken little interest in encouraging and developing local cultures. To build state capacity, particularly in the regions, South Sudan would be advised to adopt another Ethiopian innovation, namely a civil service college that could train the skilled local administrators needed to realise local autonomy objectives. A second legislative house more along the lines of Ethiopia's House of Federation would also be valuable to South Sudan, as a mechanism that promotes the resolution of inter-ethnic disputes.

Notes

1   This chapter was first published as 'Ethiopian ethnic federalism: a model for South Sudan?' by John Young in the *Ethiopian Journal of Federal Studies* at the Center for Federalism and Governance Studies, Addis Ababa University. It is reprinted with permission from the *Ethiopian Journal of Federal Studies*.

References

Aalen, Lovise (2006), 'Ethnic federalism and self-determination for a semi-authoritarian state: The case of Ethiopia', *International Journal on Minority and Group Rights* 13, no. 2–3: 243–61.

Abrahamsen, Rita (2001), *Disciplining Democracy: Development Discourse and Good Governance in Africa* (New York, NY: Zed).

African Union (2015), 'Final report of the AU Commission of Inquiry on South Sudan'.

Asnake, Kefale (2013), *Federalism and Ethnic Conflict in Ethiopia: A Comparative Regional Study* (New York, NY: Routledge).

Balcha, Berhanu G. (2007), 'Restructuring state and society: Ethnic federalism in Ethiopia', PhD diss., Aalborg University.

Chapman, Malcolm (1993), *Social and Biological Aspects of Ethnicity* (Oxford: Oxford University Press).

Clapham, Christopher (2001), 'The political framework: Controlling space in Ethiopia', in Wendy James (ed.), *Remapping Ethiopia: Socialism and After* (Oxford: James Currey).

— (2013), *Ethiopia: Federalism and the Developmental State*, Centre of African Studies, University of Cambridge.

Elazer, Daniel J. (1987), *Exploring Federalism* (Tuscaloosa, AL: University of Alabama).

Fiseha, Assefa (2005), *Federalism and the Accommodation of Diversity in Ethiopia: A Comparative Study* (Nijmegen: Wolf Legal Publishers).

— (2012), 'Ethiopia's experiment in accommodating diversity: 20 years' balance sheet', *Regional and Federal Studies* 22, no. 4: 435–75.

— (2014, November 5), author interview, Addis Ababa.

— (2015), 'Ethiopia: Development with or without freedom?', *International Studies in Human Rights* 111: 99–138.

Fleiner, Lidija R. B. (2000), *Can Ethnic Federalism Work?*, presented at the Facing Ethnic Conflict Conference, Center for Development Research, Bonn.

Geertz, Clifford (1963), *Old Societies and New States: The Quest for Modernity in Africa and Asia* (New York, NY: Free Press).

Gudina, Merera (2003), *Ethiopia: Competing Ethnic Nationalism and the Quest for Democracy, 1960–2000* (Maastricht: Shaker Publishing).

Horowitz, Donald L. (1985), *Ethnic Groups in Conflict* (Berkeley, CA: University of California Press).

— (1994), 'Democracy in divided societies', in Larry J. Diamond and Marc Plattner (eds), *Nationalism, Ethnic Conflict, and Democracy* (Baltimore, MD: Johns Hopkins University Press).

IGAD (2015), Agreement on the Resolution of Conflict in the Republic of South Sudan, Addis Ababa.

International Crisis Group (2009), *Ethiopia: Ethnic Federalism and Its Discontents*, Africa Report No. 153.

Lijphart, Arend (1994), 'Prospects for power-sharing in new South Africa', in Andrew Reynolds (ed.), *Elections '94 South Africa: The Campaigns, Results and Future Prospects* (London: James Currey).

Lipset, Seymour M. (1983), *Political Man: The Social Basis of Politics* (Baltimore, MD: Johns Hopkins University Press).

Markakis, John (1974), *Ethiopia: Anatomy of a Traditional Polity* (Oxford: Clarendon).

— (1994), 'Ethnic conflict and the state in the Horn of Africa', in Fukui Katsuyoshi and John Markakis (eds), *Ethnicity and Conflict in the Horn of Africa* (London: James Currey).

Mazrui, Ali A. (1975), *Soldiers and Kinsmen in Uganda: The Making of a Military Ethnocracy* (London: Sage Publications for the Inter-University Seminar on Armed Forces and Society).

Nordlinger, Eric A. (1972), *Conflict Regulation in Divided Societies*, (Cambridge, MA: Center for International Affairs, Harvard University).

Ottaway, Marina (1995), 'The Ethiopian transition: Democratisation or new authoritarianism?', *Northeast African Studies* 2, no. 3: 67–87.

Proclamation No. 7/1992, 'Proclamation to Provide for the Establishment of National/ Regional Self-Governments', *Negarit Gazeta*, Addis Ababa.

Proclamation No. 1/1995, 'Proclamation of the Constitution of Federal Democratic Republic of Ethiopia', *Negarit Gazeta*, Addis Ababa.

Smith, David (2014), 'Ethiopia, 30 years after the famine', *Guardian*, https://www.theguardian.com/world/2014/oct/22/-sp-ethiopia-30-years-famine-human-rights.

Stalin, Josef (1913), 'Marxism and the national question', first published in *Prosveshcheniye* 3–5, March–May 1913, English version at https://www.marxists.org/reference/archive/stalin/works/1913/03a.htm.

Sudan Tribune (2015), 'Former rebel spokesperson arrives in Juba after defection', 20 February, http://www.sudantribune.com/spip.php?article54045.

Tewfik, Hashim (2010), *Transition to Federalism: The Ethiopian Experience* (Ottawa: Forum of Federations).

Tronvoll, Kjetil (2000), *Ethiopia a New Start?*, Minority Rights Group International.

World Bank (2001), *Ethiopia Focusing Public Expenditures on Poverty Reduction: Public Expenditures Review of Oromiya Region, Volume III: World Bank Report 23351-ET* (Washington, DC: World Bank).

— (2015), *Ethiopia Poverty Assessment Report 2014: World Bank Report* (Washington, DC: World Bank).

Young, John (1997), *Peasant Revolution in Ethiopia: The Tigray People's Liberation Front, 1975–1991* (Cambridge: Cambridge University Press).

— (2006), *The South Sudan Defence Forces in the Wake of the Juba Declaration*, Geneva, Switzerland: Small Arms Survey.

CHAPTER 8

Assessing the Merits of Decentralisation as a Conflict Mitigation Strategy[1]

Joseph Siegle and Patrick O'Mahony

Introduction

We live in a golden era of decentralisation. Support for shifting power to local tiers of government has never been higher. This perspective is grounded in the belief that doing so will increase government responsiveness and accountability to citizens, increase government flexibility to address the diverse needs of often highly heterogeneous populations, reduce corruption through enhanced oversight, and foster dispersal of power from what have often been highly monopolised political structures. In the process, it is argued, decentralisation will augment greater political legitimacy while strengthening a sense of citizen ownership of their government.

Increased popular participation and a belief that citizen actions can help shape the nature and priorities of government are also commonly thought to foster greater social and political stability. If citizens believe the government is concerned about and responsive to their needs, and they have recourse when grievances have occurred, then there is little cause for armed struggle. Similarly, if decentralisation fosters more space to exercise local customs and religious beliefs without fear of persecution, the risk of inter-group strife in ethnically diverse societies can be minimised. After all, the vast majority of a citizen's daily interactions with government are at the local level. If local government can be representative of and sensitive to the needs of citizens, would-be tensions can be proactively addressed.

Sceptics contend, on the other hand, that decentralisation increases the risk of ethnic and civil strife. Loosening central control triggers an inevitable sequence of ever-greater demands for autonomy, ratcheting up the centrifugal pressures on the state. Rather than building a stronger sense of ownership and affinity with the state, decentralised authority accentuates differences between regions, fosters citizen identification with ethnic or geographic groups rather than the state, and emboldens demands for particularised services by minority groups. By weakening incentives to consider national interests, decentralisation encourages local politicians to stake out hard-line positions in defence of regional priorities, deepening political polarisation.

The heightened focus on decentralisation is an outgrowth of the ongoing global democratisation movement. Over the past two decades, more than a hundred countries have taken meaningful steps towards democracy, 80 per cent of which are in the developing world. This has resulted in a sea-change of global governance norms. In the late 1980s, two-thirds of the world's states were 'not free' according to Freedom House's annual tabulation. Today, that ratio is reversed. This has dramatically expanded the opportunities to pursue decentralisation, and has also placed a large segment of the decentralisation debate in the context of countries undergoing macro-level political and economic transitions.

The policy implications stemming from better understanding the relationship between decentralisation and intra-state conflict are far-reaching. How much of a risk does decentralisation pose? Should decentralisation continue to be a prominent feature of democracy promotion efforts? In which contexts is decentralisation most destabilising? Are there instances where decentralisation should not be pursued? Given that intra-state conflict has direct negative economic consequences for a country's neighbours and spills across borders a third of the time, there are also regional security implications. Moreover, since industrialised democracies are often the sponsors of decentralisation efforts, they are faced with the dilemma of intervening in intra-state conflicts that have spun out of control.

Definitive answers to these questions remain elusive and the debate over decentralisation's destabilisation risks continues to be largely driven by anecdotes. Through a review of existing research and fresh cross-sectional analysis, this chapter attempts to sift through what is currently known about this relationship, to help provide policymakers and practitioners with some empirically grounded guidance on these issues.

Types and dimensions of decentralisation

The decentralisation literature identifies three major types of power-sharing arrangements with sub-national governments: devolution, deconcentration and delegation.

Devolution is the increased reliance upon sub-national levels of elected government with some degree of political autonomy. Sub-national levels of government are substantially outside direct central government control, yet subject to general policies and laws, such as those regarding civil rights and the rule of law (USAID, 2000).[2] This is generally considered the most expansive form of decentralisation, entailing a considerable shift towards political and operational control by locally elected officials.

Deconcentration is the transfer of power to an administrative unit of the central government at the field- or regional office-level. Local officials are typically not elected but appointed by the central government. This is often considered to be a limited form of decentralisation since the national government retains control over resources and priorities. Since independent local governments do not exist in many countries, deconcentration is often the form of decentralisation that takes place (Litvack et al., 1998). It is also the mechanism pursued by central governments focused on enhancing state penetration, rather than local autonomy and citizen participation.

Delegation is the transfer of managerial responsibility for a specifically defined function outside the usual central government structure. Depending on how it is implemented, this type of decentralisation could represent widely different aims. It could be a means of building the capacity of local government officials in preparation for a subsequent move towards devolution. In this sense, it would be a starting point for decentralisation. Alternatively, it could simply be a means by which central authorities maintain the status quo, while claiming a commitment to shared governance with sub-national tiers (Ellison, 2004).

Decentralisation typically proceeds along three main dimensions of national and sub-national power-sharing:

Political decentralisation involves the transfer of political authority to the local level through the establishment of elected local government, electoral reform, political party reform, authorisation of participatory processes and other reforms.

Financial or fiscal decentralisation refers to the transfer of financial authority to the local level. It involves reducing conditions on the inter-governmental transfer of resources and giving local jurisdictions greater authority to generate their own revenue. As with most aspects of public sector administration, the allocation of resources is a revealing barometer of an initiative's priority.

Administrative decentralisation entails the full or partial transfer of functional responsibilities to the local level (e.g. healthcare services, the operation of schools, the building and maintenance of roads and garbage collection).

The wide range of possible combinations of types and dimensions of decentralisation (it is rarely implemented in pure form) adds further complexity to assessing the potential impact of centralisation and decentralisation on internal conflict. Yet the debate is still largely carried out in a dichotomous tone of 'decentralisation v. centralisation'. A survey of the decentralisation experience in Africa is illustrative of the potential for misinterpretation (Ndegwa, 2002). While nearly all African countries claim to have pursued decentralisation since the democratisation wave swept the continent in the early 1990s, objective assessments reveal only a third exhibit functioning decentralised structures. There has also been a pattern of administrative decentralisation without political decentralisation, reflecting the preferred form of decentralisation in non-democratic countries. Perhaps most revealingly, local governments control less than 5 per cent of national public expenditure in two-thirds of African countries. All African countries (except South Africa) have posted shares of local expenditures below 14 per cent, which is the average for developing countries.

The more practical analysis would be to examine the appropriate balance between layers of government. Jonathan Rodden discusses an emerging view of decentralisation as 'an organic, intertwined transfer of political, fiscal, and policy autonomy' (Rodden, 2003: 481). He calls for more nuanced analysis based on the complexity and diversity of several alternative forms of federalism and decentralisation. Fiscal and policy decentralisation often do not entail a shift from the centre to regional or local governments, but rather an adding of new layers or resources or responsibilities to existing lower-tier governments.

A theme that emerges from these considerations is that decentralisation is a collaborative process. Effective decentralisation is dependent on the cooperation of, and coordination with, the central government. Central government officials must be willing and committed to sharing some of their authority and resources if decentralisation is to be effective. Local government leaders, in turn, must be capable of managing additional authority while accepting central government oversight.

Decentralisation and internal conflict in the post-Cold War era

Recent trends in intra-state conflict

Intra-state conflict accounts for nearly all episodes of armed conflict observed in the twenty-first century (Afghanistan and Iraq being stark exceptions). This continues a pattern seen since the 1980s and which accelerated with the end of the Cold War. The frequency and intensity of armed intra-state conflict has declined by 60 per cent since the early 1990s (Marshall and Gurr, 2005). Rather than ushering in an era of instability and ethnic violence that many predicted, the end of the superpower rivalry has given way to a period of comparative historic calm (Marshall, 2002). The powerful effect that the Cold War had on fomenting and sustaining internal conflicts in the developing world raises an important intertemporal cautionary flag to analysis attempting to identify causal factors of contemporary civil and ethnic conflict. Cross-national analysis drawing heavily on the pre-1990 period is subject to misinterpretation and misapplication in the twenty-first-century context.

Another powerful determinant of internal conflict is income level. Poor countries have been more prone to intra-state conflict in the post-Cold War period than relatively better-off countries. Specifically, countries with per capita incomes below US$2,000 have been eight times as likely to engage in intra-state conflict in the post-Cold War period as countries with per capita incomes above US$4,000. Understanding how decentralisation may affect conflict, therefore, must take place within a developing-country framework. While the close link between poverty and conflict is well accepted, the reasons for this are less clear. The legacy of the Cold War and the spate of long conflicts in the developing world it generated, the tendency for these conflicts to persist once started, competition for limited resources, weak power-sharing and peace-building institutions, a history of autocratic political structures and use of repression, the relative ease with which small bands of rebels can destabilise weak states and contagion from conflict in neighbouring countries all contribute to this outcome.

The fact that the dramatic decline in armed conflict occurred concurrent with the period of unprecedented democratic expansion is also highly relevant. The idea that democracies rarely fight each other appears to have more bearing on internal conflicts than previously assumed. Established democracies are several times less likely to descend into violent civil conflict than non-democratic systems (Gurr, 2000). Research has shown that the risk of conflict in low-income democratisers is declining more rapidly in the post-1990 period relative to low-income autocracies (Halperin et al., 2005). The life expectancy of autocracies, in contrast, has been declining and is shorter than that of democracies (Przeworski et al., 2000). While fledgling democratic systems are more vulnerable to conflict than established democracies, the surge in the number of democratisers in the past two decades has not altered the steady downward trend in global conflict.

Whether this trend can be sustained remains to be seen. Counter-forces to these positive trajectories include the legacy of a large number of countries with weak capacity recovering from societal conflicts during the Cold War, the increased access to war matériel and personnel by subnational actors, the growing resonance of Islamic radicalism in non-Arab societies fanned by funding from ultra-conservative Wahhabi dogmatists, the spike in energy prices that is deepening the natural resource curse (the vortex of autocracy, underdevelopment and instability), and the resurgence of China and Russia on the global stage (Marshall and Gurr, 2005; Siegle, 2005; Carothers, 2006). Internal conflict also tends to be regionally concentrated, with more than half of all episodes occurring in sub-Saharan Africa. The Middle East, North Africa and South Asia are also disproportionately represented. These competing global trends underscore the fluidity of this subject area, adding further caution to any analysis.

This review now turns to the theory and empirics surrounding two broad drivers of internal conflict and their relationship with decentralisation: ethnic divisions and political polarisation. It then appraises insights generated from two specific contexts that have garnered increased attention in the post-Cold War period, namely post-conflict and natural resource-rich developing countries.

Ethnic divisions

The conflict-mitigating rationale for decentralisation in ethnically diverse societies is that, by ensuring minority group representation, decentralisation provides political channels through which differences can be reconciled. The prospect for formal power within the national structure represents an incentive for minority group cooperation with the central state. Greater local control over the issues that affect the vast majority of citizens' daily routines provides assurances to minority groups that their priority concerns will be considered. In this way, decentralisation is seen as a flexible institutional mechanism to accommodate the varied priorities of diverse populations within a single state.

Greater levels of minority participation in the public sphere is seen as a stabilising force. Similarly, by providing more layers of government, decentralised systems diffuse competition (and fears) away from a single, winner-takes-all prize. Supporters of decentralisation in ethnically diverse societies tend to view the state, rather than another ethnic group, as the greatest potential security threat to a given group (Rummel, 1994; Horowitz, 1985; Saideman et al., 2002). Accordingly, devolving state power is a mechanism for reducing this threat. Federal and unitary states differ significantly in how they approach decentralisation in ethnically diverse populations. In unitary states, governments tend to use decentralisation as a tool for eroding ethnic identity and solidarity. Federal states, in contrast, explicitly recognise the rights of ethnic groups in the belief that accommodation augments stability and unity (Schou and Haug, 2005).

The principal concerns over decentralisation in ethnically diverse societies are that it encourages ethnic identification, accentuates inter-group differences and fosters discrimination against local minorities, which all increase the likelihood of ethnic strife. It is also argued that decentralisation in ethnically diverse societies with weak central governments encourages inter-ethnic competition and collapsed states (Posen, 1993). Moreover, the process of decentralisation increases the probability that the dominant ethnic group or political party affiliation at local levels will differ from those at the national level. This potentially antagonistic equation can amplify tensions between central and sub-national government authorities, particularly during elections (Schou and Haug, 2005).

Some research does find a positive relationship between the degree of ethnic diversity and probability of conflict (Easterly and Levine, 1997), however, this linkage is not robust. Subsequent analysis finds a parabolic relationship: countries with either highly diverse or homogeneous populations are remarkably stable (Collier and Hoeffler, 2004). In homogeneous societies, no threat from a competing group is felt; in highly diverse societies, no one group is large enough to impose its will on the others and the mutual recognition of this reality leads to greater inter-ethnic assimilation. The greatest threat of ethnic conflict comes from societies where there is a dominant group comprising between 45 and 90 per cent of the population (Collier and Hoeffler, 2004). In these cases, minority groups fear they will be permanently excluded from politics and are inherently vulnerable to discrimination. At the same time, they are large enough to assert their priorities and be perceived as a threat to the majority. This is consistent with studies showing that societies with more concentrated minority populations are more susceptible to ethnic conflict (Saideman and Ayres, 2001; Gurr, 1993).

Empirical comparisons find that minorities in federalist states are significantly less likely to engage in violence and that federal states experience half the number of armed rebellions compared to unitary states (Bermeo, 2005). Similarly, Saideman et al. (2002) find that federalism is associated with more protest but less rebellion. Federalism is also credited with controlling secessionist demands in the Russian Federation, which has 89 potentially problematic autonomous units and over 100 ethnic groups (the exception being the brutal conflict in Chechnya). Nigeria and India are also cited as examples of countries with large numbers of ethnic minorities where federalism is credited with reducing conflict.

Democracies that use proportional representation are found to be particularly effective at reducing ethnic tensions, even in societies with significant minority ethnic group concentrations (Saideman et al., 2002). A related finding is that ethnic diversity appears to be more problematic in autocratic states. Specifically, economic growth in ethnically diverse societies with autocratic governments is 3 percentage points lower than the norm. In contrast, ethnic diversity is associated with no adverse effects in democratic states (Collier, 2001). This is explained by the fact that autocratic governments have a narrow base of core supporters, which in ethnically diverse societies often breaks down along ethnic lines.

Decentralisation is more likely to be observed in countries that started out as federations or were the result of merging distinct ethnic and religious groups, and is less prevalent in countries that began with highly centralised political systems, or where there were large inflows of migrant populations who became territorially integrated and demanded some peripheral autonomy and more resources (Sambanis, 2002; Fearon and Laitin, 2001). Vital to development and conflict mitigation, comparative studies show that decentralisation contributes to enhanced popular participation (Crook and Manor, 1998), though the depth of this participation may be limited (Blair, 2000).

Dawn Brancati (2005) concurs that political decentralisation is more successful in reducing ethnic conflict and secessionism, provided that regional parties do not dominate the political system. Regional parties are more likely to precipitate ethnic conflict and the drive to secession by mobilising constituencies on ethnic or geographic grounds. Regional parties may also produce legislation that threatens other groups in a country, or block legislation that can alleviate tensions already present in a society (Brancati, 2005).

Researchers in this area have come to significantly different conclusions about the stabilising effects of decentralisation (Bermeo, 2005). Those sceptical of federalism serving a conflict-mitigating function base their arguments largely on the Eastern European experience, where decentralisation policies generated conflict and promoted secession or partition and greater intolerance towards minority groups left behind (Roeder, 1991; Snyder, 2000). Proponents of federalism, on the other hand, tend to cite successful examples from Asia, Africa or Latin America to show how political decentralisation reduces ethnic conflict.

Arild Schou and Marit Haug (2005) conclude that decentralisation fulfils a conflict-mitigating role when it (i) broadens popular participation, including for minority groups, (ii) brings sub-national groups into a bargaining process with the government, (iii) increases state legitimation through broadened local popular participation, (iv) establishes state outreach and control in remote areas, (v) builds trust between groups that participate in local governance institutions and (vi) redistributes resources between regions.

Decentralisation risks increasing conflict potential when it increases competition between local and national power-holders. This may entail sub-national actors using decentralised resources for political mobilisation, including the capacity of groups to break away. In response, central governments may attempt to undermine devolved powers to regain authority. A shortcoming of this literature is the limited number of large sample-size cross-national studies of developing countries (Schou and Haug, 2005). This has led to an over-reliance on anecdotal findings and highly varied perspectives on the relationship between decentralisation and ethnic conflict.

Political polarisation

Given their limited ability to accommodate diverse interests, ethnic factionalism is a major vulnerability of autocratic systems. Conversely, because they rely on cooperation and compromise, political factionalism (being the polarisation of distinct political or social groups) is a risk predominantly faced by young democracies (Marshall and Gurr, 2005). Decentralisation may accentuate this risk, because incentives under decentralised structures may reward incompatible or uncompromising political platforms, advancing parochial interests and creating a contentious atmosphere in which negotiated solutions to policy differences are difficult to achieve (Marshall and Gurr, 2005). In other words, sub-national political leaders in decentralised systems may find it expedient not to seek compromise with the central government, and if this dynamic is replicated across sub-national regions in a country, there is little middle ground in which to govern in the national interest.

Decentralisation is also considered a vulnerability in transitional political systems because local structures often lack accountability mechanisms, making them particularly prone to local élite capture (Bardhan, 2004). Local élite capture, in turn, tends to be related to a lack of local democratic practices due to uneven political participation and competition, as well as a lack of information available to citizens, central government oversight and an independent media. Moreover, while most decentralisation theory assumes citizen 'mobility', being the ability and willingness of individuals to move to better-performing jurisdictions if dissatisfied, this mechanism of accountability generally does not apply in developing and transition countries where many households do not have the resources or employment prospects to allow a move. Decentralisation by itself is unlikely to be a panacea for problems of accountability.

Some scholars link decentralisation to greater inequality, posing a potential source of relative deprivation, grievance and instability (Linz and Stepan, 2002). However, these studies do not specify whether these disparities are a reflection of the greater economic productivity of certain regions (consistent with decentralisation theory), or an outcome of privileged positions afforded some groups over others. This also needs to be compared with the systematic inequities between ethnic and political groups that has been a hallmark of centralised autocracies and a prime source of intra-state strife. Similarly, Daniel Treisman (2002) finds that states with more tiers of government tend to be perceived as having higher levels of corruption. Yet it is unclear how the relatively more visible petty corruption encountered at the local level under decentralised arrangements compares to the often unseen, grand corruption that can occur in centralised structures.

Decentralisation is also believed to increase vulnerability to external influences by opening up ready cleavages that outside actors can exploit. Of particular risk are contexts in which an ethnic group engaged in sectarian conflict has a strong base of support just across the border. Indeed, secession is more likely if the groups are located close to international borders (Lake and Rothchild, 2005). There is also some evidence linking countries with large diasporas (i.e. countries that have had a long history of conflict) with sustained internal conflict due to the additional access to resources this represents (Collier, 2000). Similarly, there are indications that ideologically motivated funding from the ultra-conservative Wahhabi-sect of Islam targeting youth in Muslim cultural centres, youth organisations, schools, madrassas and mosques has contributed to the increasingly militant views of previously moderate Muslim populations (seen, for example, across the Sahel). Inter-religious tensions and demands for greater autonomy and the supplanting of secular law with Sharia law is likewise on the rise in these societies (Berman, 2003; Lyman and Morrison, 2004).

Proponents counter that decentralisation helps mitigate civil conflict by facilitating the dispersal of power from the centre to the periphery, compensating for historically highly centralised power structures established under autocratic governments. Decentralisation, therefore, builds additional checks and balances into a political structure, while attempting to establish a more stable political equilibrium between the centre and periphery. Spreading power among a wider array of actors, furthermore, provides them with greater incentives to participate and cooperate, helping to reduce grievances, moderate extremist or violent positions, and incorporate them into the political process. In this way, decentralisation can build a national dialogue, cohesion and state legitimation. The greater responsiveness and accountability of a government that is closer to citizens also facilitates more active participation, an important contributor to stability.

An empirical study of 28 ethno-federal states finds that federalism reduces the threat of secession (the extreme outcome of self-determination) and violent partition *with the notable exception of federal states that contain a 'core ethnic region'*, defined as a region with an outright majority or a population that exceeds the second largest group by 20 per cent or more. Seven of 14 such cases ultimately collapsed, including Czechoslovakia in 1990–92, the Mali Federation in 1960, the USSR in 1990–91 and Pakistan in 1970–71

(Hale, 2004). A broader sample of countries also finds multinational federations to be highly vulnerable, with additional failures in Kenya, Uganda, Tanganyika, Nigeria, Ethiopia, Indochina and Burma (Schou and Haug, 2005). Important qualifications emerge, however. Ethno-federal states lacking a core ethnic region have proved very resistant to secessionism and collapse. Of the 13 cases that were so categorised between the Second World War and 1999, not a single one collapsed (Hale, 2004). Imposed federalist systems also have a poor track record. Every federalist country that split apart or turned towards unitarism in the twentieth century was imposed by an outside power (Bermeo, 2002). The bad track record of multinational federations, accordingly, owes as much to the fact that (i) they were forced together and were autocratically governed (e.g. the USSR and Yugoslavia); (ii) they did not genuinely accommodate national minorities; (iii) they were dominated by certain ethnic groups; and (iv) the extreme ethno-national diversity in the communist federations made them particularly unstable (McGarry and O'Leary, 2004; Schou and Haug, 2005).

These results dovetail with a growing literature on secession that rejects the notion that separatist demands are inevitable outcomes of autonomy. Rather, secession is likely to be pursued only if all of the following conditions occur: (i) groups have a distinct cultural identity; (ii) groups are territorially concentrated; (iii) there is significant group-level grievance, possibly driven by economic inequality, political discrimination or a threat of cultural annihilation; (iv) the economic benefits of membership of the state are not significant for the aggrieved group; (v) cleavages are not cross-cutting and the conflict is concentrated between the government and a single ethnic group; (vi) the political benefits of membership for the group's élites are smaller than their expected political gains within a new state; and (vii) there are no security benefits to remaining in the state (Sambanis, 2002). Secession, meanwhile, is not necessarily a stable outcome, since successful secession (partition) does not reduce the risk of war recurrence (Sambanis, 2002).

Post-conflict

The literature on decentralisation in post-conflict environments is limited. A rationale for pursuing decentralisation in post-conflict environments is that it represents an opportunity to break away from what are often highly centralised and repressive power structures of a recently displaced regime. The domestic political logic of decentralisation for stronger or more dominant groups in post-conflict contexts is that it signals to weaker parties a willingness to compromise and accommodate, establishing a basis for transition towards peace. At the same time, a dominant party's offer of decentralisation could be interpreted as a sign of weakness, and could provide a political platform for local leaders to compete for national political power or pursue secession. Decentralisation in post-conflict contexts is considered especially difficult, as the requisite levels of trust and reciprocity required for this system to work effectively are particularly lacking in such environments.

It is also complicated by the fact that certain regions may be armed. Pursuing decentralisation in these contexts is tantamount to ceding the central government's monopoly over the legitimate use of coercion. Since this also increases the risks of secession, it is an option central authorities will likely only pursue as a last resort (Sambanis, 2002). On the other hand, minority representation in police forces is a necessary element of negotiated post-civil-war settlements as a means to increase confidence and effective monitoring of violations of the peace (Sambanis, 2002).

According to Lake and Rothchild (2001), there are highly restricted contexts in which political decentralisation after civil war has been successful: multiple groups compete for political influence at the national level, none can dominate the state, each is led by moderates tolerant of the desire for autonomy of the others, and democracy is robust. Perhaps it is unsurprising, therefore, that of the 55 civil wars that have reached a successful settlement since 1945, none had territorial decentralisation included as part of the settlement (Lake and Rothchild, 2005). The more frequently observed tendency is towards greater centralisation after civil war, seen for example in Argentina, Nigeria, Pakistan and Venezuela (Lake and Rothchild, 2001).

Rentier states[3]

There is a growing recognition of the deleterious effects on development resulting from economies that are heavily dependent on exportable natural resources, the aptly named 'natural resource curse'. This phenomenon is generally studied in the context of corruption. However, 'resource rents' both undermine and perpetuate poor governance. Public scrutiny is generally weaker in countries with high natural resource rents because of lower taxation and a higher probability of patronage politics (Collier and Hoeffler, 2005). Once economies are dominated by the logic of extraction, they are even less inclined to invest in the institutions necessary for capitalist development, creating a pernicious path dependency for rentier states (Acemoglu, 2001; Dauderstadt, 2006). Oil, for example, has transformed the institutional structures of many countries in the Middle East, the Gulf of Guinea, Central Asia, Latin America and South-East Asia (Oliveira, 2006).

Democracies with relatively stronger political and economic institutions are comparatively immune from the resource curse (Robinson et al., 2002; Mehlum et al., 2005). Sequence matters, though. Countries that have developed stable democratic institutions prior to the discovery of the resource wealth are much more likely to realise the developmental benefits of these resources. Even so, natural resource-dominated economies tend to undermine weak democratic institutions, particularly electoral competition. Strengthening the checks and balances of democratic systems, notably a free press, are vital for negating these adverse effects (Collier and Hoeffler, 2005).

Resource-rich countries are also significantly more conflict-prone than others. Much depends on the structure of the economy and the type of resource. When resources are geographically concentrated and difficult to exploit (i.e. 'point source resources'), it is easier for the central government to control the revenues (often with the help of multinational enterprises that possess the necessary technology). Resource-rich countries with point source resources tend to be more oppressive and not respect human rights (de Soysa, 2006). The combination of revenues and oppression tends to make these authoritarian systems durable, however. When resources are scattered and cheap labour is needed for exploitation, revenues are more difficult to control. If regulated legitimate markets do not emerge, conflicts are very likely to flare up in countries lacking strong political institutions (Dauderstadt, 2006). These contexts provide ripe opportunities for local warlords to emerge and finance their operations by controlling these resources, such as diamonds in Sierra Leone, coltan in the Democratic Republic of the Congo, timber in Cambodia, or drugs in Afghanistan or Colombia (Rubin, 2006).

Disputes over natural resource management at the local level have led to demands for greater community participation through decentralisation reforms. Yet a common thread in cases of decentralisation and local natural resource management is the volatility of the process. While granting local communities more control over natural resources should facilitate greater accountability and equity of the revenues generated, the institutional infrastructure and regulatory environment needed to manage this process are often lacking at the local level. Disputes over land tenure, boundary issues and licensing can quickly accelerate into full-blown conflicts.

Regan Suzuki (2005) argues that decentralisation in natural resource-rich local environments is more likely to deepen rather than mitigate tensions and conflict. Decentralisation-related conflict is more likely when decentralisation reforms are 'indeterminate', such as when there are conflicting institutional frameworks, a lack of clear roles and responsibilities, and a weak legislative structure. This opens the door to local élite capture, which undermines the enforcement of enabling legislation, stymieing the decentralisation process and causing it to lose legitimacy. Territorial delineation, furthermore, is vulnerable to exploitation by external economic and political interests.

A study of decentralised forest management in Indonesia similarly indicates that the changes brought about by decentralisation have spurred intra- and inter-group conflict. Decentralisation encouraged a boom in small-scale timber harvesting, dramatically increasing the number of actors competing for these resources. The ensuing competition fanned existing tensions and created new sources of conflict (Sudana, 2005). The problem has been worsened by local governments issuing as many permits as possible, with the goal of generating additional local revenue. Protests, sometimes violent, have become a new phenomenon among local communities.

At the same time, reforms have created opportunities for local communities to demand a share of the benefits. The resulting competition for compensation paid by mining and logging companies has triggered jurisdictional boundary disputes between communities, as well as within communities. Uncertain government policy, the lack of appropriate conflict-resolution approaches and the low conflict-management capacity of both communities and local government have resulted in prolonged and increasingly bitter rivalry between ethnic groups. The majority of instances of conflict observed in this area occurred after decentralisation in 2000–2002 (Sudana, 2005).

Cross-sectional analysis

For the purposes of this chapter, details of the methodology and results of the cross-sectional analysis conducted by the authors will not be discussed. However, a brief overview of the data used for this analysis and key study findings are outlined here.

Data used

As far as cross-national data on decentralisation is concerned, the key constraint to reliable data is the shortage of comparable measures across a sufficiently large sample of countries to enable meaningful generalisations. Since most intra-state conflict and contemporary democratisation are occurring in low-income countries, coverage for this group of countries is particularly important. Yet most available data on decentralisation focuses on the OECD countries. An exception is a decentralisation dataset of 166 countries covering the mid-1990s created by Treisman. Treisman (2002) defines and constructs a dozen variables on six facets of decentralisation (vertical, decision-making, appointment, electoral, fiscal and personnel) from some 130 constitutions and more than 200 publications on the structure of local governments.

Another cross-national measure of decentralisation that provides a degree of 'ground-truthing' of the Treisman measures is a variable of 'centralisation of state authority' generated by the Polity III regime-type and political authority index (Jaggers and Gurr, 1995). Covering 147 countries, Polity's measure of centralisation is based on the degree of geographic concentration of decision-making authority. States are scored as unitary, intermediate or federal.

Data on episodes of conflict were drawn from the 'Major Episodes of Political Violence 1946–2005' dataset compiled by the Centre for Systemic Peace. This dataset provides annualised information of 316 conflict episodes, listing all civil and ethnic conflicts initiated since 1995 as well as those that were ongoing as of 2005. Civil conflicts are defined as major episodes of armed conflict involving rival political groups. Ethnic conflicts are armed conflicts between ethnic groups or involving a distinct ethnic group and the state.

Key findings

Data analysis reveals that the relationship between decentralisation and intra-state conflict is more complex than can be captured in any single summary statement. Rather than finding that decentralisation is always a stabilising or exacerbating factor to internal conflict, the results of this research show wide divergences depending on types of decentralisation, conflict and context.

Most fundamentally, the effects of decentralisation on conflict outcomes were far more apparent for ethnic than civil conflict. While there are cases of overlap between ethnic and political conflict, the underlying grievances and motivations of the two conflict types differ. For post-1995 ethnic conflict, the effects of the various decentralisation indicators were highly differentiated, demonstrating both beneficial and deleterious effects. Relatively greater levels of sub-national expenditures, employment and percentage of elected sub-national tiers were statistically linked to lower levels of new ethnic conflict. In other words, decentralisation that was marked by greater degrees of legitimacy, control over expenditures and capacity seemed to have mitigating effects on ethnic conflict. These findings are consistent with arguments that when local leaders are answerable to the general public, when they have the discretion to pursue identified local priorities, and are empowered with a base-level of financial resources and staffing, the results will be more responsive government, better service delivery and greater stability.

Interestingly, the two measures of fiscal decentralisation considered – share of local expenditures, and taxes – behaved very differently in explaining ethnic conflict. More extensive local government expenditures were linked to a lower propensity of ethnic conflict, whereas greater levels of local taxes were associated with more frequent ethnic conflict. This pattern suggests that it is local government control over expenditures rather than the source of revenues that improves government responsiveness to local citizen priorities. Indeed, it may be that a relatively greater share of local expenditures originating from national sources serves a valuable conflict-reducing function by strengthening the bond between the national and sub-national levels of government, particularly in the many developing and democratising countries where national identity is weak. Local governments that raise a large share of their own resources, on the other hand, may feel comparatively less affinity with and need for national structures. Greater levels of local government control over revenues may also heighten inter-regional tensions when large disparities in access to local resources emerge, such as in many natural-resource-rich contexts. Regions with marginal natural resource endowments demand redistribution, while better endowed regions chafe at the need to subsidise their poorer counterparts. This, in turn, may fuel sectarian tensions, especially if the geographic boundaries mirror ethnic cleavages. Sizeable locally generated revenues controlled by the local élite also empower them to pursue policies of discrimination against local minorities.

Measures of legal provincial autonomy, meanwhile, are consistently linked to higher levels of ethnic conflict. Systems where federalism was formalised or provincial governments were granted some degree of autonomy were consistently linked to higher probabilities and magnitude of post-1995 ethnic conflict. This result supports the thesis that local autonomy affords local élites greater leeway to accentuate ethnic distinctions and limit the rights of local minorities. Emboldened by their autonomous designation, provincial leaders may attempt to assert more authority than they actually have, heightening tensions between national and provincial leaders. Alternatively, a federal structure may raise expectations of provincial leaders to effect change, but if they lack the resources and capacity to do so, this could be a source of disappointment and potential grievance that may eventually lead to conflict. Importantly, provinces in many non-federal systems have greater discretion over policy and finances than those in some federal structures. Accordingly, rather than encouraging legal structures of provincial autonomy, this analysis points to the relatively greater importance of decentralisation initiatives that enhance the legitimacy, spending discretion and capacity of local authority – expenditures, employment and elected leaders.

Civil conflict has few stable explanatory factors, decentralisation or otherwise, suggesting a greater degree of case-specificity. Civil conflicts do more closely mirror income levels, consistent with the well-established poverty-conflict nexus. Relatively poorer countries are more subject to the onset of civil conflict. The median per capita income level of countries that succumbed to civil conflict over the past decade (US$449) was lower than that of countries engaged in ethnic conflicts (US$632). Thus, ethnic conflict may pose a relatively greater risk to lower-middle income countries than civil conflict in the post-1995 period. Accordingly, the risk of ethnic conflict may persist even for countries making good progress developmentally.

In sum, the relationship between decentralisation and intra-state conflict does not fit neatly into any single summary classification. We cannot say, for example, that political decentralisation is superior to administrative decentralisation, as the data does not allow for this. Nor are we able to weigh in authoritatively on preferences on the delegation/deconcentration/devolution spectrum, partly because this is complicated by the hybrid approaches commonly employed in practice. Rather, the important distinction seems to have more to do with the value of enhancing local government service delivery capacity (both resources and personnel), coupled with legitimately elected local leaders. Local governments with this combination of qualities are apparently better able to respond to community needs, thereby contributing to greater stability.

These findings recognise that decentralisation is not an unmitigated good. Under certain circumstances, decentralisation can be a contributing factor to higher rates of ethnic conflict and, to a lesser extent, civil conflict.

What are these circumstances under which decentralisation heightens the risks of conflict? Several contextual risk factors were identified, including:

- Highly inequitable local revenue sources, typically from natural resources but increasingly from illicit sources such as drugs or unreported customs fees;
- Countries with a history of ethnic conflict;
- Provinces where the central government does not have control over security;
- Political parties organised along ethnic or geographic identity lines;
- Societies where there are large concentrations of minority groups; and
- Countries with comparatively higher rates of corruption for their income cohort.

The focus on context underscores the reality that two-thirds of ethnic and civil conflict is occurring in non-democratic political environments. It is crucial to distinguish between decentralisation occurring in democratic settings and decentralisation implemented in closed systems. The greater legitimacy and local government responsiveness that apparently contributes to lower levels of ethnic conflict through political and fiscal decentralisation cannot be assumed to materialise in non-democratic settings. Thus, promoting decentralisation as a conflict-mitigating tool regardless of context, even in democratic settings, is imprudent. At best, decentralisation on its own is unlikely to overcome the conflict-augmenting effects of an inhospitable environment. Worse, it could have a detrimental impact.

Parallel to an assessment of contextual risks is the need for institutional risk assessments. This analysis has highlighted the non-trivial share (25 per cent) of new intra-state conflicts occurring among relatively established, lower-middle income democracies and democratic backsliders such as India, Indonesia, Nigeria, the Philippines, Sri Lanka, Thailand and Turkey. Colombia is illustrative. It ranks near the top of certain decentralisation measures such as sub-national employment and expenditures. However, Colombia's weak accountability structures contributed to the long-lasting civil conflict there. Accordingly, decentralisation strategies need assess not only whether a political context is democratic but also whether there is sufficient accountability. On one 0–50 point accountability scale, we see that low-income countries that succumbed to ethnic or civil conflict in the past decade average accountability scores four points lower than those that do not experience conflict – a statistically significant difference. This accountability divergence holds up with regards to ongoing civil or ethnic conflict even among countries considered democracies. In the Philippines, we see the undercutting impacts that chronic corruption has had on democracy's conflict mitigating tendencies.

Creating accountable, legitimate political structures at the national and local levels will augment the conflict-mitigating potential of decentralisation strategies. Building mechanisms of vertical (vis-à-vis citizens) and horizontal (between branches of government) accountability would also limit some of the most acute risks of conflict from decentralisation (e.g. pseudo-democratisation/decentralisation, local élite capture of the decentralisation process, or rentier economies taking hold at the local level). This has a direct bearing on the decision to pursue decentralisation rather than other priorities.

The most stable decentralisation tends to be in cases where the central state is legitimate, relatively capable, accountable and subject to a system of checks and balances. Similarly, decentralisation on its own is not a panacea to the risks of internal conflict. Policies guarding against the politicisation of ethnic cleavages, cultivating national pride and identity, ensuring adequate protections for minority groups and redistributing resources to marginalised areas are all initiatives best orchestrated from the centre.

Decentralisation is a dynamic process that often unfolds over a period of years. Qualitative analysis suggests that devolving power in a slow, incremental manner promotes stabilisation. This favours the gradual assumption of responsibilities at the local level, capacity building and a shared appreciation of the complementary roles that local and central authorities play in effective governance.

Finally, a cautionary reminder. This analysis is only as strong as the underlying data that supports it. Few large cross-national datasets of decentralisation have even been compiled. The Treisman decentralisation data used in the quantitative analysis of this study is the best and most complete decentralisation dataset of which we are aware. Nonetheless, it still has limited data coverage for certain important variables. Recognising this, conclusions have been limited to only those patterns that are consistently observed. For example, the decentralisation factors that were found to be most relevant, namely federalism/regional autonomy and local government expenditures and taxes, were corroborated by variables independent of Treisman's dataset. Still, until the body of decentralisation data can be expanded in quality and breadth, these results should be considered exploratory.

Policy implications

These findings present a nuanced perspective on the relationship between decentralisation and conflict. No overarching generalisations are appropriate, and more comparative research, supported by more complete and refined decentralisation data, is needed to substantiate the distinguishing features of decentralisation that are stabilising or risk-inducing. This should be complemented by longitudinal studies that help sort out not only superior decentralisation structures but the most appropriate timing and approaches for attaining them. That said, this analysis indicates that, *on the whole*, decentralisation within low-income countries is *not* subject to higher rates of civil or ethnic conflict than more centralised systems. In fact, this analysis finds that relatively higher levels of sub-national expenditure and employment as well as authentic political decentralisation are linked to a lower probability of ethnic conflict. Nonetheless, real risks exist, particularly in cases where provinces are accorded some form of legal autonomy or control a relatively high share of tax revenue (often from natural resources). These risks are compounded in societies with a history of ethnic conflict, pervasive corruption, poverty, uneven access to natural resource revenues, high inflation, concentrations of minority groups and geographically based political parties, among other factors. Based on these observed patterns, several priorities emerge:

Conflict risk analysis. Recognising that decentralisation initiatives can pose risks, decentralisation strategies should be accompanied by a comprehensive conflict risk analysis that closely examines the two main drivers of internal armed conflict, namely ethnic divisions and political polarisation. Risk assessment findings should guide policymakers in deciding whether to support decentralisation and, if so, how best to minimise potential vulnerabilities.

Focus on local expenditures over tax revenues. Local control over tax revenues provides a firm basis for planning and implementing local priorities and, thus, is seen as the lifeblood of meaningfully advancing decentralisation. Yet these fiscal, administrative and governance objectives must be weighed against broader nation- and state-building processes. Fiscal independence (especially at the regional level) in the absence of other unifying processes can strengthen societal divisions and fan secessionist aspirations, particularly if ethnic group demarcations strongly coincide with geographic jurisdictions. Policymakers should focus on enhancing local government control of expenditures relative to revenue collection, which should remain a primary responsibility of the central government. Concurrently, greater attention should be given to improving the transparency and fairness of allocations of national tax revenues among local governments. As national identity and cohesion is solidified, the viability of greater levels of local revenue generation can be re-examined.

Central government control over the security sector. Transferring control of resources and administrative and political authority to provinces where the central government is not in control of the security sector is a recipe for disaster. Central government resources will be used to fund insurgent activities. Accordingly, ensuring a central government monopoly over the use of force should precede decentralisation. This guidance may lend itself to asymmetric decentralisation in contexts where control of the security sector varies. Similarly, a focus on security sector reform, and the creation of democratic legitimacy of the armed forces that will facilitate central government control, may be needed before significant decentralisation can be considered.

Avoid establishing autonomous regions. Federal systems and those that provide 'residual authority' to sub-national legislatures have been comparatively more likely to experience new outbreaks of ethnic conflict in the post-1995 period. The factors underlying these conflicts are no doubt varied and complex. However, promoting regional autonomy appears to be a high-risk strategy for accommodating ethnic or geographic differences. Decentralisation efforts would be better directed at strengthening sub-national government capacity, control over expenditure, political legitimacy, and ties with the national government.

Democratic accountability. Decentralisation occurs within a broader political context. It matters greatly whether this backdrop is advancing vertical and horizontal accountability, checks on national and local executives, the rule of law, norms of transparency, civil society oversight and a free press, among other mechanisms of shared power. To the extent that these processes are in place or advancing, the stabilising effects of decentralisation are most likely to be realised. If these accountability structures are not in place and there appears little commitment to establishing them, the effects of decentralisation are likely to be dramatically different. Decentralisation is one potential avenue of democratic accountability. It is not a substitute for it.

Efforts to enhance democratic accountability should precede decentralisation much as a house's foundation precedes its frame. Via this course, decentralisation can be confidently pursued as a genuine reform initiative. Making decentralisation contingent on a degree of democratic accountability, of course, creates a dilemma over what to do in low-accountability environments. Decentralisation proponents may argue that decentralisation can be an important incremental step towards establishing accountability. While this may be true in some cases, the risk of decentralisation being hijacked by local élites or exploited by polarising political parties under these circumstances appears to be higher.

Anti-corruption. Closely linked to the emphasis on democratic accountability is the finding that societies with stronger controls over corruption were less prone to civil conflict. Perceptions of injustice, relative deprivation and the self-enrichment of public officials at citizen expense are potential radicalising stimulants. Addressing the legacy of corruption and patronage norms inherited from years of closed governance is a major challenge for contemporary democratisers that threatens to foment disillusionment and undermine popular support for the democratic process. This is true at the local as well as national level. Conflict-mitigating decentralisation efforts, accordingly, should include an assertive anti-corruption strategy if the decentralisation process is to achieve its intended objectives of creating a more efficient, responsive and stable public sector.

Need for multi-tiered decentralisation strategy. An important observation highlighted by this analysis is that the threat of decentralisation-influenced internal conflict is present even in well-established and relatively better-off democratisers such as Colombia and the Philippines. This is somewhat counter-intuitive, as the focus in the conflict literature is mostly on low-income, typically non-democratic fragile states. There are, therefore, different classes of countries at risk of conflict. Conflating them is likely to obscure important differences in the causes and challenges that each faces. Recognising these differentiated risks can facilitate a more appropriate multi-tiered decentralisation strategy. For example, in autocratic contexts where the fact that power is not shared is little disguised (a position often enforced through repression), decentralisation efforts almost always follow a form of deconcentration and are generally aimed at strengthening the central government's presence at the local level rather than supporting greater autonomy. The pace of decentralisation will necessarily vary widely between contexts, and those with weaker democracies may need considerable time before adequate accountability institutions are in place. External actors should be sensitive to this and careful not to rush these processes prematurely.

Decentralisation that strengthens ties with the centre. Too often debates over decentralisation are cast in a 'decentralisation v. centralisation' framework. This is a particularly common tendency with regards to decentralisation and conflict risk. In fact, decentralisation is not a zero-sum game. Effective decentralisation is closely tied to a capable, supportive central authority committed to the process. It is not a matter of either/or, but of the appropriate distribution of responsibilities and resources among the various levels of government. Decentralisation initiatives should be mindful of simultaneously incorporating unifying initiatives into their strategies as a means of strengthening the connection of the sub-national regions to the whole. There are numerous formal and informal mechanisms by which this objective can be accomplished. For example, structural remedies that maintain strong incentives for inter-regional cooperation (e.g. requiring minimum vote-shares from multiple provinces to encourage cross-ethnic and cross-regional cooperation), and building multi-directional accountability to ensure there are layers of reinforcing incentives for local leaders to pursue the public good and curb abuses. Some means by which this may occur include regular federal audits, central government control over all natural resource and customs revenues, and pursuing national unity campaigns that strengthen national pride and social cohesion.

In conclusion, decentralisation offers numerous advantages to developing countries. Yet decentralisation is not a risk-free endeavour. Unconditional decentralisation can easily play into dynamics of group identification and political polarisation that are major contributors to internal conflict. Accordingly, despite their many potential benefits, decentralisation initiatives should only proceed with constraints, recognising the context, conflict risks and need for concurrent efforts to strengthen ties between sub-national and national political structures.

Notes

1   This chapter is an extract of a paper that was prepared for USAID's Office of Democracy and Governance, as a supporting study to the revision of the *Decentralisation and Democratic Local Governance Programming Handbook*. A copy of the original paper can be found at https://pdfs.semanticscholar.org/f240/a47a91ff48e86ce030192edaca2c7dd88f90.pdf.
2   All definitions in this section are derived from USAID's *Decentralisation and Democratic Local Governance Handbook*.
3   Rentier economies are societies in which a large proportion of income is gained from the manipulation of rents (being the difference above equilibrium prices resulting from monopolistic control over a good or service), rather than in the form of wages and profits resulting from work and productivity enhancement. Similarly, in rentier states a large share of government revenue is derived from rents rather than taxes.

References

Acemoglu, Daron, Simon Johnson and James A. Robinson (2001), 'The colonial origins of comparative development: An empirical investigation', *The American Economic Review* 91, no. 5: 1369–401.

Bardhan, Pranab (2004), 'Decentralisation of governance and development', *The Journal of Economic Perspectives* 16, no. 4: 185–205.

Berdal, Mats and David M. Malone (2000), *Greed and Grievance: Economic Agendas in Civil Wars* (Boulder, CO: Lynne Rienner).

Berman, Paul (2003), 'The philosopher of Islamic terror', *New York Times Magazine*, 23 March, http://www.nytimes.com/2003/03/23/magazine/the-philosopher-of-islamic-terror.html?mcubz=0.

Bermeo, Nancy (2002), 'A new look at federalism: The import of institutions', *Journal of Democracy* 13, no. 2: 96–110.

— (2005), *Position Paper for the Working Group on Federalism, Conflict Prevention and Settlement*, prepared for the International Conference on Federalism, 3–5 March, Brussels.

Blair, Harry W. (1998), *Spreading Power to the Periphery: An Assessment of Democratic Local Governance: USAID Program and Operations Assessment Report No. 21*.

— (2000), 'Participation and accountability in the periphery: Democratic local governance in six countries', *World Development* 28, no. 1: 21–39.

Brancati, Dawn (2005), 'Decentralisation: Fueling the fire or dampening the flames of ethnic conflict and secessionalism', *International Organisation* 60, no. 3: 651–85.

Carothers, Thomas (2006), 'The backlash against democracy promotion', *Foreign Affairs* 85, no. 2: 55–68.

Collier, Paul (2000), 'Ethnicity, politics, and economic performance', *Economics and Politics* 12, no. 3: 225–45.

— (2001), 'Ethnic diversity: An economic analysis', *Economic Policy* 16: 128–66.

Collier, Paul and Anke Hoeffler (2004), 'Greed and grievance in civil wars', *Oxford Economic Papers* 56, no. 4: 563–95.

— (2005), 'Resource rents, governance, and conflict', *The Journal of Conflict Resolution* 49, no. 4: 625–33.

Crook, Richard C. and James Manor (1998), *Democracy and Decentralisation in South Asia and West Africa: Participation, Accountability and Performance* (Cambridge: Cambridge University Press).

Dauderstadt, Michael and Arne Schildberg (eds) (2006), *Dead Ends of Transition: Rentier Economies and Protectorates* (New York, NY: Campus Verlag).

de Soysa, Indra (2006), 'Resource curse: The empirical evidence', in Michael Dauderstadt and Arne Schildberg (eds), *Dead Ends of Transition: Rentier Economies and Protectorates* (New York, NY: Campus Verlag).

Easterly, William and Ross Levine (1997), 'Africa's growth tragedy: Policies and ethnic divisions', *The Quarterly Journal of Economics* 112, no. 4: 1203–50.

Ellison, Kenneth (2004), *An Overview of Decentralization: Causes, Trends, and Challenges*, USAID's Center for Democracy and Governance.

Fearon, James D. and David D. Laitin (2001), *Ethnicity, Insurgency, and Civil War*, paper prepared for the Annual Meetings of the American Political Science Association, San Francisco, CA.

Gurr, Ted R. (1993), *Minorities at Risk: A Global Survey of Ethnopolitical Conflicts* (Washington, DC: US Institute of Peace).

— (2000), *Peoples Versus States: Minorities at Risk in the New Century* (Washington, DC: US Institute of Peace).

Hale, Henry E. (2004), 'Divided we stand: Institutional sources for ethnofederal state survival and collapse', *World Politics* 56, no. 2: 165–93.

Halperin, Morton H., Joseph T. Siegle and Michael M. Weinstein (2005), *The Democracy Advantage: How Democracies Promote Prosperity and Peace* (New York, NY: Routledge).

Hegre, Havard et al. (2001) 'Toward a democratic civil peace? Democracy, political change, and civil war 1816–1992', *The American Political Science Review* 95, no. 1: 33–48.

Horowitz, Donald L. (1985), *Ethnic Groups in Conflict* (Berkeley, CA: University of California Press).

Jaggers, Keith and Ted R. Gurr (1995), 'Tracking democracy's third wave with the Polity III data', *Journal of Peace Research* 32, no. 4: 469–82.

Lake, David A. and Donald Rothchild (2001), 'Containing fear: The origins and management of ethnic conflict', in Michael E. Brown et al. (eds), *Nationalism and Ethnic Conflict*, revised edn (Cambridge, MA: MIT Press).

— (2005), 'Territorial decentralisation and civil war settlements', in Philip G. Roeder and Donald Rothchild (eds), *Sustainable Peace: Power and Democracy After Civil Wars* (Ithaca, NY: Cornell University Press).

Linz, Juan and Alfred Stepan (2000), *Federalism, Democracy, and Inequality: With Special Reference to the Classic Outlier - the USA*, paper presented at the International Political Science Association, 1–5 August, Quebec City.

Litvack, Jennie, Junaid Ahmad and Richard Bird (1998), *Rethinking Decentralisation in Developing Countries: Sector Studies Series* (Washington, DC: The World Bank).

Lyman, Princeton and Stephan Morrison (2004), 'The terrorist threat in Africa', *Foreign Affairs* 83, no. 1: 75–86.

Marshall, Monty G. (2002), 'Measuring the societal impact of war', in Fen Osler Hampson and David M. Malone (eds), *Reaction to Conflict Prevention: Opportunities for the UN System* (Boulder, CO: Lynne Rienner).

Marshall, Monty G. and Ted R. Gurr (2005), *Peace and Conflict: A Global Survey of Armed Conflicts, Self-Determination, Movements, and Democracy* (College Park, MD: University of Maryland).

McGarry, John and Brendan O'Leary (2004), *Federation As a Method of Ethnic Conflict Regulation* (Ottawa: Forum of Federations).

Mehlum, Halvor, Karl Moene and Ragnar Torvik (2005), 'Institutions and the resource curse', *Economic Journal* 116, no. 508: 1–20.

Ndegwa, Stephen N. (2002), *Decentralisation in Africa: A stocktaking survey: World Bank, Africa Region Working Paper Series No. 40.*

Oliveira, Ricardo M. S. Soares de (2006), 'Context, path dependency and oil-based development in the Gulf of Guinea', in Michael Dauderstadt and Arne Schildberg (eds), *Dead Ends of Transition: Rentier Economies and Protectorates* (New York, NY: Campus Verlag).

Oneal, John R. and Bruce M. Russett (2001), *Triangulating Peace: Democracy, Interdependence, and International Organisations* (New York, NY: Norton).

Posen, Barry R. (1993), 'The security dilemma and ethnic conflict', *Survival* 35, no. 1: 27–47.

Przeworski, Adam et al. (2000), *Democracy and Development: Political Institutions and Well-Being in the World, 1950–1990* (Cambridge: Cambridge University Press).

Robinson, James A., Ragnar Torvik and Thierry Verdier (2002), 'Political foundations of the resource curse', *Journal of Development Economics* 79: 447–68.

Rodden, Jonathan (2004), 'Comparative federalism and decentralisation: On meaning and measurement', *Comparative Politics* 36, no. 4: 481–500.

Roeder, Phillip G. (1991), 'Soviet federalism and ethnic mobilisation', *World Politics* 43, no. 2: 196–232.

Rondinelli, Dennis A. (1999), 'What is decentralisation?', in Jennie Litvack and Jessica Seddon (eds), *Decentralisation Briefing Notes* (Washington, DC: World Bank Institute).

Ross, Michael L. (2004), 'How do natural resources influence civil war? Evidence from Thirteen Cases', *International Organisation* 58, no. 1: 35–67.

Rubin, Burnett R. (2006), 'Transforming protectorates: Building effective, accountable states', Michael Dauderstadt and Arne Schildberg (eds), *Dead Ends of Transition: Rentier Economies and Protectorates* (New York, NY: Campus Verlag).

Rummel, Rudolph J. (1994), *Death by Government* (New Brunswick, NJ: Transaction).

Saideman, Stephen M. (2001), *The Ties that Divide: Ethnic Politics, Foreign Policy, and International Conflict* (New York, NY: Columbia University Press).

Saideman, Stephen M. and R. William Ayres (2001), 'Determining the sources of irredentism: Logit analyses of minorities at risk data', *Journal of Politics* 63, no. 4: 1126–44.

Saideman, Stephen M. et al. (2002), 'Democratisation, political institutions, and ethnic conflict: A pooled time-series analysis, 1985–1998', *Comparative Political Studies* 35, no. 1: 103–29.

Sala-i-Martin, Xavier and Arvind Subramanian (2003), *Addressing the Natural Resource Curse: An Illustration from Nigeria; NBER Working Paper No. 9804.*

Sambanis, Nicholas (2002), *Preventing Violent Civil Conflict: The Scope and Limits of Government Action*, background paper for the *World Development Report 2003*.

Schou, Arild and Marit Haug (2005), *Decentralisation in Conflict and Post-Conflict Situations*: *NIBR Working Paper No. 139.*

Siegle, Joseph T. (2001), 'Democratisation and economic growth: The contribution of accountability institutions', PhD diss., University of Maryland.

— (2005), *Spreading Democracy and Development*, paper prepared for the conference on 'Terrorism, security, and America's purpose: Towards a more comprehensive strategy', 6–8 September, Washington, DC.

Snyder, Jack (2000), *From Voting to Violence: Democratisation and Nationalist Conflict* (New York, NY: Norton).

Sudana, Made (2005), *Winners Take All: Understanding Forest Conflict in the Era of Decentralisation in Indonesia*, Center for International Forestry Research, Bogor, Indonesia.

Suzuki, Regan (2005), *The Intersection of Decentralisation and Conflict in Natural Resource Management: Cases from Southeast Asia* (Ottawa: International Development Research Center).

Treisman, Daniel M. (2002), *Defining and Measuring Decentralisation: A Global Perspective* (Los Angeles, CA: University of California).

USAID (2000), *Decentralisation and Democratic Local Governance Programming Handbook: Technical Publication Series* (Washington, DC: Center for Democracy and Governance).

CHAPTER 9

Decentralisation and the Logic of the Political Marketplace in South Sudan

Alex de Waal and Naomi Pendle

Introduction

Decentralisation is both a technical exercise in governance and an exercise in using and allocating political power. This chapter is concerned with the latter; hence, we deal only in passing with the normative, legal-constitutional and technical aspects of decentralisation. Instead, we focus on how political decisions to decentralise, and the contours of that decentralisation, serve political purposes. South Sudan's decisions in 2015 and 2017 to decentralise were taken in the midst of considerable political turmoil, and a short-term political calculus may have been uppermost in the minds of those making decisions.

The political rhetoric of decentralisation is that it brings government closer to the people, that it is an unalloyed public good. There is considerable technical expertise required in the design and implementation of fiscal, administrative and constitutional decentralisation, including through federal constitutions. Kent Eaton et al. (2010) elaborate on how decentralisation can in theory bring government closer to the people, improve the efficiency of public service delivery and the quality of democracy, increase rates of civic engagement in politics and, therefore, generate more responsive and accountable local government. They detail three dimensions of decentralisation: fiscal, administrative and political, as outlined in the previous chapter by Joseph Siegle and Patrick O'Mahony. Eaton et al. (2010) also usefully distinguish between decentralisation (in which authority is devolved, at least in principle, to local levels) and deconcentration, which can constitute the proliferation of local administrative units without greater local involvement.

However, decentralisation is never solely, or even principally, a disinterested technocratic exercise. Paul Smoke observes that, despite 'unambiguous proof of its desirability', decentralisation is not favoured because of political reasons (Smoke, 2003: 7). Decentralisation is almost always enacted from the centre, with the goals of stabilising or consolidating central power by means of reorganising the provincial political landscape. The proliferation of administrative units on the local level can serve the purposes of a central state that does not wish to dilute its power. Rulers can take political and economic advantage of the opportunities afforded by administrative reorganisation, to recruit new governmental personnel and get rid of others or reduce their powers, and redraw boundaries. Across Africa, decisions to decentralise are routinely taken by governments that have limited democratic credentials or intent (Grossman and Lewis, 2014). Decentralisation can be pursued to strengthen the centre's influence on the local level, or it can be a way of generating disorder and uncertainty amid turbulent politics, working for the benefit of the ruler (Chabal and Daloz, 1999).

The logic of decentralisation varies across countries and political circumstances. In some cases, decentralisation can be the result of protracted public deliberations aimed at strategically restructuring national governance. At the other extreme, it can be the product of opportunistic political manoeuvring for tactical gain. Central authority penetrates local political topographies to differing degrees and can be resisted, co-opted or shaped by provincial political élites. Therefore, the actual effects of top-down attempts to reshape the core–periphery linkage vary significantly across a country depending on the local context. Decentralisation is thus also a political strategy fraught with the possibility of unintended consequences. The centre is likely to use different strategies in different places based on calculations about the peripheral élite (Boone, 2003). In exploring this contested political landscape, we draw on Catherine Boone's framework of political topography of local governance in Africa, in which she identifies four 'ideal types' of centre–local government relations:

(i.) Institutionalised power-sharing, in which indigenous élites wield local non-state power but are economically dependent on the centre; under these conditions the centre and the local élites reach formulae for accommodation.

(ii.) Administrative occupation, in which the state apparatus is suspended above rural society and the centre uses administrative deconcentration or subdivision (not decentralisation), whereby its agents retain or regain control over new local institutions.

(iii.) Usurpation, which involves the displacement of influential local élites, so that institutions are deconcentrated while political power is concentrated. Typically the old élites lurk in the wings as a counter-élite, seeking to make a comeback.

(iv.) Non-incorporation or abandonment of peripheral areas.

Boone's typology is based on historical analysis of the evolution of patterns of local administration in several West African countries, although the analysis is highly appropriate to elsewhere in Africa. We introduce some additional elements, however, to take into account the way in which power relations have been disrupted by protracted armed conflict and economic transformations, prompting the emergence of new local power relations, including revolutionary élites and military aristocracies in the case of South Sudan (Pinaud, 2014).

Another consideration is that, while decentralisation is a policy measure appropriate primarily for geographically dispersed populations where there are pre-existing local administrative units, it can also be enacted in the context of a shifting political topography, including instances of mass displacement and rapid urbanisation. Conflict-related humanitarian crisis is, in demographic terms, a form of accelerated traumatic urbanisation (de Waal, 2009). In this context, decentralisation can intersect with and potentially exacerbate conflicts over land, identities and local jurisdictions.

In this chapter, we adapt Boone's framework to accommodate the logic of the political marketplace, defined as a system in which political allegiances and services are exchanged for material reward in a competitive manner (de Waal, 2015). In such systems, successful leaders at all levels of the state apparatus are able to finance and manage their political budgets and deploy symbolic resources in order to minimise the risks of disloyalty and rebellion. Their strategies must be adaptive to changing circumstances, including fluctuations in their political budgets (the material resources they can spend on patronage and buying political services), changes in the prevailing price of loyalty, and other eventualities in the turbulent world of real politics in countries such as South Sudan (de Waal, 2015).

The power base of local élites is also changing, including not only kinship-based affinities, but also more innovative forms of locally organised allegiances based upon 'moral populism'. Moral populism refers to a system in which the logics of political alliances are based on the instrumentalisation of social identities and moral norms. When political marketplace dynamics prevail at a national level, local power brokers often make use of moral populist agendas to organise their constituencies. There is a need to analyse decentralisation when the real politics include a penetrating political marketplace and the use of moral populism, conditions that prevail across much of the continent and that are evident in the case of South Sudan.

Comparative examples from neighbouring countries

Demonstration of the complex politics of decentralisation initiatives can be found among South Sudan's neighbours, beginning with Sudan itself (which, of course, included Southern Sudan until 2011). These comparative cases reveal common themes and also demonstrate how examples from neighbouring countries may have influenced South Sudanese thinking on decentralisation. The Somali case also has instructive parallels when it comes to understanding the functions of a federal system in a weak state dependent on its neighbours and international aid donors.

Sudan

Colonial authorities governed Sudan through a combination of direct administration in the major towns, and indirect rule or native administration in the peripheries. Provincial chiefs served as brokers between the administration and the population (Leonardi, 2013). While many administrative districts mapped onto units of native administration, others (notably the Abyei district) were designed to instead bring groups that were often in conflict under a single colonial administrator, and such districts were tasked with preventing and resolving inter-communal disputes. Post-colonial Sudan undertook three major exercises in decentralisation (in 1981, 1994 and 2005), as well as far-reaching local government reform (1970) and the establishment of an autonomous regional government in southern Sudan (1972). Each of these exercises reflected bargaining between provincial and national élites, with various power interests at play. Rarely, if ever, did the state design its local government units with a view to effectively facilitating local conflict resolution.

The 1970 reform abolished the native administration system, revoking the powers of chiefs established by colonial-era ordinances and creating a professional, bureaucratic civil service. This created an administration suspended over Sudanese rural society, an 'usurpation' of local élites. This system failed as provincial aristocrats were only temporarily displaced and rapidly penetrated the weakened system. A notable feature of the 1972 creation of the autonomous region of southern Sudan, using regional devolution rather than decentralisation, was that, for the first time, southern Sudanese could wield political power in Khartoum.

The significant political influence exerted by the southern bloc was one reason that Nimeiri undertook the first of Sudan's decentralisation initiatives in 1981, which included two parallel actions. The first was the redivision of southern Sudan into three regions, a step widely known by the Bari word *kokora*. The literal meaning of *kokora* is 'to divide' but it can also imply 'to share', such as when one loaf of bread is divided to be shared (Willems and Deng, 2015). Amid fears about a Dinka-dominated southern government, this redivision was welcomed by Equatorians and other southern Sudanese leaders who had felt excluded from the southern regional government. The logic behind the Sudanese government's promotion of *kokora* was to generate political pressure within the southern area for further subdivision, as groups that found themselves minorities in the new administrative units pressed for further re-districting. These new divisions prevented the creation of a unified southern regional government that would have been more able to challenge Khartoum's agenda.

Nimeiri's second step was the creation of seven new regions in the north, notably in Darfur, Kordofan and Eastern Sudan. This action was intended to divert the political energies of those northern politicians with regional power bases by directing them into competition with one another over power in the regional capitals of Al-Fashir, Al-Obeid and Kassala. In this regard it was successful, and the political rivalries it engendered in Darfur helped set in motion that region's slide into armed conflict in 1987. Notably, the decentralisation in the early 1980s occurred at a time of economic and fiscal crisis, and the administrative units that were set up were almost entirely without funds or functioning departments.

The second decentralisation initiative in 1994 saw the creation of 26 states, 16 in the north and ten in the south. This was also undertaken at a time of extreme austerity, alongside other socio-political initiatives that empowered quasi-governmental Islamist organisations and strengthened neo-traditional authorities. Decentralisation took markedly different forms in different locations: in Darfur it divided the Fur among three states, and generated a violent dispute over the control of Western Darfur state. Among Nuba and southern Sudanese communities in the newly created jurisdictions and in displaced settlements in the vicinity of Khartoum, the socio-political initiatives had the unintended consequence of invigorating local leaders' celebration of non-Islamic cultural heritage. Due to the financial crisis, however, many of the states were little more than empty shells.

The third decentralisation, undertaken with the implementation of the 2005 Interim Constitution of Southern Sudan (consequent to the Comprehensive Peace Agreement), was a very different affair. It took place in the middle of Sudan's oil boom, when the national budget increased ten-fold over a seven-year period. For the first time, state administrations had budgetary resources and it was an era of unprecedented fiscal expansion, particularly in Southern Sudan, where the incoming administration of the Sudan People's Liberation Movement (SPLM) was building institutions and payrolls from scratch.

The bulk of new expenditure lay in salaries. The public wage bill grew, as chronic underpayment of public servants was addressed and Sudan's ruling party was keen to demonstrate the material rewards of political loyalty. The World Bank's 2007 Public Expenditure Review found major problems with public expenditure management at state level, attributing it to poor information, weak capacity and political pressure to spend more and to inflate expected state revenues to match projected spending (World Bank, 2007). Spending on the public wage bill crowded out other spending, including on productive investments. For many Sudanese, the peace dividend came in the form of salaried employment: it was a payroll peace.

Sudan's three decentralisations were all instances of institutionalised power-sharing whereby indigenous élites that had long wielded local non-state power gained formal positions in the administration, becoming economically dependent on the centre for financial reward.

Uganda

Colonial Uganda was marked by highly uneven manifestations of the local state, which typically took the form of decentralised despotisms in which government-appointed chiefs served as executive officers and judges, and often also as the principal sources for interpreting customary law (Mamdani, 1996). Although giving the appearance of homogeneity, the native administration system had great regional variation depending on economic and security interests, and the capacity and political stature of chiefly authorities. Successive post-colonial governments repeatedly reconfigured these power relations. Indeed, each of Boone's four 'ideal types' of centre-local government relations (power-sharing, administrative occupation, usurpation and abandonment) can be found in the modern history of Uganda.

Scholars who have studied the decentralisation undertaken by President Yoweri Museveni, including Elliott Green (2010, 2015) and Janet I. Lewis (2014), show how reforms and reorganisation of local government have served to reinforce the power and reach of the political centre: it has in fact been *de facto* recentralisation. Creating new districts has been an opportunity to increase patronage. This has occurred at a time of economic growth, which has enabled expanding administrative expenditure even while the national budget has come under increasing scrutiny from the public and aid donors, thereby reducing scope for diverting public funds into political budgets. The expansion in the number of districts in Uganda (from 34 in 1990 to 56 in 2000 and 112 in 2010) has not only increased the public wage bill, but also presents recurrent opportunities for reconfiguring patronage networks. Grants to districts have been conditional, allowing the centre to dictate how money is spent locally (Francis and James, 2003). Green demonstrates that establishing new districts has been popular locally and has helped Museveni to win elections.

Ethiopia

Ethiopia's 1995 constitution is remarkable in that it gives far-reaching powers to the states, each of which is defined around a cultural-linguistic group. This arrangement was adopted during the 1991 transitional period due to the political challenges facing the country, notably the collapse of the military dictatorship and the triumph of the Ethiopian Peoples' Revolutionary Democratic Front (EPRDF). For 25 years, the terms of decentralisation in Ethiopia have been determined exclusively by the EPRDF and its political and economic calculations.

Although widely known as 'ethnic federalism' (Turton, 2006), the Ethiopian constitutional architects see it instead as a federation of 'nations and nationalities', each of which enjoys the right to self-determination (Gebrehiwot and Haftetsion, 2015). The terminology is important: 'nations' are historically constituted entities that rise, change and fall, while 'ethnic groups' are popularly understood in much of the policy literature as primordial entities. Critics of the constitution condemn it for laying the basis for the break-up of the country. Ethiopia's federation of nations has both accommodated differences in identity and allowed politicians to exaggerate ethnic cleavages for tactical reasons (Abbink, 2011). At the same time, the system has been a means for the EPRDF to maintain central control. Decentralisation of administration and budgeting, and the recognition of diverse languages and cultures, has gone alongside the standardisation of state constitutions and the centralisation of power in a single political party (Abbink, 2011; Gebrehiwot and Haftetsion, 2017). Over the last decade, the central government's development model has diminished the policy autonomy of regional governments (Abbink, 2011).

The practical realisation of decentralisation in Ethiopia has depended on the relationship between the central state and the particular political élites in each location. The EPRDF has chosen different strategies to interact with different communities based on historical trajectories, informal institutions and local power dynamics (Aalen 2011). Only in the 'emerging' states that were historically peripheral to the Ethiopian empire (Afar, Gambela, Somali) do we see the power-sharing formula in operation, albeit with vigorous and sometimes violent contestation. In the highland areas, the emergence of a new class of administrators associated with the bureaucracies of the new states has led to what Gebrehiwot and Haftetsion (2015) call 'administrative nationalism': a group whose material interest and socio-cultural worldviews are shaped by the resources and status associated with these institutions.

Gambela State is particularly relevant to South Sudan. Situated on Ethiopia's western border and dominated by Anuak and Nuer peoples, Gambela is geographically and ethnically proximate to South Sudan. The movements of Nuer in and out of Gambela during periods of war and peace in southern Sudan have created ethnically based competition over which of these two groups constitutes the numerically dominant 'nation' in Gambela. Numerical dominance is politically important as it is the basis for the legal and political claim for control over the administration of the state government (Abbink, 2011). In Gambela, the central Ethiopian government has switched support between groups over time, changing the regional leadership, which has resulted in violent clashes. The frequent movement of people from South Sudan into Gambela means that many South Sudanese have direct experience of this system.

Kenya

Kenya's experience of decentralisation shows important variation from the patterns in Sudan, Uganda and Ethiopia, notably in that the current constitutional formula emerged through protracted negotiations among different political groups. It is rooted in Kenya's history of ethnic and territorial politics.

During the negotiations leading to Kenya's independence, a strong coalition, comprised mostly of the leaders of smaller ethnic groups, argued for a decentralised or federal constitution. The resulting 'Majimbo' constitution was short-lived, however, as President Jomo Kenyatta moved quickly to centralise power. *Majimbo*-ism (regionalism) gave way to *harambee*, meaning 'all working together', a call for Kenyan unity (Anderson, 2005). Smaller ethnic groups were brought into a political merger with the ruling Kenyan African National Union (KANU). After the 2002 election, decentralisation became a key issue in the national constitutional debate, with a particular focus on the potential benefits of bringing service delivery closer to the people. Calls for decentralisation became even more salient in the wake of the 2008 electoral violence that saw politicians use ethnic identity to mobilise people in an effort to gain control over the central government. The 2008 electoral violence convinced many Kenyans that the combination of competitive electoral politics and a winner-takes-all system, with largely ethnically based constituencies, was a recipe for conflict that might destroy the nation. There was a clear need for power-sharing.

Consequently, in 2010 a new constitution was adopted that reproduced the 47 independence-era administrative units and that gave new powers to county governors. Importantly, some power over land allocation at the local level was devolved to new county governments (Boone, 2012). The constitution guaranteed that a minimum of 15 per cent of the nationally raised revenue would be allocated to county governments and that 5 per cent would be used as an 'equalisation fund' to assist previously marginalised counties. Therefore, regardless of who won in a national election, local leaders would still have the same access to state resources (Kanyinga, 2016). Decentralisation has been credited with minimising the violence accompanying the 2013 election (Cheeseman, Lynch and Willis, 2014).

However, decentralisation has brought about a notable expansion of government positions in the executive, legislature and civil service positions, leading to fears of bloated county-level payrolls and accusations that it has created new forms of patronage (Kanyinga, 2016). Others argue that the system merely gives politicians another opportunity to secure a piece of the pie (D'Arcy and Cornell, 2016). However, theft of state resources is not as easy at the county level. County assemblies have proved more active in forcing their governors to be accountable, compared to their national counterparts. Some county assemblies have even impeached their governors (Kanyinga, 2016).

The Kenyan exercise in decentralisation arose through a negotiated compromise among different factions of the country's political élite and was then subjected to a national referendum, rather than being the executive decision of a central authority. As such, it holds the promise of being more durable than other decentralisation formulae in the region.

Somalia

Somalia's history of decentralisation shows a markedly different trajectory from the cases just discussed. For the independence generation, Somalia was seen as a nation in search of a state, an ethnically homogenous people divided into five territories by colonial powers seeking a 'Greater Somalia' that encompassed them all (Laitin and Samatar, 1987). The impulse was for centralisation and unification, but this has not been possible. Instead, pressure for a federal system arose through an internationally mediated peace process which, in 2012, finally resulted in the formation of a federal government in Somalia.

Federalism was adopted in part because of repeated failures to establish a central government in Mogadishu. Focusing on the provinces was seen as a workable alternative. A federal Somalia was also pursued, in part, because neighbouring countries, especially Ethiopia, were wary of a centralised Somali state. Support for the federal system is uneven across Somali political society: some are principled enthusiasts, many support it for tactical reasons, and others are vocally opposed. One of the consequences of the federal formula is that the presidents of each of the federal states are able to seek international assistance in their own right. In practice, this has included security cooperation and assistance. An unintended outcome is that state presidents can obtain aid from Arab countries, generally with few strings attached, to strengthen their political autonomy and build patronage systems.

The Somali experience of decentralisation is therefore quite unlike other cases in north-east Africa. Somali federalism was not initiated from the centre as part of a cogent governance strategy, but was a template promoted from the outside. It is a weak-state decentralisation, a mechanism for post-conflict reconstruction and designed around the modalities for external aid and a peace-support operation.

South Sudan's decentralisation

South Sudan's decentralisation does not closely follow the experiences of its neighbours, though it has echoes of several of them. In particular, following the model of the 1981 and 1994 decentralisations in Sudan, President Salva Kiir has used his executive powers to divide and weaken provincial powers at a time when his financial patronage capacity has been strained. South Sudan's decentralisation policy has been implemented at a time of civil war and economic crisis, both factors that have led to massively reduced government spending and smaller political budgets with which to reward clients. Expanding the number of states was not the outcome of a national public debate, but a unilateral decision taken by the president, with all indications suggesting that it was a tactical response to immediate political pressures.

At independence in 2011, South Sudan inherited the ten states of the CPA. Important provisions of the CPA included that concerning the direct election of state governors. While the 2005 Interim Constitution of Southern Sudan (ICSS, 2005) outlined a decentralised federal system for Southern Sudan, the 2011 Transitional Constitution of the Republic of South Sudan (TCSS) instead established a system of government that exhibits many unitary features (Schomerus and Aalen, 2016). The TCSS has given the president the power to remove elected state governors and/or dissolve state legislatures if he believes there is a crisis that threatens national security.

Three case studies that demonstrate how decentralisation has played out in practice in South Sudan will now be explored. The first case study will outline the conflict in Pibor, and the following cases will look at the circumstances around the creation of the 28 and, later, 32 states.

The Greater Pibor Administrative Area

A local leader in Pibor, David Yau Yau, mounted a rebellion in June 2010. His militia, the Cobra Faction, was drawn predominantly from ethnic Murle in Pibor. On the eve of South Sudan's independence, Yau Yau signed an agreement with Kiir which integrated his Cobra Faction troops into the SPLA and promoted senior commanders of the faction. However, Yau Yau was discontented with the integration package as he did not receive the payoff he had hoped for (Small Arms Survey, 2013). A year later, he again defected from Kiir's government and launched another armed rebellion. Prior to his defection he visited Khartoum, and Kiir's government suspected Sudan of funding the rebellion (Small Arms Survey, 2013).

People in Pibor demanded the creation of a new state that would separate them from Jonglei State, as they felt the Jonglei State government neglected their area, only intervening with military or police action. They saw themselves as being on the periphery of the periphery and demanded a more direct relationship with the centre. This is in line with Boone's prediction that in areas that are neither politically threatening nor economically valuable, the centre is likely to opt for a strategy of non-incorporation (Boone, 2003). Indeed, during the CPA period, Pibor did not have the political or military strength to be a threat to Juba, nor the economic opportunities to capture the centre's attention. The Juba leadership calculated that they could simply offer some titbits to the rebel leaders and leave Pibor untouched as a junior unit within Jonglei State. However, this neglect empowered Yau Yau to highlight grievances with the centre and the Jonglei government based on ethnic identity. However, as soon as Yau Yau signed the first peace agreement, the political value of Pibor diminished once again and the central government had little political incentive to deliver on its promises. Failure to honour the peace agreement thus became the reason for a second revolt.

During the second rebellion, the Cobra Faction proved its military strength against the SPLA and, by 2013, a military defeat of the SPLA seemed increasingly likely. Boone argues that central government leaders make institutional choices based on their calculations about the strength of rural élites (Boone, 2003). In the political market calculus, a well-organised revolt is a signal that more attention needs to be paid to bringing unhappy élite members back into line. During the second rebellion, Yau Yau established himself as a strong local leader who could not be ignored. Circumstances had also changed. In December 2013, armed conflict erupted in Juba and elsewhere. Akobo, to the north of Pibor, was a key stronghold of the new armed opposition. For Kiir's government, Greater Pibor could act as a buffer against opposition forces or an avenue for government offensives, giving Pibor new national importance. Yau Yau's value increased accordingly. If a deal could be made with Yau Yau, he had the potential to be a key local ally for Kiir's government, and the Cobra Faction could even be used as a pro-government militia.

In January 2014, Kiir signed a ceasefire with the Cobra Faction, followed in April 2014 by a peace agreement. This agreement created the Greater Pibor Administrative Area (GPAA) and Yau Yau was appointed its chief administrator. The GPAA was a federal state in all but name, and its chief administrator had governor-like status. Power-sharing was institutionalised between the centre and the local élites who were Yau Yau's clients. At that time, creating an eleventh state in South Sudan would have required a constitutional amendment that Kiir did not want to contemplate. The compromise formula appeared to have satisfied the grievances and demands for more localised power for which many in the Cobra Faction had been fighting.

The GPAA provided a model for how the Juba government could fight its war on the cheap. Creating the new administrative unit was a means for Kiir's government to secure political services without having to pay substantial sums of money. There are several noteworthy points here. First, it is usually cheaper to buy political allegiance locally rather than centrally, as clients in provincial towns make smaller demands of their immediate patrons than they would if they travelled to the capital to make their demands of central rulers.

Second, the funds dispensed to Pibor could be taken from official government funds, not from the discretionary political budgets of the president and his aides. In South Sudan, transfers from central to state government can readily be used to buy loyalties. They are fungible across official and political budgets and constitute a significant percentage of national expenditure: some 19 per cent of the formal national budget was allocated to the states in 2016 (World Bank, 2017). After the money is transferred, however, there is no accountability requirement from the centre over how these funds are spent. At least half of the states do not even comply with the conditions and guidelines for the transfers of funds to local governments (EU-TAPP, 2016). Therefore, these transfers of money can be used at the governor's discretion. By creating a state (or unit resembling a state) and/or appointing a new governor, central government was able to reward loyalty at the state-level through gifting transfers from the centre. In turn, governors often use this money to fund their political budgets and they spend it on rewarding supporters in their state. Governors reward loyalty by putting people on the state payroll, and they have consistently paid salaries even if they have not accounted for much of the rest of the transferred money (EU-TAPP, 2016).

Third, local political units are typically organised on an ethnic basis, using kinship-based solidarity. Appealing to such identity politics is the oldest trick in the political playbook for a leader under financial and military stress. Combined with a licence to loot the resources of rival communities, it is especially effective as a means of mobilising one group to fight another, and has been referred to as 'counter-insurgency on the cheap' (de Waal, 2004).

In creating the GPAA, Kiir rewarded Yau Yau's renewed loyalty through the state budget. However, the government did not just demand peace for this payment, it also demanded the Cobra Faction's integration into the

SPLA, so that it could be used in the ongoing civil war. The Cobra Faction leaders were willing to be integrated in order to receive salaries and training, but were opposed to being deployed outside their home area. Initially, the Cobra Faction's integration took place only within the GPAA, but by late 2017 forces from Pibor were being deployed elsewhere in South Sudan, including lending support to Kiir during tensions between Kiir and his former chief of staff, General Paul Malong.

This political bargaining has, however, had unintended consequences for Kiir. Yau Yau was brought further into the national government and was appointed deputy minister of defence. Shortly after his appointment, many of his former colleagues in the Cobra Faction again rebelled and joined the SPLM/A-IO. As Yau Yau became more entangled in the national political marketplace, he struggled to maintain authority over his key military constituency. In January 2018, Yau Yau was returned to the governorship of what is now Boma State with the instruction to reduce Murle raids against neighbouring Dinka Bor communities. This period will be a test of his remaining popular appeal and the extent to which he is now reliant on the militarised force of the central state in order to govern locally.

This pattern of purchasing (or renting) loyalty as a counter-insurgency strategy has a long history in Sudan's wars. The method was honed by Khartoum's military intelligence and adopted by its rivals, including the southern Sudanese. Kiir has relied on purchasing the loyalty of groups who can provide him with military support, but who do not necessarily have a historic (or ethnic) reason for loyalty, as seen in the GPAA example. The creation of the GPAA served the purpose of appeasing a violent rebellion and reasserting central control over political patronage.

The creation of 28 states

Riek Machar, in the SPLM/A-IO's first large meeting in 2014, adopted a pro-federalism policy and proposed the division of South Sudan into 21 states based on the 21 districts of the Anglo-Egyptian condominium. More radically, the SPLM/A-IO proposal also changed the existing formula for controlling the country's oil revenues, by far the largest source of government revenues and politicians' political budgets. The existing formula was that oil revenues were paid first to the central government, which then allocated a share (2 per cent) to each oil-producing state. The SPLM/A-IO proposed reversing this so that the states would receive the money directly, keep most of it and remit the remainder to Juba. In this proposal, the state governments would have the direct relationship with actors in the global markets and the centre would no longer be the gate-keeper. The SPLM/A-IO pro-federalism policy also resonated with the popular politics of the Equatorians, who were increasingly demanding a federal system. During April 2015, Equatorian governors, armed rebels in the Equatorias and leaders of the SPLM/A-IO jointly signed a document calling for federalism. Debate around the SPLM/A-IO proposal quickly concentrated on arithmetic and boundaries of states, rather than the powers of the states in relation to the centre. Preoccupation with the number of states resonated with élite attempts to use territorially based social identities to mobilise forces for war.

Kiir initially tried to close down all discussion of federalism as he was aware that such a constitutional and fiscal reform would deliver a death blow to his patronage-based political system, and possibly the central state itself. In August 2015, Kiir, the SPLM/A-IO and others signed the Agreement on the Resolution of the Conflict in the Republic of South Sudan (ARCSS). Kiir and his then Chief of Defence, General Malong, were visibly unhappy at the pressure placed upon them by international and regional actors. They believed that they had the upper hand militarily and that ARCSS ceded far too much authority to the SPLM/A-IO. They were particularly dissatisfied that ARCSS gave the SPLM/A-IO the power to nominate the governors for Unity and Upper Nile States, South Sudan's oil-producing states. The ARCSS proposal did not change the existing formula for allocating oil revenues between state and central governments, but for Kiir it was a disagreeable step in the direction of the SPLM/A-IO's federalism attempts, which spelt the end of the government's control of the oilfields.

Two months later, Kiir unexpectedly issued a decree (Presidential Establishment Order 36/2015) increasing the number of states from ten to 28. The powers of the states were not changed, only their number and boundaries. Increasing the number of states appeared to mark a turnaround in government policy, and constituted a violation of ARCSS. It created uncertainty not only about the provisions of ARCSS, but also about the continued validity of the agreement. It briefly appeared that the sponsors of the agreement, namely the IGAD member states and their international backers, might seek to challenge and reverse Kiir's decree. However, by early 2016, the mediators had softened their position. The leaders of IGAD member states doubtless understood and sympathised with Kiir's plight, having faced comparable challenges themselves.

One key implication of redrawing state boundaries and re-dividing existing states was that the new arrangement allowed the most productive

MELUT BASIN OILFIELDS

Number of states in South Sudan	State name	Dominant political affiliation	Note
Period of 10 states	Upper Nile	GRSS	Dinka dominate at the county level around the oilfields, but Nuer and Shilluk are powerful at the state level.
SPLM/A-IO 21-state proposal (2014)	Adar	GRSS	Dinka dominate. However, SPLM/A-IO/Nuer-dominated Sobat State has a border close to the oilfields.
ARCSS (2015)	Upper Nile	SPLM/A-IO	ACRSS gives the SPLA-IO power to nominate the governor for Upper Nile.
28 states declared by Kiir (2015)	Eastern Nile	GRSS	This becomes a Dinka majority state dominated by the Padang Dinka. The creation of Latjor State to the south creates a largely mono-Nuer, pro-SPLM/A-IO state at a distance from the oilfields. This largely reflects the then-current military positions.
32 states declared by GRSS (2017)	Northern Upper Nile State	GRSS	Eastern Nile is divided into two states. This moves the oilfields into a different state from Malakal.

WEST NILE OILFIELDS

Number of states in South Sudan	State name	Dominant political affiliation	Note
Period of 10 states	Unity	GRSS	Power struggle between Taban Deng (with support from Kiir and Riek Machar) and Angelina Teny over political leadership.
SPLM/A-IO 21-state proposal (2014)	Liech	SPLM/A-IO	The SPLM/A-IO's Liech State (based on the condominium-era districts) has the same boundaries as Unity State.
ARCSS (2015)	Unity	SPLM/A-IO	ARCSS gives the SPLM/A-IO power to nominate the governor for Unity State.
28 states declared by Kiir (2015)	Ruweng State and Northern Liech State	GRSS GRSS	Ruweng State is dominated by Dinka communities loyal to GRSS. Northern Liech has been less consistently loyal to the GRSS but GRSS has significant control of parts of Northern Liech.
32 states declared by GRSS (2017)	Ruweng State and Northern Liech State	GRSS GRSS	No change

Table 9.1 Oil-producing states and their political affiliations

oilfields in Melut Basin to fall inside states that were dominated by communities loyal to Kiir's government. This minimised the SPLM/A-IO's ability to appoint a governor in these areas, and reduced the chance that the oil-producing states could form a single bloc to challenge Juba's fiscal centralism.

For Kiir, the benefit of creating 28 states was not only that it secured government control over the oilfields, but also that it offered other benefits with regard to the management of the political marketplace. The creation of the 28 states necessitated a tactical redrawing of boundaries to reconfigure local politics. Resembling a classic case of gerrymandering, the redrawing of the states' boundaries increased the fraction of the states that were dominated by communities loyal to Kiir. In contrast, communities that had supported the armed opposition were largely placed in their own states, restricting their influence and limiting the administrative power of their leaders over other communities. Kiir assumed he could instrumentalise ethnic politics to ensure Dinka loyalties.

The new state divisions left potential opponents and hostile constituencies politically weakened. For example, the division of Western Bahr el Ghazal State into Lol and Wau States divided and weakened these communities that had historically opposed the SPLA. The new Lol State included some counties with Dinka majorities that had previously been part of Northern Bahr el Ghazal State and had shown loyalty to the government. Although Wau State was still dominated by those with less loyalty to the SPLA, it lost some of its political and security significance, as it no longer had an international border or control over the resource-rich Raja region.

Increase to 32 states

In January 2017, Kiir issued a further decree that increased the number of states from 28 to 32. In the context of the continuing conflict, but also an increasingly fragmented and weak armed opposition, this was a stratagem for creating new constituencies of government support. Each new state had a particular tactical rationale.

In July 2016, after fighting had erupted in Juba, the SPLM/A-IO leader Riek Machar fled and Taban Deng, former governor of Unity State and deputy leader of the SPLA-IO, took over leadership of the SPLM-IO in government. The government recognised Taban Deng's leadership of the SPLM-IO, but many in the SPLM-IO itself, including Machar, did not. After July 2016, communities and soldiers that supported the SPLM-IO violently debated Taban Deng's legitimacy. In this context, Taban Deng used government resources to increase his support, including the creation of new states. These new states were used to reward those who had opted for peace with the government, and to solidify the power of those in the new government.

For example, the redivision into 32 states divided the new Tambura State from Gbudwe State in western Equatoria. The initial creation of Gbudwe State in 2015 had revived the Zande District (an administrative unit from the 1950s), and united an area that had been divided into Yambio and Tambura Rural Councils (Johnson, 2015). In 2015, this unusually large state appeared to be a reward to Governor Patrick Raphael Zamoi for his loyalty to the government. Zamoi had replaced the former Western Equatoria governor, Joseph Bangasi Bakosoro, earlier in 2015. Yet as this state was so large, it prompted debate locally about whether it should be divided further.

Political and military alliances also shifted after the initial creation of Gbudwe State in 2015. By early 2017, some of the armed opposition forces near Yambio and Tambura engaged directly with the government in building peace, contradicting the instructions of the rebel leader, Fatuyo, who had prohibited his forces from engaging in local church-led peace efforts. The creation of another state in this area in early 2017 can therefore be seen as a reward for some groups' co-operation with government. The division also created obstacles for further opposition collaboration. By dividing Gbudwe State, the government succeeded in redrawing boundaries to effectively demarcate the areas over which it had stronger control.

The increase in states allowed Kiir to buy the loyalty of more people through state governor appointments. However, by late 2015, central government funds were waning, inflation was surging, and the cost of the war was increasing. Sudan's history of boom-and-bust political markets has been reproduced in Southern Sudan and, later, South Sudan, since 2005 (de Waal, 2015). During the CPA period of 2005–2011, a time of high oil production and oil prices, funding political budgets became largely dependent on access to oil revenues (de Waal, 2014). By 2015, the decline in oil revenues forced Kiir to seek alternatives to manage the business of politics, and one of his strategies was to create other opportunities for rent income, such as local taxes and fees, and to shape political rivalries around access to those resources. With scarce revenues, many promised state grants were not realised, and governorship appointments came to be seen as a licence to generate state-level revenue and loot the natural resources of the state. At the time of writing, appointment to a government position at the state level still appears to buy some loyalty, even if salary payments are rarely expected. It is unclear how long this will last.

The regional and international players involved in the South Sudanese peace process have their own interests in various formulae for decentralisation and federalism. Whether they recognise it or not, they are active players in South Sudan's political marketplace. As the regional rivalries remain undimmed, especially between Sudan and Uganda, continuing contests over provincial political power inside South Sudan can be expected. Kiir's decentralisation has stirred up local dynamics, some of which were intended, and some of which were not. Regional élites have instrumentalised social identities to mobilise political support, and politicians have continued to manipulate borders and identities, often prompting conflict (Justin and de Vries, 2017). Populist logic has also been employed, with ethnic solidarity and crude xenophobic rhetoric being promoted and directed against the intrusive role of the international community.

Unintended consequences

New states were divided in areas where the government was more confident of support. This appears to have created new opportunities for peripheral élites to renegotiate their relationship with the centre. It also shows that identity politics is not always easily controlled from the centre. In 2015, for example, Warrap State, the home state of Kiir, was divided into Twic, Gogrial and Tonj States. The appointment of new governors was particularly controversial. It was assumed that the governorship was a material gift from Kiir of transfers from the state budget (when revenues are available), and also an unwritten licence to capture the state's land and resources to build local patronage networks. Local politicians took the opportunity to resurrect old disputes over land boundaries and grazing rights, and used ethnic identities linked to territory to mobilise armed youth to fight for land and resources.

After the post-CPA divisions of the counties of Warrap State, thousands died in Gogrial during armed clashes over boundaries and land rights. It required direct intervention by Kiir to bring the conflict to an end. After the re-division of the states in October 2015, the same tensions re-emerged. In January 2017, Kiir appointed his bother-in-law, Gregory Deng, as governor of Gogrial State. Residents feared Gregory Deng would use his position to capture key resources for himself and his community, including important grazing land, and armed conflict between communities in Gogrial slowly escalated. In July 2017, Kiir eventually declared a state of emergency in Gogrial in an attempt to stop the fighting, explicitly demonstrating the centre's direct control over regional dynamics. An SPLA force was sent to Gogrial, and a neighbouring state governor, acting on instructions from Kiir, was active in ending the conflict. In contrast to the conflict a decade before, Kiir's intervention did not immediately stop the fighting; rather, it was only after Gregory Deng's removal that tensions started to ease.

Conclusion

This chapter has shown that decentralisation has taken a number of different forms in north-east Africa, including variant forms in Sudan and South Sudan. The timing and nature of decentralisation has, in each case, been driven by political dynamics. These political dynamics have varied, from a national public debate on the future governance of the country to central government attempts to retain power when faced with challenges from the provinces, to accommodating national rivals in peace agreements, to responding to the dictates of regional powers, and combinations of all these. Decentralisation tends to be controversial and is often criticised. Nonetheless, in Uganda, Ethiopia, Kenya and Somalia there have been demonstrable national gains from well-considered decentralisation policies. The way in which it has been done in South Sudan, however, has made it less promising.

Since 2015, South Sudan's decentralisation has been characterised by the use of administrative reform and deconcentration as a mechanism for reconfiguring political patronage systems to the centre's advantage. South Sudan's decentralisation was initiated in the context of a bankrupt government that could no longer fund a centralised patronage payroll, ongoing civil war, and an internationally imposed peace agreement that reflects different and unresolved interests among neighbouring states and international actors. By creating 28 states, Kiir destabilised political patronage networks in a manner that was tactically useful to him. He reduced the leverage of state governors, created new political rivalries on the local level, expanded the scope for divide-and-rule manoeuvres, defused a more radical federalist agenda and proactively rather than reactively allocated patronage.

The new states and their governors have transformed local authorities into key government allies, usurping rival authorities in some instances.

These alliances have often been based on the capture of state budgets or tacit permission to loot state resources. These new relationships between peripheral élites and the centre have impacted the relationships between the peripheral élites and the people they claim to govern. For example, in Pibor, Yau Yau's co-option by the centre appears to have distanced him from the people he could formerly mobilise. In Gogrial, fears of the governor using his relationship with the centre to capture resources fostered mistrust and conflict.

For the government in Juba, the fundamental calculus is that decentralisation has meant some deregulation of local political rivalry and some locally adverse outcomes, which have been a small price to pay for a cheaper and less challenging political structure. This fits well into the framework explaining the variations in relations between central and local government developed by Boone (2003) and the political marketplace framework of de Waal (2015). These explanatory frameworks imply that South Sudan's current administrative map and its formula for the division of power between central and state governments should not be seen as a fixed settlement. Rather, it should be viewed as an opportunistic arrangement that suits the needs of the government in today's circumstances, and which will be altered, possibly transformed, as circumstances change.

This last consideration points to a slender opening for bringing together opportunistic political logic with technical expertise and normative democratic logic. The very fragility of the current decentralised arrangement in South Sudan provides an opportunity for opening the topic up to public debate and expert dialogue, ideally leading to reform. This could mean that the long-suffering people of South Sudan may be able to begin to enjoy the benefits of national independence in the form of determining the best governance arrangements for their country.

References

Aalen, Lovise (2011), *The Politics of Ethnicity in Ethiopia: Actors, Power and Mobilisation Under Ethnic Federalism* (Leiden and Boston, MA: Brill).

Abbink, Jon (2011), 'Ethnic-based federalism and ethnicity in Ethiopia: Reassessing the experiment after 20 years', *Journal of Eastern African Studies* 5, no. 4: 596–618.

Anderson, David M. (2005), '"Yours in struggle for Majimbo": Nationalism and the party politics of decolonization in Kenya, 1955–64', *Journal of Contemporary History* 40, no. 3: 547–64.

Gebrehiwot, Mulugeta and Fiseha Haftetsion (2015), 'The politics in naming the Ethiopian federation', *Journal of Ethiopian Studies* 48: 89–117.

— (2017), *The Norms and Practices of Nationalism and Self-Determination in Contemporary Ethiopia*, paper presented at workshop titled 'Nationalism and Self-Determination in the Horn of Africa', Cambridge, February 2017.

Berman, Bruce J., Jill Cottrell and Yash Ghai (2009), 'Patrons, clients, and constitutions: Ethnic politics and political reform in Kenya', *Canadian Journal of African Studies* 43, no. 3: 462–506.

Boone, Catherine (2003), *Political Topographies of the African State: Territorial Authority and Institutional Choice* (Cambridge: Cambridge University Press).

— (2012), 'Land conflict and distributive politics in Kenya', *African Studies Review* 55, no. 1: 75–103.

Chabal, Patrick and Jean-Pascal Daloz (1999), *Africa Works: Disorder As Political Instrument* (London: James Currey).

Cheeseman, Nic, Gabrielle Lynch and Justin Willis (2014), 'Democracy and its discontents: Understanding Kenya's 2013 elections', *Journal of Eastern African Studies* 8, no. 1: 2–24.

D'Arcy, Michelle and Agnes Cornell (2016), 'Devolution and corruption in Kenya: Everyone's turn to eat?', *African Affairs* 115, no. 459: 246–73.

de Waal, Alex (2004), 'Counter-insurgency on the cheap', *London Review of Books* 26, no. 15: 25–7.

— (2009), 'Why humanitarian organizations need to tackle land issues', in Sara Pantuliano (ed.), *Uncharted Territory: Land, Conflict and Humanitarian Action* (Rugby, UK: Practical Action Publishing).

— (2014), 'When Kleptocracy Becomes Insolvent: The brute causes of the civil war in South Sudan', *African Affairs* 113 no. 452, 347–69.

— (2015), *The Real Politics of the Horn of Africa: Money, War and the Business of Power* (Cambridge: Polity).

Eaton, Kent, Kai Kaiser and Paul J. Smoke (2010), *The Political Economy of Decentralization Reforms: Implications for Aid Effectiveness* (Washington, D.C.: World Bank).

EU-TAPP (2016), *Technical Assistance for Sub-National Capacity Building in Payroll and PFM in South Sudan: Project Completion Report, August 2014–February 2016*, 31 March 2016, https://europa.eu/capacity4dev/file/30071/download?token=D9FdHBqm.

Francis, Paul and Robert James (2003), 'Balancing rural poverty and citizen participation: The contradictions of Uganda's decentralization program', *World Development* 31, no. 2: 325–37.

Green, Elliott (2010), 'Patronage, district creation, and reform in Uganda', *Studies in Comparative International Development* 45, no. 1: 83–103.

Green, Elliott (2015), 'Decentralization and development in contemporary Uganda', *Regional and Federal Studies* 25, no. 5: 491–508.

Grossman, Guy and Janet I. Lewis (2014), 'Administrative unit proliferation', *American Political Science Review* 108, no. 1: 196–217.

Interim Constitution of Southern Sudan (2005).

Johnson, Douglas H. (2015), 'Brief analysis of the 28 states boundaries', Centre for Peace and Development Studies, University of Juba, https://paanluelwel2011.files.wordpress.com/2015/10/douglas-johnson-brief-analysis-of-the-boundaries-of-the-28-states-for-cpds-oct-2015.pdf.

Justin, Peter H. and Lotje de Vries (2017), 'Governing unclear lines: Local boundaries as a (re)source of conflict in South Sudan', *Journal of Borderlands Studies* 33, no. 2: 1–16.

Kanyinga, Karuti (2016), 'Devolution and the new politics of development in Kenya', *African Studies Review* 59, no. 3: 155–67.

Laitin, David D. and Said S. Samatar (1987), *Somalia: Nation in Search of a State* (Boulder, CO: Westview Press).

Lata, Leenco (1999), *The Ethiopian State at the Crossroads: Decolonization and Democratization or Disintegration?* (Trenton, NJ: Red Sea Press).

Leonardi, Cherry (2013), *Dealing With Government in South Sudan: Histories of Chiefship, Community and State* (Suffolk, UK: James Currey).

Lewis, Janet I. (2014), 'When decentralization leads to recentralization: Subnational state transformation in Uganda', *Regional and Federal Studies* 24, no. 5: 571–88.

Mamdani, Mahmood (1996), *Citizen and Subject: Contemporary Africa and the Legacy of Late Colonialism* (Princeton, NJ: Princeton University Press).

Pinaud, Clemence (2014), 'South Sudan: Civil war, predation and the making of a military aristocracy', *African Affairs* 113 no. 451: 192–211.

Presidential Establishment Order 36/2015 of South Sudan.

Schomerus, Marieke and Lovise Aalen (eds.) (2016), *Considering the State: Perspectives on South Sudan's Subdivision and Federalism Debate*, https://www.odi.org/sites/odi.org.uk/files/resource-documents/10837.pdf.

Small Arms Survey (2013), *David Yau Yau's Rebellion. Human Security Baseline Assessment for Sudan and South Sudan*, www.smallarmssurveysudan.org/fileadmin/docs/facts-figures/south-sudan/armed-groups/southern-dissident-militias/HSBA-Armed-Groups-Yau-Yau.pdf.

— (2016), *The Conflict in Upper Nile State: Human Security Baseline Assessment for Sudan and South Sudan*, www.smallarmssurveysudan.org/facts-figures/south-sudan/conflict-of-2013-14/the-conflict-in-upper-nile.html.

Smoke, Paul (2003), 'Decentralisation in Africa: Goals, dimensions, myths and challenges', *Public Administration and Development* 23, no. 1: 7–16.

Transitional Constitution of the Republic of South Sudan of 2011.

Turton, David (2006), *Ethnic Federalism: The Ethiopian Experience in Comparative Perspective* (Oxford: James Currey).

Willems, Ren and David Deng (2015), *The Legacy of Kokora in South Sudan*, Pax, https://www.paxforpeace.nl/publications/all-publications/the-legacy-of-kokora-in-south-sudan.

World Bank (2007), *Sudan: Public Expenditure Review, Synthesis Report* (Washington, DC: Poverty Reduction and Economic Management Unit).

— (2017), *South Sudan Economic Update, 2017: Taming the Tides of High Inflation* (Washington, DC: World Bank).

CHAPTER 10

African Decentralisation as a Power Calculation, and Its Relevance for South Sudan

Lovise Aalen

Introduction

Many African governments introduced provisions for decentralisation in the early 1990s, as a part of the 'third wave of democratisation' (Huntington, 1991). In the last 15 years, most constitutional reforms or new power pacts in Africa, including Somalia and South Sudan, have included decentralisation in some form. Decentralisation is defined as the transfer of power, responsibilities and finance from central to sub-national levels of government at a provincial or local level (Crawford and Hartmann, 2008). Decentralisation is thought to bring government closer to the people and reforms are seen as a means to deepen democracy, solve conflict and improve service delivery. It therefore has strong support among international policymakers, national civil society actors and across political party lines.

Still, there is great variation across states in the *implementation* of the constitutional decentralisation provisions. Some states have abandoned local government structures altogether, while others hold local polls regularly and local government structures are empowered both politically and financially. The variation in implementation is not, however, an expression of variation in democratic performance. A regime's willingness to implement decentralisation is not necessarily related to a desire to create or deepen local democracy. Decentralisation, or the lack of it, should instead be viewed as a part of the larger power calculations of a regime, where devolution of power is seen either as a way of enhancing regime survival or undermining it.

Based on analyses of several African states, including Angola, Ethiopia and South Africa, this chapter argues that decentralisation reforms are likely to be implemented and sustained in regimes that are able to use local polls and local government structures as a tool for consolidating control of the national dominant party at the local level. In regimes without this capability, decentralisation reforms are not likely to be implemented. In this chapter, this argument is discussed in the context of the introduction of decentralisation reforms in South Sudan.

The 2011 Transitional Constitution of South Sudan includes decentralisation provisions, outlining devolution of power to two sub-national levels: state, and local. Local governments have an important role to play in the redistribution of land and reintegration of returnees after the civil war and are seen as crucial for the creation of sustainable peace in South Sudan (Branch and Mampilly, 2005). To date, however, local-level legislatures have not been established and local elections have not been held. This chapter argues that the lack of implementation of decentralisation provisions is likely to be explained by the regime's power calculations, and the national ruling party's inability to use local politics to sustain its power base on the local level.

The first section of this chapter discusses the concept of decentralisation, placing this work within the pragmatic and realistic camp of decentralisation studies. Rather than considering the assumed advantages of decentralisation and its normative goals, this chapter will look at factors that explain the variation in the implementation of decentralisation reforms. The second section looks into how regimes' power calculations determine whether decentralisation efforts are sustained or not. The last section looks at South Sudan's decentralisation reforms and structures, and the preconditions for effective decentralisation that are absent in the country, namely the ruling Sudan People's Liberation Movement (SPLM)'s lack of territorial control, and the absence of effective wartime administrative structures or cohesive party organisation.

Decentralisation: the concept and state of the art

The literature distinguishes between two major kinds of decentralisation (Crook and Manor, 1998). The first is essentially an administrative process, often called deconcentration, in which power and resources are transferred to local branches of the central state. The second type is political or democratic decentralisation, which implies that power and resources are transferred to authorities who are representative of and accountable to local populations. Most studies of decentralisation reforms in Africa are based on the political or democratic understanding of the concept. These studies tend to outline the desired outcomes or normative goals of transferring power and resources to the local level.

It is assumed that decentralisation, if properly implemented, will increase public participation in decision-making and enhance the downward accountability of government officials, thereby leading to a deepening of democracy (Blair, 2000). By bringing government closer to the people, it is thought that social services and public decisions are better matched to local needs, thereby enhancing efficiency and transparency in the use of government resources (Connerley et al., 2010). Decentralisation reforms can also be a method of conflict resolution as, by allowing sub-national groups authority over local resources, territory and decision-making, demands for secession or other forms of sub-national autonomy may be mitigated (Crawford and Hartmann, 2008).

There is a well-established consensus on the benefits of decentralisation. The international donor community, civil society organisations and implementing governments all favour strengthening local governments. On the political right, decentralisation is favoured because it shrinks the power of the central bureaucratic state. This was an important justification for the structural adjustment programmes of the 1980s, where the international donor community promoted decentralisation as a way of 'rolling back the state'. On the political left, decentralisation is promoted as a way of empowering people on the ground. This has been a focal point during the 1990s and 2000s, linked to 'the third wave of democratisation', where popular participation in decision-making is seen as a key to 'good governance'.

The majority of studies of decentralised governance in Africa nevertheless share the conclusion that decentralisation has not led to better governance or economic performance, or to a deepening of democracy (Azfar et al., 1999; Connerley et al., 2010; Crawford and Hartmann, 2008; Obeng-Odoom, 2011). The main explanation for this failure is not decentralisation itself, but the lack of proper *implementation* (Crook and Manor, 1998).

A public administration or economics approach to explaining such a failure focuses on the fiscal and technical aspects of the process, specifically on how a lack of revenue transfers from the centre or limited spending autonomy impedes the local government bodies' ability to make efficient decisions (Dickovick, 2011). In contrast, the conventional political science approach would centre around the formal or legal aspects of the process. Political science would focus on how the decentralisation process is obstructed by weaknesses and complexities in institutional design or shortfalls in legal frameworks (such as a lack of guarantees in the constitution, or no specific local government laws), unclear division of responsibilities between the levels of government, or limited capacity of local administrations (Azfar et al., 1999). A solution to this would then be to keep decentralisation reforms simple, to avoid creating confusion around the division of power and resources or overstretching local governments. Capacity-building and technical assistance would be provided for both central ministries and local government bodies to enable a better understanding and handling of decentralisation processes (Connerley et al., 2010).

A more applied political analysis of decentralisation in Africa stresses not only the formal sides of central and local governance, but realises that decentralisation, even if properly designed, cannot work independently from the social and political structures in which it is embedded (Crook and Manor, 1998). In systems dominated by patronage and clientelism, local government structures are likely to be captured by local élites who, in many cases, are also part of the central government's patronage systems (Wunsch, 2001). Others have pointed out how executive dominance over legal bodies, a weak civil society and general civic apathy on the local level restrict opportunities for popular participation (Poteete and Ribot, 2011).

The solution to these failures of decentralisation would then be the introduction of genuinely accountable governments, both at central and local levels. A flaw in this argument, however, is that the preconditions for success are mixed up with the desired outcomes of the same process. As Daniel Treisman (2007) points out, the conditions required for successful decentralisation are actually benefits that decentralisation itself is supposed to produce. Decentralisation would improve accountability as long as systems of accountability were established. Furthermore, this and other preconditions for the success of decentralisation (such as transparency and the rule of law) are not specific to decentralisation. These features could make any system work, including a centralised one. These preconditions do not, in themselves, establish a presumption that one system is better than the other.

However, both the strongly normative basis and the explanation of poor implementation undermining the success of decentralisation fail to link the lack of desired outcomes to *governments' motivations* for decentralisation. They conceal that decentralisation, in most cases, is implemented for a number of more pragmatic and strategic reasons, far different from normative goals. As noted by Christopher Clapham (1995), since colonisation leaders in Africa have been preoccupied with state survival, and have made state survival a matter of regime survival. They have invariably aimed at introducing reforms which retain and even consolidate their power and control of resources (Crawford and Hartmann, 2008). Decentralisation should also be understood in this context.

The first wave of decentralisation in Africa happened during colonialism, when indirect rule was a means to penetrate and manage the rural hinterland. After independence, most governments aimed at strengthening the central state and building the nation, and if power was transferred to the local level, it was to deconcentrate centralised administrative tasks rather than to empower local communities. From the 1980s onwards, decentralisation became a part of international donor policies, first linked to the neo-liberal structural adjustment programmes and, later, as a way of enhancing 'good governance' (Hyden, 2007).

In response to this, African governments adopted the rhetoric of decentralisation, not necessarily because of a change of heart, but for strategic reasons. First, this fulfilled the conditions placed on them by donors and, second, and potentially more importantly, it was seen as a way of strengthening the incumbent's legitimacy in the eyes of his citizens. The issue of incumbents' legitimacy has become particularly important in the 'hybrid' or 'electoral authoritarian' regimes in Africa today. Liberal democratic institutions, including decentralised governance, have been introduced and elections are held, yet incumbents use these mechanisms to sustain their own power rather than enlarge the space for opposition or popular participation (Diamond, 2002; Schedler, 2006).

Similar to the way in which elections can be instruments of political control rather than devices of liberalisation, decentralisation can be an efficient tool for consolidating ruling party dominance, rather than enhancing local governments' efficiency, accountability and transparency. As Catherine Boone (2003) argues, regimes manipulate local power relations to their own advantage and avoid moves that could foment local challenge. In the implementation of decentralisation, central actors not only fail to execute reforms, but deliberately resist the loss of power. Despite excellent institutional design, such regimes are able to employ 'a repertoire of domination' to effectively circumvent or neutralise formal policy changes (Poteete and Ribot, 2011).

This process of 'centralising decentralisation' within hybrid regimes has not been well covered in the literature. One exception is J. Tyler Dickovick's 2011 study of recentralisation in the developing world, in which he explores why decentralisation happened in the first place and, thereafter, why recentralisation occurs. He starts with the pragmatic assumption that presidents and chief executives prefer not to decentralise. If they do, it is because of an electoral defeat or a general reduction in executive power. Based on Kathleen O'Neill's (2003) argument that democratic decentralisation is often adopted as an electoral strategy in circumstances where weakened politicians seek to maximise control over political and fiscal resources, Dickovick argues that sub-national autonomy varies in inverse proportion to the power of the chief executive. For example, if an economic crisis takes place, it presents an opportunity for the executive to centralise power again. Changes in the national political economy therefore explain recentralisation.

A problem with Dickovick's analysis is that he assumes that when states introduce decentralisation reforms they are actually decentralising. To recentralise, there must have been a genuine decentralisation in the first place. However, in many African states, this is not the case. Dickovick argues that

the existence of decentralisation with lack of recentralisation, as in Senegal, does not mean that central states are weak relative to sub-national governments, rather it means that central states have institutionalised ways to withhold power from the sub-national governments. Even in an age of decentralisation, the centre can hold. (Dickovick, 2011: 176)

Another argument against his hypothesis of weakened executives leading to decentralisation is that if executives have too little control on the ground they are unlikely to introduce decentralised governance as it is too risky even if not properly implemented. As pointed out by Ragnhild Muriaas (2008), promoting local democracy can be more problematic for parties with less solid roots in society than in contexts with a dominant party and strong organisation to rely on. An important implication of this is that the more competitive a political system is, the less chance there is for the introduction and implementation of decentralisation reforms.

Decentralisation as a way of consolidating national dominance

This inductive analysis of three post-conflict cases – Angola, Ethiopia and South Africa – suggests that one factor explaining this variation is élite discontinuity, seen when an insurgent group gains power in the aftermath of conflict (Aalen and Muriaas, 2017). Decentralised systems adopted by new governments with an extensive social base derived from an insurgency, as in South Africa and Ethiopia, have proved relatively robust. By contrast, where there is no change in the executive after a conflict ends and the ruling party continues to be challenged by one or more rival armed groups, as in Angola, decentralisation has remained unimplemented.

Ethiopia, which has held regular elections throughout the post-conflict period, is by no means a democratic regime. Rather, it has used sub-national elections as a tool for consolidating control of the national ruling party at the local level. Even in the relatively more democratic context of South Africa, sub-national elections are clearly a part of the ruling African National Congress (ANC)'s power calculus to enhance its nationwide presence and control.

It is argued that, in post-conflict settings, the emergence of new élites with electoral confidence and territorial control is a likely *precondition* for implementing decentralisation reforms and routinising local elections. These new regimes favour decentralisation because it enables them to gain control over local authorities that may be aligned with the former government. It may also work as a channel for political mobilisation.

In contrast, regimes that do not represent new élites or a clear victor and that cannot be confident of winning elections across the national territory at the point when decentralisation provisions are introduced, are not going to implement sub-national elections regularly, even if sub-national polls are required by the constitution. A government that remains in power after being challenged by armed groups with domestic regional support, or after the end of war, has few incentives to build decentralised structures which may serve to formalise the wartime social networks of insurgent groups.

Decentralisation, as opposed to centralisation, is a useful tool for con-solidating dominance for two reasons. First, decentralisation increases a regime's legitimacy in the eyes of both international donors and domestic constituencies. The introduction of local government, even if not properly implemented, can be justified by referring to the normative ideals of bringing government closer to the people, making government more effective and mitigating sub-national conflict. Second, decentralisation facilitates control and mobilisation at the local level, which a centralised system could not do.

In dominant party states, which often have a blurred division between party organisation and state administration, establishing local government opens up new channels for party recruitment in local areas. Also, even if the opposition could win pockets of power in local elections, the opposition is generally weaker at the local level than at the national level, making it easier for the ruling party to out-manoeuvre and contain the opposition at the local level. Local structures might also result in local cadres being paid salaries and allowances that make them dependent on the continued survival of the ruling party. In this way, decentralisation may, in fact, further patronage. In a competitive system, these incentives are weakened or disappear as there is greater uncertainty about who is going to win the local elections (Muriaas, 2008).

In the literature on post-conflict states, increased attention is being given to the impact of how conflicts end and how institutions develop in the aftermath of conflict. How conflict ends is thought to affect prospects for democracy (Gurses and Mason, 2008), the characteristics of post-conflict party systems (Ishiyama and Batta, 2011), the process of building post-war party organisations (Reilly, 2013) and the credibility of post-war parties (Lyons, 2016). However, little research has considered how the process of routinising sub-national elections is affected by how conflict ends.

Lyons (2016) argues that the victors of war shape the post-war political order, and that victorious insurgents can consolidate and expand their political power by building on their wartime structures of command and control. When insurgent groups win power after long, intense conflicts, they may have developed experience in administering liberated territory and managing top-down relationships with the peasantry (Lyons, 2016). In such circumstances, introducing local governance structures and sub-national elections would make it possible for a national party to govern by formalising wartime structures where such networks are present, and building institutions in communities where such networks don't already exist (Lyons, 2016).

Rachel Riedl and J. Tyler Dickovick (2014) contend that robust decentralisation (covering administrative, fiscal and political decentralisation) occurs where national governments perceive regime survival advantages in implementing decentralisation. According to this argument, hegemonic parties in an authoritarian setting are most likely to decentralise if these parties believe they can extend the party-state to the local level, increase patronage opportunities and deepen links between the party-state and citizens.

This chapter builds on these arguments, by contending that having the ability to use wartime structures of command and control can both build powerful party organisations and affect the commitment of post-conflict governments to implement constitutional decentralisation provisions. This is so regardless of the democratic credentials of post-war governments.

The prospects of implementing and sustaining decentralisation in South Sudan

The experiences of other post-conflict states in Africa show that decentralisation is most likely to happen where there is a clear victory, and where the regime has territorial control and an ability to use local government structures for ruling party mobilisation and control. In light of this, what are the prospects for decentralisation in South Sudan? The following discussion assesses developments around local governance in South Sudan since the end of the last civil war in 2005, including the move to independence in 2011.

The South Sudanese government, led by the SPLM, has expressed support for decentralisation. Local government reforms are also supported by the international donor community, who see decentralisation as a way to resolve conflict and improve service delivery in South Sudan (UNDP, 2012). The Interim Constitution of 2005 prescribes a decentralised system with three levels of government: national, state and local.[1] At the time, South Sudan was divided into ten states. President Salva Kiir later unilaterally increased the number of states to 28. Local government has three layers: county, *payam* (having a minimum population of 25,000) and *boma* (a village or ward).

County governments are responsible for tax collection, among other things. At the *payam* level, traditional leaders play a role in the judicial system, applying customary law. In *bomas*, authority is divided between the *boma* administrator (appointed by the SPLM) and the traditional chief (appointed by a council of elders). The Local Government Act (2009) permitted traditional authorities to be integrated into local councils, continuing a practice established under colonial indirect rule.

Despite these provisions, decentralisation has remained largely unimplemented in South Sudan. The 2011 Transitional Constitution reneged on some of the decentralisation provisions included in the 2005 Interim Constitution, creating a more centralised state. In most of the country, county legislative assemblies do not exist, county commissioners are largely appointed from the centre, borders between the local administrations are not demarcated, and there is no clarity on how local government can raise revenues or receive transfers from the centre to provide local service delivery (De Simone, 2013). The return to armed conflict in December 2013 has further lessened the chances that the South Sudanese government may implement a genuinely decentralised system of governance. Devolution of power, particularly through a federal system, also became controversial for a time as one of the main demands put forward by the main opposition party, the Sudan People's Liberation Movement-in-Opposition (SPLM-IO).

Therefore, it's unlikely that South Sudan will implement a complete system of local governance soon. As the SPLM is seeking regime survival, it is inclined to consolidate central power and national territorial control before decentralisation is carried out. What follows here demonstrates that South Sudan lacks what other decentralising post-conflict regimes in Africa have had, namely territorial control, a legacy of effective wartime structures to administer the local population, and a central party organisation capable of and interested in using local administration to contain opposition and mobilise support for the national regime.

Lack of territorial control

The current political regime in South Sudan came out of a larger political settlement in the wider Sudan, the 2005 Comprehensive Peace Agreement (CPA). Although the SPLM took control of the Southern Sudan government in 2005, it did not have full territorial control as there were competing militias and factions of the SPLM that challenged the central power in Juba. The SPLM had to gain control of these militias and gradually incorporate them into the national army.

The South Sudan Defence Forces (SSDF), which were integrated into the national army in 2006, were the largest of these militias, almost comparable in size with the SPLM itself (Sørbø, 2014). The arrangement is therefore not an outcome of one side's victory, as in Ethiopia for instance. Rather, it is similar to that of post-civil-war Angola, where the ruling People's Movement for the Liberation of Angola (MPLA) was challenged by the National Union for the Total Independence of Angola (UNITA) in certain areas of the country. This led to the MPLA viewing the empowerment of local authorities in UNITA-dominated areas as a threat. Decentralisation, including local elections, was therefore never implemented in Angola.

Despite the apparent success of militia integration, old fault-lines, often ethnically based, have remained within the new national army. Combined with low discipline and informal chains of command, the arrangement has allowed previous militia leaders to mobilise their old power bases in times of crisis. These power bases reach down to the local level, with significant militarisation of civilians and links to local power structures and agendas (Oosterom, 2014). This arrangement makes it possible for state governors and divisional army officials to run policies independently from the centre (de Waal, 2014). Since the SPLM lacks nationwide territorial control and does not hold a monopoly over violence, it is likely that the regime would perceive genuine, country-wide decentralisation as a threat to its hold on power. After all, holding local elections in areas outside SPLM control may result in resources and power being extended to local leaders outside the SPLM, potentially strengthening the opposition's base and threatening the SPLM regime's survival.

Weak wartime structures

Post-conflict regimes that have their roots in victorious insurgencies can use decentralisation to consolidate and expand their political power by building upon their pre-existing wartime structures of command and control. For example, the Tigray People's Liberation Front (TPLF) in Ethiopia built administration systems for the civilian population in areas they controlled during the struggle against the Derg regime (Young, 1997). Therefore, when the TPLF took power in Addis Ababa in 1991, it already had a civilian support base in the north, had gained invaluable experience in administering local communities, and could use its local wartime structures as a model for creating new local administrations nationally. Decentralisation was therefore not perceived as a risk for the TPLF, as it could count on its wartime experience and structures to ensure that newly appointed local governors did not turn against it.

In South Sudan, there were also attempts to establish local governments during the civil war (Rolandsen, 2005). After the TPLF assumed power in Ethiopia in 1991, the Sudan People's Liberation Army (SPLA), the SPLM's military wing, lost vital external support from Ethiopia. Consequently, the SPLM tried to create local civilian administrations, particularly in non-Dinka areas, to nurture support for the insurgency (Johnson, 2003). During the 1990s, the SPLM was also pressurised by NGOs and the international community to establish political structures and cede to local peace and reconciliation initiatives.

The National Convention of 1994 made civil authority a priority, and the Civil Authority of South Sudan was established in 1996, incorporating traditional leaders into the SPLM administration as mediators between guerrilla forces and local populations. However, traditional leaders had suffered under guerrilla control – their authority had been undermined and their constituencies dispersed, and they were challenged by new chiefs appointed by the SPLM or the government (Branch and Mampilly, 2005).

The SPLM leader John Garang's leadership was based on personal alliances with loyal officers who were dependent on his personal support, and he tried to use the new initiatives to co-opt new actors into the party machinery (Rolandsen, 2005). Since Garang's death in 2005, no undisputed leader has replaced him. The old Garang faction has remained weak and the party's organisation remains factionalised (Rolandsen, 2015).

Another factor that contributed to the SPLM lacking efficient wartime administration structures was that the SPLA depended on NGOs as the main service providers in SPLA-controlled areas and relied on neighbouring states and the UNHCR to accept and take care of displaced populations. This external support meant that SPLA civilian administration was not essential and did not develop. The historically strong position of NGOs as service providers in South Sudan has undermined the legitimacy and capacity development of local governments and, consequently, hampered decentralisation.

There is, therefore, limited evidence for how local SPLM/A administrative structures worked in practice, or whether they could serve as a basis for post-war decentralised administrations. Contrary to the case of the TPLF in Ethiopia, the SPLM/A does not appear to have the efficient wartime administrative structure needed to facilitate decentralisation.

In want of a cohesive dominant party

When examining decentralisation patterns in Africa, it becomes apparent that dominant party states provide a particularly good basis for implementing decentralisation reforms. In such states, division between party organisation and state administration is often blurred. Establishing local government bodies enables the party to recruit in local areas. This allows the ruling party to extend the party-state to the local level, increase patronage opportunities and deepen links between the party and citizens. Decentralisation reforms, therefore, favour the national dominant party and, as such, are likely to be sustained. Both the ANC in South Africa and the Ethiopian People's Revolutionary Democratic Front (EPRDF) have efficiently used local government structures to extend their power base and have actively exploited local elections to challenge or remove local remnants of the old regime.

The SPLM has the potential to become a dominant ruling party, both due to its historical legacy as the liberation party and because the opposition is divided. As in other dominant party states, the boundaries between the SPLM and the state are blurred and the SPLM is willing and able to use state resources to sustain its power. In practice, however, the SPLM has not utilised the state to build a stable party apparatus. With only two national conventions, in 1994 and 2008, internal party democracy is minimal. Compared to the ANC or the EPRDF, the SPLM does not have a strong party organisation and has not made adequate effort to build such an organisation. Instead of employing state resources and public funds to build the party organisation, officials exploit party positions for personal enrichment and to maintain personal patronage networks. This practice extends back to the colonial administration, when political power was seen as a way of accessing resources. Similarly, at independence, SPLM officials rushed to secure access to resources.

During the military struggle, looting food and other kinds of aid was a military strategy. The Sudanese government used aid and resources as part of a divide-and-rule strategy to control the southern insurgents. Financial patronage became the mechanism for conflict management, both in the north and the south. During the CPA years (2005–2011), both the National Congress Party in the north and the SPLM in the south spent excessively on rival patronage systems (de Waal, 2014). These patron–client networks are, however, constantly subject to renegotiation, and violence is the means of bargaining. Instead of building up local party and administrative struc-tures, the patronage system results in national leaders facing 'rent-seeking rebellions', the mutiny of army commanders or local political leaders with armed constituencies as they seek a larger share of government resources (de Waal, 2014).

During the process of bargaining between national patrons and local clients, decentralisation is a resource that local leaders try to exploit, with destructive effects. As pointed out by Marieke Schomerus and Tim Allen, 'decentralisation, while theoretically the best way to govern South Sudan, has in reality often become an instrument to entrench "tribal" lines over competition for resources, manifesting itself in the proliferation of new counties' (Schomerus and Allen, 2010: 9). Local political élites use decen-tralised governance systems to claim land ownership for their communities, and ethnic communities ask for county boundaries to be drawn along tribal lines, all further entrenching ethnic identities and social divisions (Oosterom, 2014). With the SPLM's policy of appointing local governors with a military background, this leads, in practice, to military-controlled tribal local administrations (Schomerus and Allen, 2010).

Conclusion

Despite the failure of decentralisation in South Sudan to date, discussions about the devolution of power have continued, and decentralisation and federalism remain highly contested issues. Many think that decentralisation is the only system that can manage South Sudan's ethnic diversity and facilitate efficient and broad-based service delivery. The SPLM-IO made federalism its political platform, while the SPLM initially saw it as subversion and disloyalty, likening it to the *kokora* system that it does not want to return to (Johnson, 2014). The SPLM-IO demanded a federation with 21 states to accommodate ethnic claims. While the SPLM at first rejected the idea of so many states, President Salva Kiir announced the creation of 28 states in 2015. Some have argued for a unitary state, while others have urged against it, reminding of the devastating experience of centralisation in Africa, which has involved corruption, inefficiency and the oppression of minorities (Kimenyi, 2012).

It is clear that increased local governance, possible through either decentralisation or federalism, offers many advantages for South Sudan. Such systems have the potential to accommodate ethnic diversity and enable local governments to provide improved service delivery and connect more closely with the local population. However, for decentralisation to be feasible, the necessary preconditions must be in place, namely that there must be a stable and established central power in South Sudan that has territorial control, a monopoly on violence and greater organisational cohesiveness.

Notes

1   'National' at this time meant the Southern Sudan regional bloc, as independence had not yet been achieved and Southern Sudan remained part of Sudan.

References

Aalen, Lovise and Ragnhild L. Muriaas (2017), 'Power calculations and political decentralisation in African post-conflict states', *International Political Science Review* 38, no. 1: 56–69.

Azfar, Omar et al. (1999) *Decentralisation, Governance, and Public Services: The Impact of Institutional Arrangements*, University of Maryland, Center for Institutional Reform and the Informal Sector.

Blair, Harry (2000), 'Participation and accountability at the periphery: Democratic local governance in six countries', *World Development* 28, no. 1: 21–39.

Boone, Catherine (2003), *Political Topographies of the African State: Territorial Authority and Institutional Choice* (Cambridge: Cambridge University Press).

Branch, Adam and Zachariah C. Mampilly (2005), 'Winning the war, but losing the peace? The dilemma of SPLM/A civil administration and the tasks ahead', *The Journal of Modern African Studies* 43, no. 1: 1–20.

Clapham, Christopher (1995), *Africa and the International System: The Politics of State Survival* (Cambridge: Cambridge University Press).

Connerley, Ed, Kent Eaton and Paul Smoke (eds) (2010), *Making Decentralisation Work: Democracy, Development, and Security* (Boulder, CO: Lynne Rienner).

Crawford, Gordon and Christof Hartmann (eds) (2008), *Decentralisation in Africa: A Pathway Out Of Poverty and Conflict?* (Amsterdam: Amsterdam University Press).

Crook, Richard C. and James Manor (1998), *Democracy and Decentralisation in South Asia and West Africa: Participation, Accountability and Performance* (Cambridge: Cambridge University Press).

De Simone, Sara (2013), 'Post-conflict decentralisation: dynamics of land and power in Unity State – South Sudan', *UNISCI Discussion Papers*, no. 33: 35–56.

de Waal, Alex (2014), 'When kleptocracy becomes insolvent: brute causes of the civil war in South Sudan', *African Affairs* 113, no. 452: 347–69.

Diamond, Larry J. (2002), 'Thinking about hybrid regimes', *Journal of Democracy* 13, no. 2: 21–35.

Dickovick, J. Tyler (2011), *Decentralisation and Recentralisation in the Developing World: Comparative Studies from Africa and Latin America* (University Park, PA: Pennsylvania University Press).

Gurses, Mehmet and T. David Mason (2008), 'Democracy out of anarchy: The prospects for post-civil-war democracy', *Social Science Quarterly* 89, no. 2: 315–36.

Hyden, Goran (2007), 'Challenges to decentralised governance in weak states', in G. Shabbir Cheema and Dennis A. Rondinelli (eds), *Decentralising Governance: Emerging Concepts and Practices* (Washington, DC: Brookings Institution Press).

Interim Constitution of Southern Sudan of 2005.

Ishiyama, John and Anna Batta (2011), 'Swords into plowshares: The organisational transformation of rebel groups into political parties', *Communist and Post-Communist Studies* 44, no. 4: 369–79.

Johnson, Douglas H. (2003), *The Root Causes of Sudan's Civil Wars* (Oxford: James Currey).

— (2014), *Federalism in the History of South Sudanese Political Thought*, research paper, Rift Valley Institute.

Kimenyi, Mwangi S. (2012), *Making Federalism Work in South Sudan*, Brookings Institute, Africa Growth Initiative.

Local Government Act of 2009.

Lyons, Terrence (2016), 'The importance of winning: Victorious insurgent groups and authoritarian politics', *Comparative Politics* 48, 2: 167–84.

Muriaas, Ragnhild L. (2008), 'Affection and defection: Local perspectives on the pull towards the government party in Malawi, South Africa and Uganda', PhD diss., Department of Comparative Politics, University of Bergen.

O'Neill, Kathleen (2003), 'Decentralisation as an electoral strategy', *Comparative Political Studies* 36, no. 9: 1068–91.

Obeng-Odoom, Franklin (2011), 'Decentralisation in developing countries: Global perspectives on obstacles to fiscal devolution', *The Journal of Australian Political Economy*, no. 67: 157–9.

Oosterom, Marjoke (2014), '"It may approach as quickly as a bushfire": Gendered violence and insecurity in South Sudan', *Institute of Development Studies (IDS) Research Report 78*.

Poteete, Amy R. and Jesse C. Ribot (2011), 'Repertoires of domination: Decentralization as process in Botswana and Senegal', *World Development* 39, no. 3: 439–49.

Reilly, Benjamin (2013), 'Political parties and post-conflict peacebuilding', *Civil Wars* 15, no. 1: 88–104.

Riedl, Rachel B. and J. Tyler Dickovick (2014), 'Party systems and decentralization in Africa', *Studies in Comparative International Development* 49, no. 3: 321–42.

Rolandsen, Øystein (2005), *Guerrilla Government: Political Changes in South Sudan During the 1990s* (Uppsala: Nordic Africa Institute).

— (2015), 'Another civil war in South Sudan; the failure of a Guerrilla Government?', *Journal of Eastern African Studies* 9, no. 1: 163–74.

Schedler, Andreas (2006), *Electoral Authoritarianism: The Dynamics of Unfree Competition* (Boulder, CO: Lynne Rienner).

Schomerus, Marieke and Tim Allen (2010), *Southern Sudan at Odds With Itself: Dynamics of Conflict and Predicaments for Peace* (London: Development Studies Institute, London School of Economics and Political Science).

Sørbø, Gunnar M. (2014), *Return to War in South Sudan*, NOREF policy brief.

Transitional Constitution of the Republic of South Sudan of 2011.

Treisman, Daniel (2007), *The Architecture of Government: Rethinking Political Decentralization* (Cambridge: Cambridge University Press).

UNDP (2012), *Decentralisation Roundtable: Key Government Officials Discussed Status and Implementation of Decentralisation*.

Wunsch, James S. (2001), 'Decentralization, local governance and "recentralization" in Africa', *Public Administration and Development* 21, no. 4: 277–88.

Young, John (1997), *Peasant Revolution in Ethiopia – The Tigray People's Liberation Front, 1975–1991* (Cambridge: Cambridge University Press).

CHAPTER 11

The Challenges of Macroeconomic Stabilisation and Poverty Alleviation in South Sudan[1]

Nora Dihel and Utz Pape

Introduction

The Republic of South Sudan emerged in 2011 from decades of conflict as the world's newest independent country, with huge state- and peace-building challenges and extreme institutional and socio-economic deficits. Six years after independence, South Sudan remains one of the world's most conflict-affected and fragile countries, seemingly unable to emerge from cycles of violence. The escalation of the war has displaced a large share of the population, particularly since November 2016. The famine declared in February 2017 underscores the severity of the humanitarian crisis.

By August 2016, South Sudan displayed all the signs of macroeconomic collapse, with output contracting, and inflation and parallel exchange market premium spiralling. While the lack of reliable information on the current state of the economy makes it difficult to precisely assess it, the economy is estimated to have contracted by about 11 per cent in Fiscal Year (FY) 2016/17 due to the conflict, oil production disruptions and below-average agriculture production. On the demand side, exports and household consumption declined while government consumption increased due to spending on defence and security operations. Real GDP is projected to further contract by 3.5 per cent in FY2018/19, following the contraction of about 6.9 per cent in FY2017/18.

Declining oil production and prices have put additional pressure on the economy already weakened by the 2012 oil export shutdown (linked to a dispute with Sudan about pipeline transit fees) and the civil war. Oil production decreased to about 120,000 barrels per day in FY2016/17, down from around 140,000 barrels per day in FY2015/16, 165,000 barrels per day in 2014 and a peak of 350,000 barrels per day before independence in 2011. In June 2017, lower Transitional Financial Arrangement (TFA) fees were negotiated and agreed between the Government of the Republic of South Sudan (GRSS) and Sudan, making transit fees dependent on the global price of crude oil. Nevertheless, production has been on the decline due to the war as well as a poor return on investment (see Figure 11.1).

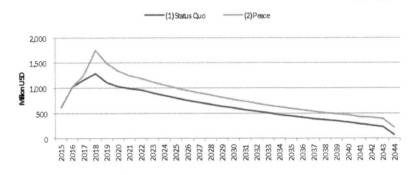

Figure 11.1 Oil revenue projections

Source: Republic of South Sudan Inclusive Growth
Country Economic Memorandum, World Bank (2017)

Exchange rate and inflation

Devaluation and the move towards a managed float of its currency in December 2015 only partially remedied South Sudan's economic problems. In the short run, the decision was expected to improve the country's fiscal and external positions, by increasing oil revenues and aid inflows in local currency and reducing imports. However, devaluation alone has not resolved the fiscal situation, as some of the positive effects of devaluation were diminished by further declining international oil prices, putting significant pressure on the exchange rate and contributing to the widening fiscal deficit.

Following the move to a more flexible exchange rate arrangement in 2015, the South Sudanese Pound (SSP) depreciated on the parallel market. The SSP depreciated from SSP18.5 to the US$ in December 2015 to SSP70 by August 2016, SSP172 by August 2017 and SSP310 by June 2018. Political events drove the volatility of the SSP: the SSP initially appreciated on the parallel market when the Transitional Government of National Unity came into place, but it later depreciated steadily, in particular after new fighting erupted in July 2016. It has continued to depreciate steadily as instability across the country continues. Although the implementation of the recent Khartoum Declaration of Agreement signed in June 2018 is starting to falter, the ongoing peace negotiations have brought a relatively positive mood to the country, with the parallel exchange rate dropping from SSP310 to SSP230 to the US$ by mid-July 2018. Despite the recent exchange rate appreciation, the spread between the official and the parallel market exchange rates remains high.

The annual Consumer Price Index (CPI) increased by 480 per cent in 2016 and by 155 per cent between July 2016 and July 2017. The year-on-year annual CPI increased by 88.5 per cent between June 2017 and June 2018 (Figure 11.2). Notwithstanding the recent price deceleration, the high-inflation environment continues to put many households in both urban and rural areas under extreme stress as they are often unable to afford the minimum food basket.

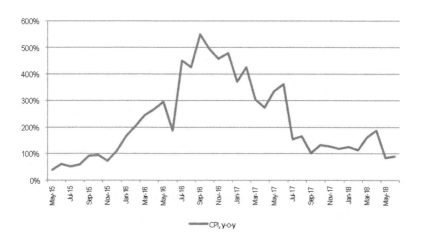

Figure 11.2 High and volatile inflation (year-on-year)

Source: South Sudan National Bureau of Statistics

Fiscal policy

In the absence of real-time data, the fiscal deficit is tentatively estimated at about 14 per cent of GDP in FY2016/17. The FY2017/18 National Budget Plan aims to restore macroeconomic stability but lacks credibility. It puts special emphasis on controlling public expenditure, increasing non-oil revenues, encouraging investment and economic diversification and removing subsidies to the national oil company, Nilepet. The plan also recommends that GRSS refrains from borrowing from the Bank of South Sudan (BSS) to bring down inflation and prevent further depreciation of the currency.

Although the FY2017/18 draft budget foresees a two-fifths cut in expenditure in dollar terms compared to the 2016/17 budget, it is unlikely that enough cash will be available to execute all budgeted items. While it is difficult to predict the prioritisation of expenditures, it is likely that the government will continue to protect security spending and core executive functions. With these expenditure cuts, the population will become even more dependent on humanitarian relief and donor-funded development projects for access to basic services. Even if the economy showed some recovery starting in 2018, poverty projection suggests poverty will continue to rise through 2019 as population growth is likely to exceed GDP growth.

The current account deficit is estimated to have narrowed to about 1.6 per cent in FY2016/17 from about 6.1 per cent of GDP in FY2015/16. Export revenues decreased due to declining oil prices and lower oil production. Imports decreased even more rapidly, however, thereby narrowing the current account deficit.

Despite moderate levels of external debt, the combined impact of civil conflict, a large fall in oil prices and high levels of fiscal spending has left South Sudan in debt distress. By June 2016, the stock of domestic and external debt owed or guaranteed by the central government amounted to about US$1.4 billion (38 per cent of GDP), while foreign exchange reserves had dwindled to about US$70 million (about two weeks of prospective imports). This crisis has caused payment delays on international obligations, civil servant salaries and other government obligations.

Outlook and challenges

The growth outlook for FY17/18 remains dire. In FY17/18, real GDP contracted by 6.9 per cent, and is projected to contract by a further 3.5 per cent in FY18/19. The fiscal deficit is projected to increase. Continued exchange rate depreciation and volatility will likely be associated with increasing dollarisation.

A key priority for the government is to address the underlying causes of the country's current macroeconomic collapse and food insecurity. It urgently needs to restore peace and security and implement comprehensive macroeconomic reforms. The latter includes measures to unify the official and parallel exchange markets and reduce inflation, as well as longer-term action to boost employment, build infrastructure and diversify the economy, with special emphasis on agriculture development.

Prior to adopting an adequate anchor to address high inflation, the government needs to pursue fiscal consolidation by limiting expenditure and raising revenues. The government can limit an imminent economic crisis scenario and start stabilising the economy by committing to improve the fiscal situation as a key priority. Falling revenue coupled with rising spending, in extremely high magnitudes, constitutes a major problem in South Sudan. Therefore, strong commitment to fiscal discipline is key to recovery. A credible fiscal consolidation requires the implementation of the following elements:

- **Revenue reforms**, which would include increasing non-oil revenues by reviewing the tax base (including customs duties) and introducing incentives to increase compliance, increasing transparency of oil revenues through full and transparent enactment of the Petroleum Revenue Management Act, and effective implementation of a single US$ account system to better account for US$ spending at the Ministry of Finance and Economic Planning and BSS; and
- **Spending reforms**, which would include reviewing the civil servant salary payment system and cleaning up the payroll, implementing states' transfer reductions, reductions in current operational spending and restructuring Nilpet operations, rationalising the usage of explicit and implicit subsides currently in use, and passing into law and implementing the Public Procurement and Disposal of Assets Bill.

Complementary Public Financial Management (PFM) reforms related to transparency around budget execution and oil revenues remain critical, especially as regards the activities of Nilepet and the Ministry of Finance and Economic Planning, and the link of oil revenues to foreign exchange management and on-budget revenues. The government would need to improve the PFM framework, particularly by establishing a cash management committee and requiring the immediate transfer of revenues from government accounts in commercial banks to the treasury accounts.

Longer-term measures should include social protection programmes to develop resilience against future shocks and create jobs for more sustainable livelihoods, as well as measures to build infrastructure and diversify the economy, with special emphasis on development of the agricultural sector. Trade and deeper regional integration with the East African Community (EAC) neighbours can become an effective instrument for ensuring food security and facilitating longer-term market development. It is likely that immediate measures will focus on working with humanitarian actors on delivering emergency food to communities in need, although ongoing conflict could derail this effort. In any event, without the government's real commitment and proactive action to end the conflict and stabilise the economy, it is difficult to engage in realistic discussions about sustainable post-conflict stabilising and development trajectories.

Poverty, food insecurity, and perceptions in a high-inflation environment

The macroeconomic collapse, high inflation and increasing food prices have led to a sharp increase in monetary poverty in urban areas, from 49 per cent in 2015 to 70 per cent in 2016. The urban poverty gap increased from 22 to 36 per cent between 2015 and 2016, meaning that the average poor urban household went from consuming 22 per cent less than the international poverty line in 2015 to 36 per cent less in 2016. Inequality among the poor also worsened, and the poverty severity index doubled from 0.10 in 2015 to 0.20 in 2016. Urban households are more reliant on markets, and have less recourse to their own production of food when faced with shortages and rising prices. They are also more likely to earn their livelihood through wages and salaries or through their own business enterprise, compared to rural households. Hence, stagnant wage levels and a general slowdown of economic activity will have led urban households to experience a real decline in purchasing power and heightened food insecurity as food prices rise relative to income levels.

The large loss of wages' purchasing power has driven many households relying on salaried work or on their own business enterprise into poverty. Although households supported primarily by wage earners remain among the richest groups in South Sudan's population, the decline in purchasing power caused many of these households to fall into poverty. Poverty among wage-earning households more than doubled from 28 per cent in 2015 to 62 per cent in 2016. Similarly, poverty among households drawing on their own business enterprise for their livelihood saw a marked increase, from 43 to 61 per cent between 2015 and 2016 (Figure 11.3).

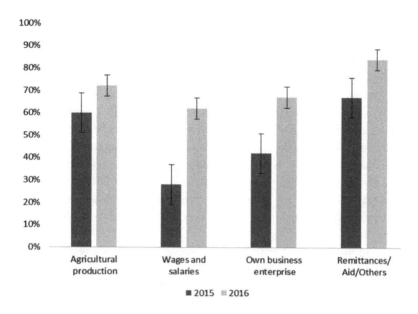

Figure 11.3 Poverty headcount by source of livelihood, urban

Source: Authors' own calculations based on HFS 2015 and 2016 urban data

Farming, hunting and fishing on own account became a more common type of employment, in particular among the richest households. In 2015, the non-poor were much more likely to be employed as salaried workers (29 and 28 per cent for the top and fourth quintile, respectively), or to help in or run a non-farm business (46 and 52 per cent for the top and fourth quintile, respectively). Economic decline has changed this, and many households in those quintiles have turned to agricultural production. Between 2015 and 2016 the number of households relying on agricultural production in the top two quintiles doubled from 18 to 36 per cent for the top quintile, and from 19 to 42 per cent for the fourth quintile. This shift in employment pattern is consistent with business income or wages and salaries becoming less reliable sources of income, forcing people to enter agricultural production to sustain themselves.

South Sudan's unprecedented level of food insecurity is the most alarming signal of the country's larger economic collapse, including high inflation. Despite great agricultural potential, the rural population has been continuously affected by food insecurity in the last few years. As of February 2015, 2.5 million people, or about one fifth of the population, were in either 'crisis' or 'emergency' levels of food insecurity, more than double the number recorded in December 2013 when the fighting broke out. A further 3.9 million people are in a state of food security stress, and likely to slip further down the rankings should livelihood support, security and markets fail. Predicted changes in climate, both in terms of more intense rainy seasons as well as hotter and drier dry seasons, could heighten future food insecurity nationally. Heightened tensions and renewed clashes across the country following the July 2016 conflict have further aggravated already overwhelming needs. Nearly 3.6 million people were estimated to be severely food insecure between October and December 2016, the highest levels experienced in South Sudan at harvest time. In both rural and urban areas, the food-insecure population has at least doubled compared to the same time last year.

Food production shortfalls are substantial. Preliminary results of the FAO/WFP Crop and Food Security Assessment Mission (CFSAM) state that overall food production for 2016 (the last harvests of which came in January 2017) is estimated at about 10 per cent below the already low and insufficient long-term average of 826,000 tons. With the exception of Warrap, all states faced deficits of cereals in 2017. The largest 2017 deficits were forecasted in the three most conflict-stricken states of Jonglei, Unity and Upper Nile states, with an aggregate shortfall in cereal of over 300,000 tons.

For the poorest urban households, hunger increased sharply between 2015 and 2016. The likelihood of experiencing hunger 'often' (more than 10 times per month) increased from 2 per cent to 13 per cent for the poorest quintile of households, while the incidence of experiencing hunger 'often' or 'sometimes' (3 to 10 times per month) increased from 26 to 44 per cent for the second poorest quintile. In 2016, households in the poorest quintile were more than ten times more likely than households in the top four quintiles to have experienced hunger 'often' in the past month (15 v. about 1 per cent respectively). While richer households may be able to respond to a rise in food prices by adjusting their diets towards more staple and less expensive foods, the poorest households' diet may already consist primarily of staple foods, and as prices increase they are unable to afford even basic sustenance. Households in the poorest quintile in 2016 were much more likely to report going entire days without food as their primary hunger-coping strategy than households in the other four quintiles (52 v. 18 per cent respectively). This figure increased sharply between 2015 and 2016 from about 15 to 52 per cent.

Many households perceive that economic conditions will continue to deteriorate. In 2015, about two thirds of South Sudanese residing in urban areas felt that economic conditions in their country were bad or very bad; in 2016 this figure increased to almost 90 per cent. The people of South Sudan are not optimistic about the future. In 2016, more than three in four stated that in three months' time the economic situation would be worse or much worse, with a notable 47 per cent of households believing the latter. This pessimism with regards to the future of economic conditions in South Sudan increased between 2015 and 2016, and the share of households believing that conditions in three months' time would be worse increased from 38 in 2015 to 65 per cent in 2016.

Economic and political volatility negatively affected households' perceptions of the performance of government and other public institutions. Households in urban areas do not think that the central government and other domestic public institutions are effective in improving their living standards. The central government, in particular, is consistently perceived to be among the least effective of institutions. Households' perception was already negative in 2015, with half of all households believing that the central government is ineffective or very ineffective in improving the daily life of its constituency. In 2016, almost 75 per cent of households held a negative view of the central government's effectiveness, up from 50 per cent in 2015.

While awaiting government's commitment to a political settlement and macroeconomic reforms, the population will likely be forced to engage in creative survival and coping strategies, often in the informal sector. There is a risk that South Sudanese citizens are already engaged, or will be forced to participate, in informal and often illegal activities. The majority of the population in rural areas will continue to rely on subsistence agriculture, facing dire conditions especially given the volatile security situation. There is little evidence that remittances from the diaspora have a significant role in coping with high inflation in South Sudan. Rather, it is expected that the number of refugees will increase, putting additional pressure on receiving neighbouring countries.

A key economic priority for the government is to restore peace and security, and implement urgent macroeconomic measures to reduce high inflation. Observed inflation over recent months has considerably deteriorated the purchasing power of households. If the macroeconomic imbalances are not managed in an effective and timely manner, poverty could rise even further. In the absence of reforms, South Sudan will spiral further towards being a failed state.

Taming the tides of high inflation: policy options for South Sudan

A key policy priority for South Sudan is to curb inflation. What can the country do in this regard? Countries have historically tamed extreme inflationary situations using Exchange Rate-Based Stabilisation (ERBS) plans and Money-Based Stabilisation (MBS) plans. Monetary or inflation targeting has been popularly adopted by many central banks around the world as a strategy for monetary policy, with the expectation that the adoption of such a monetary regime would reduce inflation and inflation volatility. Under a spiralling inflationary situation, an exchange rate anchor may be another option, in combination with a broader set of stabilisation programmes that combine fiscal prudence with a tighter monetary regime of varying forms.

Political will is critical to the pursuit of any stabilisation plan. Peace and security remain a crucial precondition for any macroeconomic stabilisation. Moreover, any reform plan requires credible commitment to take concrete steps to address the economic issues. Effective programmes have sequenced the initial stabilisation programmes with structural and institutional reforms. The latest economic and security developments in South Sudan seem to indicate that, despite the urgent need for fiscal consolidation and exchange rate adjustment, the government continues to focus on conflict-related policy choices that delay any meaningful reforms. Without clear political commitment, any stabilisation plan will be meaningless.

Which stabilisation path for South Sudan? Although there is a clear agreement that South Sudan needs to reform, vested interests and rent-seeking behaviour from politicians with access to foreign currency at the official rate are preventing or delaying the reform process. There is also a lack of agreement on the specifics of the reform to support lower inflation. For example, it is not clear whether the country would be most suited to adopting a currency board approach or a full dollarisation, or continue with a floating regime. Finally, reforming the monetary regime involves a major change in the economic environment, and a major shock for the economy. The uncertainty surrounding the impact may add to the reluctance to reform.

All stabilisation plans need a nominal anchor to lower inflation, and they differ among each other depending on which nominal anchor is used. Nominal anchors play a fundamental role in successful stabilisation plans. First, setting a predetermined path for the exchange rate or the amount of money helps pin down prices and controls inflation expectations. Second, a nominal anchor limits political pressures to pursue expansionary monetary policies that could fuel inflation. Third, nominal anchors send a strong signal to the market that the policy regime has shifted and the government is credibly committed to fighting inflation.

Experiences with stabilisation plans suggest that they vary in the speed at which inflation is reduced, the business cycle they create and their sustainability over time. Specifically, when choosing a stabilisation plan, policy-makers are confronted with trade-offs regarding 'speed versus sustainability' and likely 'recession now versus recession later'. On the one hand, ERBS is very successful at reducing inflation quickly, even in countries where inflation is exceptionally high. In addition, immediately after its implementation it creates an economic boom. However, over time the economic expansion is followed by a recession. The economic downturn, which might include a financial crisis, can trigger the collapse of the stabilisation plan and the re-emergence of inflation. As a result, ERBS is relatively short-lived, sometimes only being in place for four or five years before it is abandoned. On the other hand, MBS decreases inflation only gradually while initially creating a contraction of economic activity. However, once this downturn is passed, economic growth returns and inflation continues to slow down. As a result, MBSs are more sustainable over time.

A common feature of ERBS and MBS is that both require a strong institutional framework to be implemented successfully. Whether the central bank is targeting the exchange rate, the growth rate of money or the inflation rate, the monetary authority needs to send clear signals to the public that its main goal is to comply with the target. This requires, among other things, that the central bank be independent, has a legal mandate to control inflation, is free from political pressures and has adequate disclosure standards. If the public does not believe that the central bank is committed to fighting inflation, the stabilisation plan is unlikely to succeed. Another important precondition for the successful adoption of ERBS and MBS is fiscal discipline. A country that implements a stabilisation plan but fails to control fiscal deficits is more prone to pursuing an expansionary monetary policy. For countries under an ERBS, expansionary monetary policies would sooner or later lead to a fall in reserves that could force the central bank to abandon the peg. Likewise, in countries under an MSB, an increase in the money supply beyond the target would undermine the credibility of the central bank. In both cases, this will weaken the main pillar of the stabilisation plan, which is the nominal anchor supposed to endure in the long term.

The main challenge for developing economies, particularly for countries emerging from conflict, is to establish the credibility of the chosen monetary regime through a nominal anchor. The empirical evidence is not conclusive about whether this can be done more successfully through inflation targeting or a hard currency peg or a crawling peg with a narrow band. Monetary policy becomes more effective when central banks are successful in leading inflation expectations and can credibly alleviate the traditional short-term trade-off between inflation and unemployment. The success of any monetary regime is directly associated with forward-looking behaviour, which, in turn, highlights the relevance of credibility. This aspect is particularly relevant for developing and post-conflict economies (see Box 11.1). A strong and credible commitment to maintaining low inflation through any monetary regime credibility thus fosters an environment that stimulates output growth.

Under South Sudan's current managed floating exchange rate regime, a monetary policy regime without an exchange rate anchor would require an explicit and clearly understood alternative nominal anchor. Theoretically, the country could initially implement a plan based on targeting the growth rate

---

BOX 11.1: MONETARY POLICY AND EXCHANGE RATE
REGIMES IN POST-CONFLICT COUNTRIES

Does the choice of exchange rate regime matter for aid effectiveness in restoring macroeconomic stability?

Based on the experience of 38 countries emerging from war and conflict, Elbadawi and Soto (2013) suggest that post-conflict performances of the fixed and managed regimes were very similar, and were superior to those of floating regimes. While inflation was in single digits under the fixed and the managed floating regimes, it was more than 16 per cent under the floating regime.

More in-depth empirical analysis confirms that in post-conflict economies both the fixed and managed regimes have direct stabilising effects on inflation. Aid does not seem to have a direct effect on post-conflict inflation under the fixed and managed regimes, while it was found to have a stabilising impact under the floating regime.

Therefore, it seems that the free-floating exchange regime may not be appropriate for countries emerging from wars and conflict situations. The managed floating regime seems to have the edge on two critical areas of economic performance: (i) aid promotes post-conflict demand for money balances and (ii) the monetary reconstruction role of aid is likely to be more effective under this exchange rate regime.

Source: Elbadawi and Soto (2013)

of money and then, over time, transition to inflation targeting. Compared to inflation targeting, using the growth rate of money as the nominal anchor can be implemented by a central bank with relatively less independence. Targeting the growth rate of money imposes some limits to the discretionary actions of the central bank, because it requires this institution to follow a specific rule. The public can easily observe the compliance of this rule, so any deviation would result in an increase in inflation expectations and the collapse of the plan. This path was followed by some countries in Latin America, such as Mexico and Peru, which started targeting the rate of money growth and after a few years moved to inflation targeting.

If South Sudan decided to adopt MBS, it would need to ensure that the exchange rate regime is compatible with macroeconomic fundamentals and would have to close the gap between the official and the parallel rate. However, there are several difficulties with this.

The first challenge would be to deepen the foreign exchange market to make it more liquid for an adequate determination of the exchange rate. The challenge for BSS will be to supply the market without signalling an intention to defend a particular exchange rate level to maintain commitment to a floating exchange rate. By limiting its participation to frequent or periodic interventions (daily or weekly) using transparent and market allocation mechanisms such as auctions, BSS could promote the development of the foreign exchange market. While an auction mechanism is already in place, challenges to determine the exchange rate remain.

The second challenge would be to build an adequate system to monitor public and private sector exchange rate risk. Since July 2015, the commercial banks' balance sheets are showing negative net foreign assets. With the 500 per cent depreciation of the SSP in December 2015, the net foreign liabilities (negative net foreign assets) of the commercial banks has increased to more than four times their capital, representing a rather high exchange rate risk exposure. BSS would need to enforce prudential requirements to safeguard the integrity of the banking system.

The third challenge for the government would be to identify appropriate intervention measures in the foreign exchange market to ensure stability. International experience shows that central banks could intervene in the exchange market when they detect exchange rate misalignment or destabilising volatility. These interventions could be on a discretionary basis or regular, pre-announced and rule-based to support the information flow to the market and reduce noise. In the case of South Sudan, it seems that BSS will continue to supply the foreign exchange market with foreign currency because of its role as banker to a government that receives revenues from oil, borrows from abroad and receives grants in foreign currency. The government has issued new guidelines for the implementation of the regulation within a floating exchange rate regime instituting an auction mechanism that is in line with international standards. However, given the low level of foreign currency reserves, the government should be very selective in its interventions, to build its credibility and promote market confidence.

The fourth challenge would be to find an alternative nominal anchor for its monetary policy. Despite the weak relationship between monetary aggregates and inflation, money targeting can serve as an alternative nominal anchor for monetary policy. Many countries shifting from a fixed to a flexible exchange rate regime have favoured an inflation targeting framework over money targeting. Many of them adopted inflation targeting over long term horizons, taking the time required to fulfil the institutional requirements and macroeconomic conditions. It is too early for South Sudan to adopt inflation targeting, given the weakness of the financial sector and low government capacity. Monetary targeting combined with tight coordination with fiscal policy would be a more appropriate framework. Reducing the central bank financing of the fiscal deficit should be an intermediary target of the monetary policy, and more appropriate than direct price administration.

Considering the limited institutional capacity, the lack of independence of its central bank and significant credibility problems in recent history, it is highly unlikely that South Sudan has the capacity to follow an MBS. Credibility issues associated with high inflation, governance problems at the central bank and fiscal dominance, as well as a low level of financial development and significant weaknesses in statistical databases (both precluding reliable monitoring and forecasting of macroeconomic indicators) make MBS an unlikely choice at this stage.

Another option would be to follow an ERBS. Given the high inflation in South Sudan and the lack of credibility of monetary policy, inflation could be tamed through a hard peg of the SSP to the US$. The disadvantage of hard pegs is the loss of an autonomous monetary policy, but at the current state of institutional development in South Sudan such autonomy might not be beneficial. The key decision to make in this case is to identify the anchor currency. The International Monetary Fund (2010) suggests that this choice should be contingent on whether the anchor currency country meets the criteria for an optimal currency area: (i) higher trade, (ii) symmetric shocks, (iii) higher labour mobility, and (iv) higher fiscal transfers within the region.

If South Sudan decided to pursue the ERBS path, full dollarisation may be an option. Dollarisation may indeed be a stronger arrangement than a currency board, as it eliminates the risk of future currency crises and reduces the costs of international transactions. Credibility of dollarisation can be boosted by political backing from the country whose currency is adopted and with an agreement on seigniorage sharing. A currency board could, in principle, impose much stricter discipline on the monetary authority than dollarisation, but given the history of governance problems with BSS and the failure of an earlier fixed exchange rate regime, establishing the credibility of a currency board arrangement without externally imposed safeguards could be difficult. Further, more time might be needed to garner political support for adopting a central bank and fiscal responsibility legislation consistent with international best practice. Additionally, ERBSs are typically short-lived because they are prone to runs on the currency and to real effective exchange rate appreciations that are corrected by devaluations. By eliminating the domestic currency, dollarisation eliminates currency crises and increases exit costs. As a result, dollarisation can be sustained over a longer period of time.

Dollarisation might help improve some of the macroeconomic weaknesses present in South Sudan. It would eliminate the possibility of financing the fiscal deficits by printing money and, thus, could promote fiscal discipline. Moreover, halting discretionary monetary policy could help to lower inflation expectations. The elimination of exchange rate risk might increase capital inflows, which could improve the external balance. An additional and important consideration is that dollarisation is not irreversible, and the government could decide to introduce a domestic currency and move towards an MBS if it desired. In practice, hard pegs, including dollarisation, have proven to be easier to abandon than originally believed, by, for example, issuing quasi-monies or official money accepted for tax collection (de la Torre et al., 2003).

Upon stabilisation, South Sudan would need to implement structural and fiscal reforms to enhance efficiency and to prevent recurrence of high inflation. Once the inflation situation stabilises, South Sudan should prepare to implement a broader set of structural and fiscal reforms along with price and exchange rate liberalisation to prevent recurrence.[2] To unlock affordable credit lines from international capital markets, South Sudan needs to manage its public debt, improve export competitiveness and also offset the negative repercussions from the appreciation of the currency of the country from where it sources its imports against the US$. Attracting both debt and non-debt-creating capital flows, notably foreign direct investment, would require supportive measures such as the alignment of the country's investment laws and procedures to international best practices, investor-friendly policies, better enforcement of the rule of law and respect of property rights. The government should also strive to improve its relations with the international community to deal with negative perceptions that have tended to increase the country's risk, making borrowing from offshore sources very expensive, even for private sector entities.

Notes

1 This chapter is based on the first South Sudan Economic Update, prepared by Nora Dihel (senior economist) and Utz Pape (economist) with input from Facundo Abraham (consultant), Arti Grover (senior economist), Luca Parisotto (consultant) and Sergio Schmukler (lead economist). Zerihun Getachew Kelbore (research assistant) provided statistical assistance.

2 The importance of structural reforms cannot be overemphasised, even for countries that do not have their own currency. For example, the crisis in Greece was fuelled by the lack of supportive policies to keep the budget deficit under control, which undermined confidence in the country's ability to remain within the European Monetary Union.

References

de la Torre, Augusto, Eduardo L. Yeyati, and Sergio L. Schmukler (2003), 'Living and dying with hard pegs: The rise and fall of Argentina's currency board', *Economia – Journal of the Latin American and Caribbean Economic Association* 3 (Spring): 43–107.

Elbadawi, Ibrahim and Raimundo Soto (2013), 'Exchange rate regimes for post-conflict recovery', *Economic Research Forum Working Paper 748*, revised April 2013.

International Monetary Fund (2017), *Republic of South Sudan Staff Report for 2016 Article IV Consultation – Debt Sustainability Analysis*.

World Bank (2017), *South Sudan Economic Update, 2017: Taming the Tides of High Inflation*, Macroeconomics and Fiscal Management and Poverty and Equity Global Practices, October.

— (2017b), *Poverty, Livelihoods and Perception in a High Inflation Environment*, Poverty and Equity Global Practice.

— (2015), *Republic of South Sudan – Systematic Country Diagnostic*, October.

CHAPTER 12

South Sudan's Civil Service Challenges

Barbara Nunberg

Introduction

South Sudan's relatively newly established government has only a short history of sovereignty and negligible prior state-organised service delivery or policymaking experience. The task of building a state that can shepherd the country beyond conflict is made that much more difficult by overwhelming developmental challenges, including low food security, constrained infrastructure, low rates of adult literacy and high levels of ethno-linguistic diversity. Additionally, continuous violence – both with regard to the renewed conflict since 2013 and ongoing, localised disruptions – has resulted in massive human displacement and poses an incalculable burden on government institutional capacity.

To deal with these problems, the country's rebel and military leadership will need to transform itself into a coherent body of public policymakers at the helm of a public administration with an institutionalised civil service that can govern credibly and sustainably. This need for a qualified, well-performing government is recognised in the 2011 Transitional Constitution of the Republic of South Sudan (TCSS), which sets out the basic formal provisions for the establishment of the civil service. Getting there will require a strategy to fill experience gaps as well as programmes to build government capacity for the medium term while addressing immediate demands to reward and re-purpose long-serving combatants and more recent militia who comprise a large portion of current government employment. Recent events and deteriorating fiscal conditions create daunting challenges to this agenda. The implosion of Government of the Republic of South Sudan (GRSS) revenues with the halt of oil production in 2012 and the resultant debt overhang, even with resumption of production in 2013, have put strains on an already high public wage bill. Moreover, the large share of recurrent spending devoted to the expanding security sector has crowded out other spending – on social services, for example – which affect GRSS's ability to deliver the 'peace' or 'independence' dividend needed to redress citizen disaffection, already stoked by widespread reports of rent-seeking by government officials (World Bank, 2015). This is the backdrop to this chapter's discussion. The analysis that follows seeks to identify key constraints on civil service development and, drawing on international experience, to suggest possible directions for remediation.

Current civil service problems: the three bottlenecks

South Sudan faces three main civil service bottlenecks that must be dealt with over the immediate and longer term. First, government spending on public sector wages in the aggregate is comparatively high, while average wages to public employees are low. Second, wage expenditures are largely allocated to security-related employment, which appears to have crowded out spending on staff in other developmental sectors, particularly health and education. This employment composition needs to be rebalanced to deliver services appropriate to a peacetime society and economy. Third, the quality and capacity of those civilian employees in the civil service is low, requiring both a short-term policy for raising the functional standard to meet immediate post-war needs, and a long-term strategy for building skills for a professional civil service to address the country's ongoing developmental challenges. Below, each of these bottlenecks is discussed in turn.

Bottleneck 1: high wage bill but low wages

GRSS's wage bill spending has steadily increased over the last decade. From 2006 to 2013/14, the wage bill averaged almost 40 per cent of total government expenditure, with the value in South Sudanese Pounds (SSP) increasing by 207 per cent over this period, from approximately SSP3.75 million in 2006 to SSP11.5 million in 2014/15. The result is a wage bill that is too high, from two perspectives.

First, it represents a relatively large proportion of total government spending (reaching a high of 47 per cent in 2012/13). This is nearly twice the average for low-income countries (26 per cent) and outstrips even Afghanistan's wage bill spending. Only Liberia emerged from conflict with a larger wage bill. An aspirational comparator is Timor-Leste, which, in the decade since its independence war, managed its wage bill down to 14 per cent of total expenditures.[1] Second, the wage bill has become unsustainable in relation to revenues, particularly given high reliance on fluctuating oil revenues.

The worsening wage-bill-to-revenue situation in South Sudan is strongly tied to volatile revenues, as Figure 12.1 shows. This is largely about oil. Figure 12.1 shows the government's heavy reliance on oil revenue since 2005. Oil accounted for a staggering 97 per cent of revenues in 2011/12, and shutting off oil production brought that share down to 5 per cent by 2012/13. Even with production largely resuming in April 2013, the dramatic decline in international oil prices (by over 50 per cent) in recent years has taken its toll on revenues. Wage bill growth can no longer be sustained by government revenues, as it had been in earlier years.

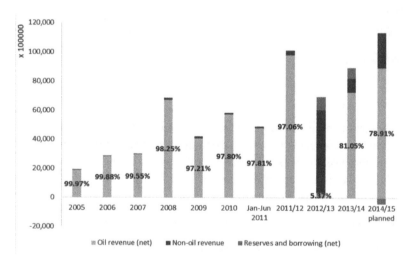

Figure 12.1 South Sudan oil revenue as a % of total revenue (SSP)

Source: GRSS Approved Budget Tables FY2014/15

Despite the high aggregate wage bill, real average wages have been declining steadily since 2007. Indeed, salaries were essentially halved between 2005 and 2012. Some relief came with the introduction and then temporary rise in housing allowances, but this did not disrupt the overall downward trend in compensation. Austerity measures further reduced salaries by 50 per cent in 2012.

South Sudan's low average wage to GDP per capita ratio also compares unfavourably to countries in the region, as shown in Table 12.1.

Country	Average salary per public service employee per annum (US$)	GDP per capita (current US$)	Wage/GDP per capita
South Sudan (GDP, 2011)	3082*	1858	1.66
South Sudan (GNI, 2011)		984	3.13
Kenya	4,065	770	5.28
Malawi	997	290	3.44
Mozambique	2,303	370	6.22
Rwanda	2,805	410	6.84
Tanzania	1,999	440	4.54
Uganda	1,820	420	4.33
Zambia	3,855	920	4.19

Table 12.1 Public service salary to GDP per country comparison (various years).[2]

*Grade 11 base salary (SSP533/month) at the 2008 exchange rate.
At an exchange rate of SSP3:US$1 the value drops to US$2,132.

The phenomenon of high aggregate wage bills with low average wages and surplus staffing is a familiar one in the region and in the low-income world more generally (see Box 12.1) But as we see below, the problem in South Sudan is also about the *composition* of the staffing, particularly as the country emerges from conflict.

BOX 12.1: LOW-INCOME COUNTRY PUBLIC PAY AND EMPLOYMENT SYNDROME

(i.)   Low human resource endowment

(ii.)   State is employer of first resort

(iii.)   Employment surplus to functional requirements

(iv.)   Control functions in disarray (poor information on staff numbers/profiles, ghosts)

(v.)   High aggregate wage bill, low average wage

(vi.)   Personnel spending crowds out complementary inputs

(vii.)   Compressed and low pay

(viii.) Poor performance (absenteeism, rent-seeking)

(ix.)   Opaque pay/allowance systems

(x.)   Competing markets drain talent

Bottleneck 2: staffing tilt towards security employment

The ballooning wage bill thus comes not from average remuneration increases, but from employment growth. There has been a surge in government staffing since 2005. Although this is to be expected given the establishment of a new government post-2005, later expanded post-independence in 2011, the staffing increase has largely been in the security sector as a result of the recruitment of militia groups into the armed and organised forces. Spending on staffing in the armed forces has consistently exceeded 50 per cent of total government staffing since 2005, as shown in Figure 12.2.

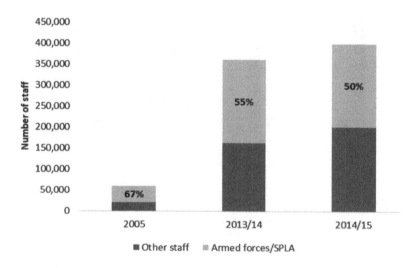

Figure 12.2 South Sudan armed forces as a % of total government staffing

Source: GRSS Approved Budget Tables FY2014/15

Civilian salary spending represents a relatively small portion (at around 38 per cent) of total personnel spending, with spending on military and organised forces accounting for the rest. General government staffing allocations across military and civilian sectors tilts overwhelmingly towards security-related positions. As Figure 12.3 shows, in South Sudan, 62 per cent of salary spending is allocated to the armed and organised forces (which includes military, police, prisons and wildlife), with only 6 per cent of staff spending allocated to education, and 3 per cent to health. When compared to other conflict and post-conflict countries, it is apparent that security-related spending in South Sudan exceeds even that in Afghanistan,[3] and is clearly crowding out staffing expenditure for other sectors, particularly the delivery of health and education. Understaffing service delivery exacts a high price from post-conflict recovery, with potentially profound developmental and political implications for years to come.

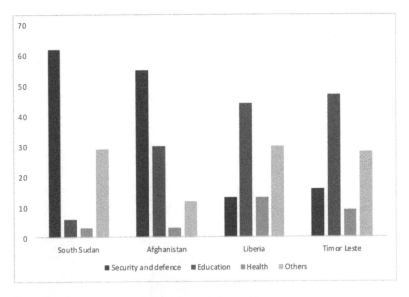

Figure 12.3 Cross-country comparison of government salary spending

Note: Figures for South Sudan for 2014/15, Afghanistan for 2013, Liberia for 2013 and Timor-Leste for 2013
Source: GRSS Approved Budget Tables FY2014/15; Srivastava (2014)

This underscores the striking finding that while there are 450 police per 100,000 people in South Sudan, there are only 1.5 doctors and 2 nurses (GRSS Ministry of Health 2015), which compares unfavourably with other post-conflict and low-income contexts (Table 12.2).

Country	Doctors	Nurses	Police
South Sudan	1.5	2	>450
Liberia	7.5	30	108
Ghana	7.1	90	94
Kenya	9.5	80	81

Table 12.2 Staffing for different key service delivery areas per 100,000 population[4]

Bottleneck 3: low-capability civil service

While the civilian portion of South Sudan's civil service may not be large on a comparative basis, previous analysis suggests that overall capacity is quite low (World Bank, 2010; World Bank, 2015). With a national literacy rate of 27 per cent, this is obviously a long-term problem that will need to be addressed with a range of measures, including fundamental human resource development at the societal level. Building civil service capacity over the longer term involves introducing sound but culturally and developmentally feasible practices for merit-based staff recruitment, pay and promotion, discipline and performance assessment. It is not for the faint of heart and requires serious, sustained, high-level political commitment and resources. It depends on raising overall qualifications of civil service staff through medium- and long-term education policies and through shorter-term training that works (evidence shows that training programmes do not always work). For very low capacity countries such as South Sudan, employing non-nationals in the private sector, in non-governmental organisations and on long-term international aid projects may be a plausible option.

There are, however, near-term capacity constraints that will make it difficult to rein in the wage bill and rebalance government spending towards service delivery in the social sectors, primarily in health and education. The first capacity constraint concerns weak human resource management. GRSS lacks the basic human resource management skills and systems to be able to effect the wage bill containment policies needed in the current environment. Absent these systems, basic information, at both central and state levels, about the number and identity of staff is missing. Weak linkages between the Human Resources Management Information System (HRMIS) and the South Sudan Electronic Payroll System (SSEPS) enables the persistence of 'ghost' workers in the system, for example. The lack of integration of armed and organised forces into the e-payroll system also prevents the achievement of reasonable control over spending on these key groups. Since the wage bill is largely a problem of surplus employment rather than high salaries, getting a clear picture of who these staff are and how they might be removed from the payroll or redeployed to other functions is key to reducing wage expenditures.

Weak capacity also manifests itself in low staff qualifications, which undermines service delivery effectiveness. Again, long-term education policies that improve the capacity of national candidates are needed. There are also some short-term practices that could improve the competency of current civil servants and new recruits. In particular, specifying and tightening job-specific qualifications and establishing checks to ensure staff recruitment is done according to clear merit-based criteria (even if these are applied selectively within existing patronage networks) could help boost the commitment and performance of front-line civil service staff.

What is to be done? Some standard approaches to easing the wage bill bottleneck

There are some common techniques used around the world to reduce staff numbers and contain the wage bill. One basic step is to collect clean data on the numbers and location of actual civil service employees through a Civil Service Census and then feed those data into a robust HRMIS linked to an electronic payroll system. Some elements of this system seem already to be in place in South Sudan, but they appear to be embryonic and incomplete. For example, they do not cover large parts of the public sector payrolls (including security-related personnel) and contain many unverified files, which would need to be validated before input into the system. A number of countries, even low-income countries, have introduced smart technology, such as electronic ID cards or biometric identification, for validated civil servants to maintain ongoing control over government spending.

Other approaches to tightening wage bill management include monetisation of salaries by eliminating non-wage benefits and allowances, which can be exceedingly difficult to calculate and to administer. Beyond this, wage bill containment is frequently achieved through programmes designed to selectively separate staff. One such programme might involve a straightforward policy to enable retirement of over-age staff (an estimated 10 per cent of the civil service in South Sudan is over the set retirement age of 65). This would require developing a credible, affordable pension plan to incentivise departures.

In addition, voluntary departure schemes, perhaps designating particular groups, such as senior age cohorts, have been designed elsewhere with well-targeted severance conditions that seek to avert the adverse selection problems that have been known to accompany voluntary separation arrangements. Finally, involuntary retrenchment schemes, also designed with appropriate severance compensation, can be introduced, particularly in conjunction with 'functional reviews' of government organisations to determine which types of employees should be made redundant. It has sometimes proved useful to pair such programmes with post-employment training as well as credit assistance, followed up with tracer studies to ensure optimal absorption into alternative labour markets.

Standard disarmament and reintegration programmes

Given the need to reduce the weight of security sector employment in South Sudan's public sector, the general civil service approaches just discussed would need to be undertaken in conjunction with broader military demobilisation and reintegration initiatives. A substantial literature on Demobilisation, Disarmament and Reintegration (DDR) suggests that the tendency to reintegrate warring factions into security sector positions within government may have the (admittedly important) short-term effect of buying peace but, in the longer-term, risks bloating the public service with inappropriately skilled personnel and at considerable cost. The remedies for transitioning soldiers into civilian roles depend on the absorptive capacity of private formal and/or informal labour markets.[5] There are many difficult challenges. Vocational (re-)training programmes may or may not be able to match the supply of (generally low) skills with market demand. Without jobs, the potential conversion of armed troops into criminal gangs is a danger. The design of departure incentive packages is complex politically and technically. Selection for demobilisation (who, how many) has important implications for future political stability. Assigning a value to a separation package involves a difficult calculus about the reservation price for peaceful exit from the government payroll, but also the perception of an appropriate pay-off by the larger citizen public.

The manner in which these decisions are made largely depends on the nature and stage of the conflict from which the country is emerging, the status of combatants within society, and the resources available for demobilisation compensation. Figure 12.4 depicts a framework developed by the World Bank for analysing the policy options for demobilisation. According to this conceptualisation, in countries where conflict has definitively terminated, combatants are held in high esteem (such as after a heroic struggle for independence) and there is an abundance of domestic revenues, cash transfers often accompany demobilisation. Where combatants are less well regarded and resources are constrained, a more modest, one-off 'golden handshake' is afforded to soldiers to remove them from public service (Srivastava, 2014).

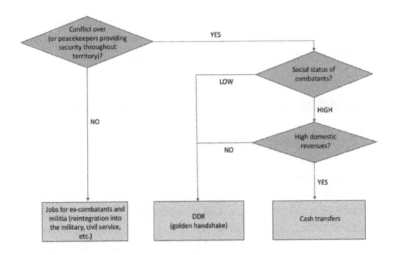

Figure 12.4 Context-contingent deals with ex-combatants

Source: Srivastava (2014)

Several countries' experience with DDR may be instructive for South Sudanese policy makers as they contemplate their own options for strategic demobilisation. In particular, Sierra Leone, Liberia and Timor-Leste have confronted DDR challenges that are comparable to those in South Sudan, as Boxes 12.2, 12.3 and 12.4 recount.

In addition to these cases, it's worth noting a few DDR approaches taken in other regions. In Bosnia and Herzegovina, a project managed by the International Organisation for Migration provided grants and individual counselling on entrepreneurship. Similarly, Serbia provided assistance to around 5,000 discharged defence personnel who were also given access to interest-free micro-loans for small business creation (International Organisation for Migration, 2012). Finally, Afghanistan pursued policy options that included public works. It employed former soldiers for 12 months to remove land mines and provide services to their own communities (IRIN, 2004).

The basic elements of these experiences are presented in Table 12.3. A few broad principles can be distilled here. First, the more costly options, including jobs on the payroll or generous cash transfers, are likely viable only in the presence of high levels of domestic revenues or significant international partner largesse. Second, the more effective employment transitions have so far focused mainly on informal economy opportunities and small enterprise generation, sometimes through access to micro-credit

BOX 12.2: SIERRA LEONE

Like South Sudan, Sierra Leone's public sector had taken on military personnel in large numbers to ensure peace as it emerged from conflict in the early 2000s. It was therefore dealing with bloated employment and a high wage bill as well as a low-paid, corrupt civil service that was failing to deliver needed social sector services. With support from donors (especially the UK and the US), a major organisational reform of the military was undertaken in 2004, offering a severance package of pension benefits to those who had served more than ten years and a one-off financial payment for those whose service had been shorter. The security sector turned its focus to internal policing rather than external threats, and the overall military establishment was reduced modestly (from 15,500 to 10,500 staff). Human resource management controls for the public service were tightened, to link personnel information systems and the payroll to further reduce the wage bill, and spending shifted dramatically towards health, education and police staffing. The programme succeeded in laying the foundation for merit-based practice in the civil service and the military, but the lack of post-service training, the limited capacity of the private sector to absorb demobilised military actors, and public controversy over rewarding perpetrators of violence through DDR benefits constrained the scale of the reduction in force.

Source: Albrecht and Jackson (2010); Sesay and Suma (2009)

BOX 12.3: LIBERIA

Liberia also emerged from its civil war with a bloated public service that included ex-combatants. Spending on health and education was low. The private sector's capacity to absorb redundant military labour was limited, with unemployment rates hovering around 85% during much of the 2000s. With significant US assistance, a DDR programme disarmed around 90,000 combatants and reduced the official military sector from 15,000 to 2,000, providing compensation in the range of US$4,000 to demobilised soldiers through a carefully designed separation programme. A significant number of military remained on the payroll, causing years of unaffordable wage bills that prompted the initiation of a more comprehensive civil service reform effort to constrain personnel expenditures and downsize staff. The initiatives were only moderately successful due to the political resistance mounted to stall reforms. But government did succeed in shifting expenditures away from defence towards health and education, whose share of spending reached close to 30 per cent by the end of the 2000s.

Source: Malan (2008); SSR Resource Centre (2005)

BOX 12.4: TIMOR-LESTE

Timor-Leste's post-conflict experience bears a marked similarity to that of South Sudan. In its post-independence period, the country faced the challenge of demobilising security personnel, managing newly discovered oil resources, and setting up national public service institutions in a context of linguistic and ethnic diversity and low human resource capacity. Government introduced a veterans' policy to demobilise independence fighters. They provided combatants with five months of transition pay and financed small livelihood generation projects, along with access to government pensions. Nonetheless, the failure of the economy to absorb many ex-combatants and the exclusion of some factions in the newly structured military establishment resulted in violent protests that nearly brought down the government in 2006. Cash transfers to former soldiers and groups of internally displaced persons on the streets of the capital, along with the reintegration of some disgruntled military officers into official positions in government, helped diffuse tensions. The government sought to protect oil revenues in a petroleum fund modelled on the Norwegian fund, but it also maintained the need for rebalancing expenditures towards social service delivery as a constant priority. As time passed, the wage bill came under pressure from patronage hiring into the civil service, but government managed to contain personnel spending, which constituted just 14 per cent of total expenditures by 2013.

Source: International Crisis Group (2013); World Bank (2008); World Bank (2014)

---

facilities. Importantly, none of the examples undertook full-scale DDR until conflicts were terminated. The reform and restructuring of the military sector went hand-in-hand with reform of the broader public service. In most cases, however, pressure to incorporate former military personnel into the public sector led to wage bill problems that continue to be a concern to governments, long after conflict has abated.

	Liberia	Sierra Leone	Timor-Leste
Reform approach	Rebuilt military from ground up and reduced force size	Rebuilt military from ground up and reduced force size	Veterans policy and large cash transfers from Petroleum Fund
Funding	External support from US	External support from UK	Petroleum Fund
Incentives	Compensation according to seniority	Pensions and compensation according to seniority	Large cash transfers, transition pay, retirement
Private sector absorptive capacity	Low	Low; limited ability to downsize and successfully reintegrate	Medium; small livelihood/ income generation projects used

Table 12.3 Summary of security sector reform elements in several post-conflict countries

From the outside: some ideas and priorities for South Sudan

In the transition to peace, and in building a public sector that can deliver on the developmental objectives South Sudan hopes to achieve in future, restructuring and reform (including rightsizing) will need to take place both in the civilian elements of the civil service and in the security-related sectors. These will need to be closely coordinated, but carried out separately. The following are an outsider's ideas on considerations policymakers may wish to take on board as they move forward with this restructuring effort.

- First, some combination of voluntary and involuntary separation programmes (both for civilian and military personnel) will likely be required. The design of programmes may differ for different types and levels of military personnel. So, for example, it may be appropriate to afford positions in the military establishment to some individuals in the higher ranks of combatant leadership, while mere 'golden handshakes' may be suited to foot soldiers.
- It may be appropriate to integrate some ex-combatants into the public sector workforce, but they should not be incorporated into the civil service proper without submission to entrance criteria that are function-related and broadly merit-based.
- Large-scale reductions in force size (voluntary and/or involuntary) and redeployment for the military will likely need to be supported with external financing, in light of current fiscal constraints. Financeable elements might include lump-sum separation payments, short-term vocational training and/or counselling, and micro-credit facilities.
- Consider redeploying security personnel to dedicated public works projects that would address short-term recovery needs such as infra-structure rehabilitation or community-based services. Such programmes could not only address immediate employment generation concerns but also advance vital short-term reconstruction and rehabilitation needs. Sunset clauses would need to be introduced with clear transition to private employment to prevent welfare dependency. To the extent that partnerships in these initiatives could be forged between the public sector and both private and non-profit entities, such projects might provide useful laboratories for future economic cooperation.
- Steps to reduce the wage bill in general will be needed in the short-term. A range of actions could be put in motion:

- Utilise an analytic tool, a variant of the Civil Service Financial Model widely employed by the World Bank to develop a strategic plan for re-dimensioning the public sector (see Figure 12.5).
- This might be coupled with a 'strategic' functional review to determine the proper functions and associated staffing for the civil service going forward.
- It will also be a near-term priority to strengthen the human resource management and e-payroll systems (HRMIS and SSEPS) to track and control public sector employment. Most likely, a civil service census will be needed to feed accurate information into these systems.

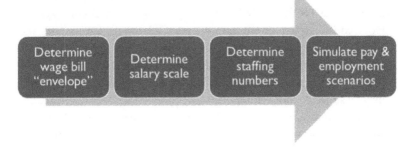

Figure 12.5 World Bank Civil Service Financial Model basic steps

Source: World Bank (2006)

- In addition to reducing and redeploying security sector employment, GRSS will need to consider how to shift staffing resources towards service delivery, particularly health and education.

  - Alternatives to direct state provision are certainly options that should be reviewed, if non-governmental or external partners are available in the immediate term, with strategies for transitioning to national provision, where appropriate.
  - To the degree that civil service staffing is to be reallocated towards front-line delivery, conditions of service that provide special premiums for these jobs, particularly in remote areas, might be put in place.

- Designing short-term programmes, likely with external partner support, to provide targeted incentives to attract non-resident South Sudanese to these critical service areas, through the UN Development Programme's

Transfer of Knowledge Through Expatriate Nationals Programme (TOKTEN) and other mechanisms to repatriate the diaspora, may be of interest.

- Finally, an organised programme to draw on the expertise and experience of other countries that have successfully engaged in post-conflict institutional reforms, such as Rwanda or some of the cases referenced in this note, could provide practical guidance to South Sudan as it navigates the difficult challenges that lie ahead.

Notes

1 Timor-Leste's wage bill may appear artificially low; however, temporary staff and other 'hidden' employment may be concealed in other budget line items that do not appear as personnel expenditures. See International Monetary Fund (2013) and Srivastava (2014).
2 Estimates by Theodore Valentine, World Bank Consultant, 2013; GRSS (2011) Budget Document; World Bank Databank.
3 The degree to which health services are supplemented by externally financed non-governmental partners in these countries is to be determined. Health workers in Liberia and Sierra Leone are financed in part by external NGOs and donors.
4 Data from UNODC (police), WHO (doctors), and WDI/WB (nurses, including midwives).
5 Studies of civil service retrenchment show better absorption into informal, small-scale activities. See Alderman et al. (1994).

References

Albrecht, Peter and Paul Jackson (eds) (2010), *Security Sector Reform In Sierra Leone 1997–2007: Views From The Front Line* (Geneva: Geneva Centre for the Democratic Control of Armed Forces (DCAF)).
Alderman, Harold, Sudharshan Canagarajah and Stephen D. Younger (1994), 'Consequences of permanent lay-off from the civil service: Results from a survey of retrenched workers in Ghana', in David L. Lindauer and Barbara Nunberg (eds), *Rehabilitating Government: Pay and Employment Reform in Africa* (Washington, DC: World Bank).
GRSS (2011), Budget Document, Juba.
— (2014), Approved Budget Tables, Ministry of Finance and Economic Planning, Juba.
— (2015), Health Sector Development Plan 2012–2016, Ministry of Health, Juba.
International Crisis Group (2013), *Timor-Leste: Stability at What Cost? Report No. 246 / Asia*.
International Monetary Fund (2013), *Democratic Republic of Timor-Leste, IMF Country Report No. 13/338*.
International Organisation for Migration (2012), 'Compendium of projects in Disarmament, Demobilisation, and Reintegration (DDR) and Security Sector Reform (SSR)'.
IRIN (2004), 'Afghanistan: Mine action for peace helps reintegrate ex-combatants', http://www.irinnews.org/news/2004/07/21/mine-action-peace-helps-reintegrate-ex-combatants.

Krauss, Clifford (2015), 'Oil prices fall to lowest since 2009', *New York Times*, 13 January 2015, https://www.nytimes.com/2015/01/13/business/energy-environment/oil-prices-fall-to-their-lowest-since-2009-recession.html.

Malan, Mark (2008), *Security Sector Reform in Liberia: Mixed Results from Humble Beginnings* (Carlisle, PA: Strategic Studies Institute, U.S. Army War College).

Ministry of Finance and Economic Planning (2014), Approved Budget Tables (Juba: Government of South Sudan).

Sesay, Mohamed G. and Mohamed Suma (2009), *Transitional Justice and DDR: The Case of Sierra Leone*, International Center for Transitional Justice, Research Unit.

Srivastava, Vivek (2014), *Rebuilding Public Services in Post-Conflict Countries: Key Issues and Lessons of Experience* (Washington, DC: World Bank).

SSR Resource Centre (2015), *SSR Country Snapshot: Liberia*, Centre for Security Governance, http://secgovcentre.org/2014/06/ssr-country-snapshot-liberia/.

Transitional Constitution of the Republic of South Sudan of 2011.

World Bank (2006), *Modeling Pay and Employment: World Bank PREM Notes 35661* (Washington, DC: World Bank).

— (2008), *Defining heroes: Key Lessons from the Creation of Veterans Policy in Timor-Leste: World Bank Report No. 45458-TP* (Washington, DC: World Bank).

— (2010), *Sudan: Strengthening Good Governance for Development Outcomes in Southern Sudan: World Bank Report No. 48997-SD* (Washington, DC: World Bank).

— (2014), *Creation of a Reformed Pension System for Civil Servants in Timor-Leste* (Washington, DC: World Bank).

— (2015), *SS Governance Review for South Sudan: Improving Human Resource Management for Strengthened Service Delivery* (Washington, DC: World Bank).

World Bank Databank.

CHAPTER 13

South Sudan's Renewable Energy Potential

A Building-Block for Peace[1]

David Mozersky and Daniel M. Kammen

Introduction

Things have not gone according to plan for South Sudan. After gaining independence in 2011 amid great hope and international celebration, South Sudan has seen stagnating economic and political progress exacerbated by civil war erupting in late 2013. International donor governments continue to support the billion-dollar-per-year humanitarian operations in the country, but humanitarian funding is under stress across the globe and the South Sudan crisis shows no signs of abating. Most donors do not want to support the current government directly because they fear that funds could be diverted to military efforts, which are likely to target civilians, and donors also recognise that short-term humanitarian programming alone will not end the crisis.

What can be done to generate new opportunities and momentum for a more peaceful future, when the outlook is so bleak? This chapter argues that a system-wide donor-driven transition to renewable energy, specifically solar power, to support humanitarian programming, is a viable way forward both now and over the longer term. Although such a transition alone will not end the conflict, it offers donors a more strategic alternative to the current practice. In the near term, a pivot to renewable energy will offer significant cost savings in a nation where electricity generation is one of the highest recurrent costs in humanitarian budgets. Over the longer term, this approach will create long-lasting, reliable energy infrastructure and could serve as a building-block for peace and development in the least electrified country in the world. At a minimum, a shift to greater domestic reliance on renewable energy will help decouple economic growth from the geopolitics of oil and gas at a time when the growing impacts of climate change highlight South Sudan's vulnerabilities (Stalon and Choudhary, 2017).

Even before the outbreak of conflict in 2013, South Sudan had the lowest electricity consumption per capita in the world and ranked near the bottom in many global development indicators (IEA, 2016).[2] The modest progress achieved during the peaceful years between 2005 and 2013 has largely been undone by the conflict since then, and much of the infrastructure, energy and otherwise, has been destroyed or looted. The electricity generation that does exist across the country is intermittent and comes almost entirely from imported diesel for generators. The lack of electrification affects all sectors of society, with government offices, hospitals and even the national parliament facing regular blackouts (Alstone et al., 2015). As the economy has collapsed and security worsened, diesel supply lines have become less reliable and more expensive. Rampant inflation has exacerbated the problem, the national consumer price index increasing more than 2100 per cent between December 2015 and July 2017, making fuel and other staple products much more expensive (World Bank, 2016).

Renewable energy offers tangible and immediate benefits that bear out over the long term. The cost of solar power in particular has dropped dramatically in recent years, and solar now is both a cheaper and a more consistent power source than alternatives in South Sudan. Solar panels can be easily scaled and can last for more than 20 years. Donor support for a solar push could help create new jobs and enhance the sustainability of local capacity. Renewable energy alone cannot end the conflict, of course, but it does offer a way to better leverage international aid flows for both short- and long-term gains.

Energy scholarship is beginning to recognise the limitations of traditional energy planning modelling, which assumes long timelines and general stability, in fragile and conflict-affected states. Adjusting long-term assumptions to reflect the unique challenges in fragile states can lead to a different set of viable conclusions, including greater emphasis on smaller-scale and renewable energy systems (Bazilian and Chattopadhyay, 2015).

Three immediate opportunities are anchored in humanitarian programming where solar investment by donors can yield benefits. One is onsite energy generation in individual NGO compounds. The second is in neutral national health institutions such as hospitals and clinics. The third involves the protection of civilians (POC) sites for internally displaced persons (IDPs) outside the destroyed regional capitals of Bentiu and Malakal; in these locations, solar systems would also create energy assets that could transition to support reconstruction and the return of IDPs to the cities in years to come.

A shift to renewable energy could also launch a far less contentious resource base than the current fossil fuel status quo. The negative impacts of a reliance on diesel have been discussed in a number of publications (for example, Alstone et al., 2015). A solar pivot could enable a poor nation to move towards sustainability. The same factors that make renewable energy a win-win approach in South Sudan also make sense for humanitarian actors and donors in other comparable conflict and crisis settings.

Energy development in South Sudan

The Southern Sudanese government received close to US$13 billion in revenue between 2005 and 2011, with oil accounting for more than 98 per cent of the total intake (GRSS, 2011). Over the same period, the international community spent approximately US$5 billion in development aid in Southern Sudan and invested another US$5.76 billion in the UN Mission in Sudan (UNMIS), which covered both Southern Sudan and parts of Sudan (Global Humanitarian Assistance, 2011).

Despite the money flowing into Southern Sudan, little energy-related infrastructure was built. Government electrification plans centred around the construction of several Chinese-built mega-dams along the White Nile, projects that never broke ground, as part of a long-term plan to build out a national grid. In the meantime, international donors, UN agencies, NGOs, the regional government and private sector actors spent hundreds of millions of dollars on generators and diesel fuel to power both aid and development efforts. Diesel was widely available from Sudan, which ran its own domestic oil refinery. The Juba government was able to pay for this fuel using Sudanese pounds received for its oil sales from the central government in Khartoum. In Juba and other southern cities, networks of diesel generators were installed or expanded to power new city grids. A Norwegian-supported hydroelectric project at the Fula rapids, near the border with Uganda, was developed to provide power to Juba, but progress was slow.

Several other projects were launched to build domestic oil refineries, but these too moved slowly and had ground to a halt by 2014 because of the economic crisis and the new civil war. None of these projects was ever completed. In March 2017, the government announced its latest plan to build a new oil refinery in South Sudan, intended to be operational by mid-2017, but by the time of writing no updates on the project had been made public (Sudan Tribune, 2017a).

When South Sudan became independent in 2011, not all terms of separation with Sudan had been agreed. The most notable outstanding issue was oil, a major economic lifeline for both Juba and Khartoum. Oil was a main economic driver of Sudan's economy and the largest source of government revenue and foreign currency, but approximately 70 per cent of the oil produced came from oil wells inside South Sudan. As a newly independent country, South Sudan no longer had to submit to the fifty-fifty revenue-sharing arrangement with Khartoum that had existed during the 2005–2013 interim period, but Juba still relied on the oil pipeline that ran through Sudan to get South Sudan's oil to market via the Red Sea. Sudan hoped to charge high transit fees for the use of the pipeline to make up for its lost oil revenue; South Sudan offered a much lower transit fee, hoping to leverage a broader transitional payment to facilitate agreements on other outstanding issues. As the negotiations continued, the oil continued to flow with no formal agreement in place.

In January 2012, after not receiving payment for the first five months after South Sudan's independence, and as the economic impact of reduced oil revenue began to bite, the Sudan government took matters into its own hands and began unilaterally offloading South Sudanese oil directly from the pipeline at Port Sudan as payment in kind, and reselling it internationally. The South Sudanese government responded by shutting down its entire oil production, rather than have its oil offloaded by Khartoum. The popular decision initially cheered in the streets of South Sudan, which viewed it as a symbol of the young nation's independence from its old oppressor. Harsh reality quickly set in, however, as the economy ground to a halt. South Sudanese officials scrambled around the region trying to find support for building an alternate pipeline to the sea, through Kenya or Ethiopia and Djibouti, but no short-term solution could be found. Meanwhile, government's foreign currency reserves began to dry up and the economic situation worsened.

Electrification suffered immediately. The diesel generators powering Juba broke down in 2012 and funding to maintain an adequate flow of diesel or to repair the generators ran short. Juba needed to use its foreign currency reserves to purchase fuel imports, and dollars were suddenly scarce. South Sudan's economy began slowly but steadily to collapse. Plans to build domestic oil refineries stalled indefinitely. The negotiations over pipeline access with Sudan continued, but bargaining power had now shifted significantly in Khartoum's favour. An agreement was eventually reached and pipeline access and South Sudanese oil production resumed in the first half of 2013. In mid-December 2013, violence broke out in Juba after a political disagreement between President Salva Kiir and former vice-president Riek Machar. Initially concentrated in Greater Upper Nile, where the country's oilfields are located, the conflict eventually spread across much of the country.

Impact of renewed conflict and economic collapse

Before war broke out in 2013, South Sudan had just 22 megawatts of operational installed electricity generation capacity, coming exclusively from diesel and heavy-fuel generators, most of them located in a handful of cities (Altai Consulting, 2014). For comparative purposes, 22 megawatts is equivalent to the electricity required to power approximately 3,600 homes in the United States. By 2017, operational generation capacity was almost certainly considerably lower, given the extent to which power generation had been disrupted or destroyed in fighting since 2013.

The impact of the precipitous drop in South Sudanese oil production caused by the closure of the Unity State oilfields was exacerbated by the dramatic drop in global oil prices. The Dar blend from South Sudan's still-operating Upper Nile fields trades at an additional discount on the international market because of its lower quality. Furthermore, the Juba government must pay other costs (such as profit-sharing and processing fees) to the oil companies, and the pipeline transit fees to Khartoum. Oil production remains the government's primary source of revenue but has brought in very little money since 2014. Inflation and divergence between the official and black market exchange rates have both spiralled, making goods, including diesel, far more expensive. The dramatic increase in the price of petrol and diesel following the devaluation of currency led to a noticeable reduction in demand, with fewer people being able to afford it (Hoth Mai et al., 2016). One effect of this trend is that internationally funded programming now offers the best entry point for renewable energy in South Sudan.

Despite the economic crisis, the government has imported fuel and heavily subsidised (by as much as 80 per cent) the domestic sale of petrol and diesel, which should be sold to the public through petrol stations for SSP22 per litre. Nonetheless, the black market for both petrol and diesel has remained active, and the price for a litre of fuel not only varies widely across the country but is also well above the official price. The black market for fuel is visible on street corners in Juba, where lines of cars waiting at petrol stations stretch down streets and around blocks. Traders have made a fortune buying up government-subsidised petrol and then reselling it on the black market for up to five times the price they paid for it (Akec, 2016). The South Sudanese government may have spent as much as 20 per cent of its entire 2017 budget on fuel subsidies, but the benefits are captured by a group of traders rather than distributed among the population at large (Akec, 2016). The deepening fuel crisis, which saw a litre of diesel fetching as much as SSP400 in Juba in late July 2017, eventually prompted government promises to end the fuel subsidies and crack down on black market trade (Radio Tamazuj, 2018). Reports in early December 2017 indicated that the government had quietly ended its fuel subsidies because it did not have the resources to back them (Sudan Tribune, 2017b), and in early 2018 the government reopened the market for private sector fuel imports.

The opportunity for renewable energy

As a global resource, renewable energy has come of age, with the sector seeing its largest annual increase in capacity in 2015. Wind power and solar photovoltaics (PV), the most popular form of solar power, seen in most solar panels today, accounted for more than three-quarters of new energy installations globally in 2015, followed by hydropower. The world now adds more renewable power capacity annually than it adds (net) capacity from all fossil fuels combined. By the end of 2015, installed renewable capacity was enough to supply almost a quarter of global electricity (REN21, 2016).

Although advances in all areas of renewable energy supply are relevant, the evolution of the solar energy sector, and in particular of solar PV, has potentially the most immediate importance for South Sudan. Solar PV is notable for its ease of installation and operation at all scales, from solar lanterns to rooftop systems for residential houses and buildings, the fast-growing area of mini-grids, and large utility-scale systems. A particularly important aspect of the evolution of solar PV energy for South Sudan is its scalability. At the bottom end of the scale, the off-grid, pay-as-you-go market has exploded in East Africa. A range of companies now offer systems in the 0–150 watt peak range that are attractively priced, often require no down payment, and can run appliances such as radios, televisions and fridge-freezers. Solar power also plays a key role in mini-grids, which can be 1 megawatt or more in size and can be powered either by solar-plus-storage systems (that is, solar panels plus batteries, which store energy for use when the sun is not shining), or by solar-hybrid systems in which solar energy is combined with diesel, wind, hydro or other technologies to provide energy for communities or businesses, or a combination of the two. This rapidly expanding sector brings many of the benefits of large utility-scale grids without the larger infrastructure costs (and vulnerabilities) that war-torn regions such as South Sudan will struggle to overcome for the foreseeable future.

Systems at each of these scales could play valuable roles in the 'green pivot' proposed for South Sudan. Because large, utility-scale solar projects are not feasible until the country is more stable, the immediate focus is on smaller-scale systems. When stability is achieved, smaller-scale systems could become a major component of a vibrant domestic and export clean-energy economy.

Advantages of solar power for South Sudan

Renewable energy, particularly solar power, has the potential to be transformative in South Sudan for several reasons. First, compared with energy produced by diesel generators, renewable energy is cheaper, cleaner and longer lasting; whereas a diesel generator requires new diesel to burn and the generator itself must be replaced every few years, a solar panel can reliably produce electricity for up to 25 years. Second, South Sudan has ample sunshine with strong solar power potential (high solar irradiance). Third, as the conflict drags on, internationally funded humanitarian programming can launch an expansion in solar power generation, offering short-term energy benefits and cost savings, while building an enduring infrastructure that will outlive the conflict and contribute to peace and stability over time.

Despite donor fatigue, large-scale international humanitarian aid funding is likely to continue in South Sudan for the foreseeable future. Currently, international donor governments cover the high energy costs for the purchase of generators and diesel for individual NGO compounds and programmes, UN agencies and peacekeeping bases, and POC camps. These costs can account for a significant proportion of programme budgets, particularly for activities outside Juba, and must be paid year after year, leaving nothing to show for the expense. Given the high price of diesel in South Sudan, renewable energy systems could quickly pay for themselves, potentially saving millions of dollars in the years to come.

Unfortunately, existing diesel usage and energy figures are not readily available from international donors or humanitarian NGOs. Some limited information about fuel usage by the UN Mission in South Sudan (UNMISS, the successor mission to UNMIS, which ended in July 2011) is publicly available, but the information is not broken down explicitly between energy and transportation usage. A late 2014 audit report shows that the peacekeeping mission signed a fuel contract in March 2014 that was capped at US\$325 million over the three-year life of the contract. During the previous three years, from July 2011 to May 2014, UNMISS had received 68.7 million litres of diesel fuel, which was used for vehicle transport and to power generators (UN, 2014). As of June 2015, UNMISS owned and operated 195 diesel generators in 22 locations across the country (UN, 2015).

The need for international organisations and NGOs to reduce costs is increasing as the gap between humanitarian funding needs and funding pledges widens. In August 2016, the then US secretary of state John Kerry threatened to halt US government aid to South Sudan if the warring leaders did not do more to end the conflict (Stevis, 2016). The US government is by far the largest donor to South Sudan, having spent more than US\$2.15 billion between 2014 and March 2017.[3] The cuts in US foreign aid proposed by the Trump administration may well affect US funding in South Sudan.

US-funded humanitarian operations, as well as those of the UN and other international actors in the country, could make better use of their diminishing resources. A few but highly instructive NGOs and individual agencies in South Sudan use solar power successfully. Internews, for example, which supports local radio stations across the country, struggled for years with expensive generator maintenance and inconsistent diesel supply lines before transitioning its more remote radio stations to 100 per cent solar-plus-storage power. Following the successful transition to solar energy at its station in Turalei in Bahr el Ghazal, Internews worked with other community radio stations to help them make a similar transition and improve their energy supply.[4]

Such success stories should not obscure the significant challenges facing widespread solar adoption in South Sudan. Looting and destruction of humanitarian agency property during the civil war have targeted solar panels (and diesel generators) in population centres and rural humanitarian outposts. This in part explains international donor hesitancy to invest in solar systems (which are more expensive to purchase initially than diesel generators). Other impediments are the limited capacity in terms of trained personnel and the economic and security environment of the solar sector. These challenges can be at least partially mitigated, however. Security risks can be minimised with the strategic placement of solar systems. Local capacity can be built and supported through donor-led investment in training and capacity building, to help ensure that the South Sudanese benefit from such a transition and that solar systems are adequately maintained.

A donor-led transition to renewable energy

The advantages of a system-wide, donor-led pivot to renewable energy for the humanitarian sector in South Sudan are many. The transition would pay for itself and begin to generate cost savings within two to five years. It would create desperately needed energy infrastructure, while supporting ongoing humanitarian operations. These long-lasting, clean energy assets could support future reconstruction and health, education and social service delivery, and would carry the additional benefit of being in place and, likely, of having already been paid for. The pivot would also create new entry points for conflict resolution and peace-building. For example, the transition from a solar system that serves a humanitarian programme to one that supplies a local institution (such as a local utility or hospital) would generate opportunities for cooperation between communities driven apart by the civil war to determine issues such as the placement, oversight, management and maintenance of the solar system. Such a shift would create physical assets for peace that could support both physical reconstruction efforts and provide new opportunities for conflict resolution.

Donor-level support for this kind of a transition is important for two reasons. First, and most obviously, donors provide the funding to sustain current humanitarian operations, including existing diesel energy budgets. Donors are thus the primary option for funding a system-wide transition to solar power. Other conflict-affected countries, Syria and Yemen among them, have seen piecemeal efforts to use solar power, but nowhere has a concerted effort to accomplish a large-scale transition been undertaken (for example, Mansoor, 2016). Second, if solar energy infrastructure is to transition to local ownership or to benefit local communities in the mid- to long-term, it needs to be managed and maintained by actors likely to remain in South Sudan over a similar period. Unlike individual humanitarian organisations, donor governments generally operate with a national or regional lens and a longer-term perspective. Their mandates and missions will evolve to support development and reconstruction when the situation allows for it. Donor-level support for a shift to solar power could thus ensure continuity and help create and anchor a framework for managing the next phase of such a programme.

Making a system-wide transition would break new ground for such a comprehensive use of renewable energy in other crisis settings. Although some humanitarian actors are beginning to explore the potential for renewable energy, it has yet to become mainstream practice. The Moving Energy Initiative, funded by the United Kingdom's Department for International Development, is an ambitious multi-organisation consortium that is exploring how to integrate renewable energy into refugee camp settings, focusing first on Kenya, Jordan and Burkina Faso. The UN has started to look at renewable energy in its peacekeeping operations under its Greening the Blue Helmets programme, but that programme is still in its inception and focused (at least initially) on reducing the UN environmental footprint rather than on the economic, local electrification or peace benefits that could come from transitioning to renewable energy.

In South Sudan, the transition to solar energy is possible in at least three distinct types of humanitarian programmes or operations in South Sudan: individual NGO compounds, hospitals and POC sites.

Individual NGO compound solar systems

Practically all electricity in South Sudan is generated by diesel generators. Internationally funded humanitarian NGOs and UN agencies run their own generators to power their compounds and programmes, as do government ministries and offices, even in the main ministerial compound in Juba. Relatively small-scale solar systems could be installed in individual NGO compounds and positioned on the ground, on rooftops or on shipping containers. As noted, solar systems are often coupled with backup battery storage, and hybrid systems include both a solar component and a diesel generator. Unlike some peace dividends that have proven elusive in post-conflict settings, a solar system would yield immediate, observable benefits by reducing diesel costs and reliance on inconsistent supply chains (Wade, 2017). More importantly, once in place, these systems could easily be extended and connected to neighbouring compounds or houses to create local mini-grids, which could eventually be connected to a larger city grid.

Donors may have to create incentives for their humanitarian grantees to make such a switch. Most NGOs are not in the business of creating access to energy, so a strong push from donors and their continued involvement will be necessary to build out mini-grids anchored around internationally funded, NGO-compound–based solar systems.

Hospitals and health infrastructure

South Sudan's health infrastructure was weak before the civil war, and has declined further since fighting resumed in 2013. The main hospitals in the regional capitals of Malakal and Bentiu have been targeted during the fighting. On the long list of needs for most hospitals and clinics, energy supplies are near the top. For example, Juba Teaching Hospital, the country's only referral hospital and the main civilian hospital in the capital, has struggled through regular and extended power outages since the Juba grid collapsed in 2012. The hospital depends on inconsistent diesel stipends provided by the Ministry of Health. During the two outbreaks of fighting in Juba in December 2013 and July 2016, the hospital was flooded with patients and struggled with blackouts because the fighting shut down diesel supply lines. Even when diesel is available, the hospital is forced to ration its fuel supplies by shutting down its generators overnight, and sometimes it must resort to purchasing additional diesel on the black market. Similar constraints have affected hospitals and health clinics across the country.

Diesel-powered generators are a dirtier form of energy than renewable energy and may cause even more pollution. A report published in September 2016 found that diesel sold in Africa was the dirtiest in the world, its average sulphur content at least four times higher than that found in any other region and 200 times higher than European levels. This variance is due primarily to lax national regulations and unscrupulous petroleum actors. It is associated with a range of negative health impacts, including increases in respiratory and cardiovascular diseases (Gueniat et al., 2016). The report did not include South Sudan, but anecdotal evidence suggests that much of the diesel being sold in South Sudan is of particularly low quality and contains many impurities, causing significant problems for running generators and leading to lower productivity and higher maintenance costs.

Support for the health sector, and service delivery more generally, is an attractive choice for international donor funding. Investment in renewable energy for hospitals and clinics could significantly improve healthcare capacity simply by providing consistent and reliable energy. Hospitals would also benefit from the same economic savings that NGO compounds with solar systems would enjoy as a part of a local mini-grid, thereby increasing energy access for the surrounding communities.

South Sudan's international partners face a dilemma: whether to support or circumvent the state. Most do not want to provide budgetary support to the government because they believe funds may be diverted to military efforts, which are likely to target civilians. At the same time, international partners appear to believe in state continuity. When Juba was at risk of falling, international partners supported the existing order, perhaps believing it to be the only alternative to state fragmentation or collapse. Many donors are managing this dilemma by switching their assistance to the humanitarian sector and disbursing aid through international organisations and local NGO partners. The problem with this approach is that the South Sudanese state has been shrinking into the space created by its own tribalised security forces. This process is further militarising society and undermining civil spaces everywhere. But civil spaces still exist. In many churches and mosques, schools and universities, and hospitals and health centres, civilians are trying to maintain public spaces and protect their shared identities.

Supporting spaces that resist the militarisation and tribalisation of society offers at least three potential peace-building gains. First, it is a way of preventing a drift towards genocide or a further violent deterioration of inter-ethnic relations. Second, it supports the survival of non-militarised social and political values and possibilities, crucial for any future peace agreement to take root. Third, it supports a decentralised version of development, which could help mitigate the centralising tendencies of the security state.

POC camps in Malakal and Bentiu

Perhaps the most compelling case for investing in renewable energy systems is in the large POC sites, IDP camps housed within UN peacekeeping bases and home to more than 200,000 civilians who have fled the violence in Juba, Bor, Bentiu, Malakal, Wau and Melut. The Bentiu and Malakal POC sites are two of the largest camps in the country, housing approximately 110,000 and 35,000 IDPs, respectively. Both camps are situated on the outskirts of regional capitals that have been destroyed during the civil war. These displaced populations are supported by large humanitarian operations powered entirely by diesel; the annual cost of powering each camp's humanitarian operations is approximately US$1 million. Malakal has relied on air shipments of diesel fuel (and everything else) for most of the last four years because of insecure road and river access; Bentiu is accessible by road for part of each year, which makes for slightly lower, but still expensive, diesel costs.

Because of the high price of diesel, renewable energy systems in these camps would offer rapid economic savings for humanitarian operations; the cost involved in installing renewable systems in Malakal would likely be recouped (by lower spending on diesel) in three years; the outlay for Bentiu would be repaid within three to four years. Large-scale civilian returns to Bentiu and Malakal are unlikely in the near term, given the ongoing conflict and continued local and national tensions, but the civilian populations will probably opt to return to their homes when adequate peace, security and stability are restored. Investment in renewable energy infrastructure today can help build the power plants of tomorrow for these cities. Continuing with the status quo of diesel power will mean that when the situation improves enough for displaced civilians to return to their homes, humanitarian actors will either pack up and leave or transition to new locations, and donors will begin to think about supporting reconstruction in the cities. Creating new solar systems for humanitarian operations now would create an energy infrastructure that can transition from camp to city to support reconstruction and returns in Bentiu and Malakal in the years to come.

In addition to being subject to broader conflict dynamics, both Bentiu and Malakal struggle with local conflict drivers that must be resolved for peace to take hold. Building these solar systems with battery storage would create pro-peace assets that could both serve as entry points for promoting local cooperation and conflict prevention, and form the core of a new local electric grid. If the security of the solar systems is a concern, the systems could remain physically located within UN bases and connected to the cities by wire. The near- and long-term advantages of solar systems for Bentiu and Malakal could also be enjoyed at other locations in South Sudan, including in the POC sites in Wau and in refugee camps hosting Sudanese civilians in Maban and Yida.

Donor funding generally operates in distinct categories: South Sudan's aid is primarily humanitarian crisis funding, which usually operates on short-term funding cycles and is distinct from reconstruction or development funding. Renewable energy can bridge these categories. It offers an immediate cost-saving strategy while creating building-blocks for future peace. The POC projects in particular have to navigate tricky political currents. UNMISS has at times been unhappy that its bases are still being used to host and protect more than 200,000 civilians. It also remains sensitive to infrastructure projects that carry any hint of 'permanence' in the camps.

The bottom line on cost

Renewable energy systems are more expensive to purchase outright, which is one reason so many humanitarian actors continue to rely on diesel.

Short-term funding cycles define most humanitarian crisis funding, creating a structural barrier to adopting renewable energy. However, although crisis funding is often short-term, many humanitarian crisis situations drag on for years. Given this grim reality, donors and humanitarian agencies need to take a longer-term view of their programming in South Sudan, making the case for renewable energy all the more compelling as the economic value of renewable energy is unlocked over time.

As noted, the cost of diesel varies in different parts of South Sudan depending on access to foreign markets, the reliability of the supply chain, and the security situation, but diesel is expensive countrywide relative to South Sudan's neighbours and most of the world. In conflict-affected, landlocked parts of the country such as Malakal, diesel is so expensive that a large-scale solar-plus-storage system to support humanitarian operations would pay for itself. The savings for a humanitarian agency on diesel fuel would pay for the full cost of the renewable energy system more quickly than in Juba, which has access to cheaper fuel by road via Kenya and Uganda. Given that solar systems have a lifespan of 20 years or more, the economic benefits of a solar system will only increase with time. In Malakal, it may take only two to three years to recoup the cost; in Juba, where diesel is less expensive, it may take four to five years.

At July 2017 prices, the cost of buying and installing a 650-kilowatt solar-plus-storage system in Malakal POC would be around US$1.8 million. The specific costs and economics of other projects across the country could be researched and assessed as part of an initial donor-supported assessment for solar transitions in the country.

How to pay for the transition

The dramatic growth of renewable energy around the world has been aided by a range of financing mechanisms, including tax credits and leasing schemes similar to home mortgages that have allowed solar developers, businesses and homeowners to pay down the cost of solar systems over time. Such credit or leasing facilities do not exist in South Sudan or in most other conflict-affected societies. Most humanitarian agencies and the vast majority of South Sudanese citizens do not have the resources to buy renewable energy systems outright.

Donors could help fund a pivot towards renewable energy in several ways. One option would be to create a funding pool for outright purchase, rationalising such a large, one-time up-front cost as the price for achieving much lower energy expenditures over time while creating a long-lasting energy infrastructure that also serves social service and peace-building goals. A second option would be to extend multi-year, lease-like payment options to humanitarian grantees or to provide guarantees of multi-year funding so that individual organisations could seek their own financing. International solar developers were actively exploring South Sudan before the resumption of fighting, and a Norwegian company, Kube Energy, is currently looking at developing a solar leasing business for humanitarian actors in South Sudan. A third, complementary option is to create a financing mechanism specifically to support renewable energy in conflict and crisis settings, such as the Peace Renewable Energy Credit (PREC).[5]

Maximising benefits and mitigating risks

As noted, solar systems have been destroyed or looted in the civil war, a fact that may discourage donors and investors from funding a switch to renewable energy. The danger should be put in perspective, however: unlike in some other conflict settings, in South Sudan solar panels are no more likely to be stolen than other forms of power generation. Furthermore, some of the potential security risks can be mitigated thanks to the nature of the three settings discussed. The POC camps are located within UNMISS bases, behind fences and protected by UN peacekeepers. Although hospitals and other components of the country's health infrastructure have suffered, certain locations, such as the Juba Teaching Hospital, have survived, perhaps because they are recognised as safe and neutral spaces. The NGO compounds are primarily walled compounds with their own security measures, and solar panels could be installed on roofs to deter theft.

To enhance the sustainability of a solar initiative, and to ensure that the South Sudanese benefit from the outset of a transition, new investment in renewable energy should be coupled with a significant commitment to fund local capacity building and training programmes in solar energy. Donor support for such a transition would help bring foreign solar developers to the country, create opportunities for the South Sudanese to get into the business of installing and maintaining solar systems, and provide a critical economic building-block through electrification capacity. Increased competition would bring a variety of benefits, including lower prices.

Conclusion and recommendations

Renewable energy is not a solution to South Sudan's myriad challenges and will not resolve the problems that drive the conflict. However, current international humanitarian funding streams do provide an opportunity to chip away at these dynamics by building cleaner, cheaper, long-lasting energy infrastructure, whether in the form of small systems for individual NGO compounds, larger systems serving hospitals and health clinics, or extensive systems in POC camps.

International donors are understandably hesitant to invest in infrastructure projects in South Sudan given that so much has been destroyed over the past few years, including significant international humanitarian assets. However, investing in renewable energy systems anchored in humanitarian activities differs from more traditional infrastructure investment in two key ways. First, donors are already funding expensive diesel systems for virtually all their humanitarian grantees. Transitioning to renewable energy would be a cost-saving strategy for future humanitarian programming. Second, these systems would generally be protected within contained compounds and could be mounted on containers or rooftops. Larger systems for POC camps would be located within the larger perimeter of the extended UN bases and well protected.

This solar energy infrastructure offers cleaner, cheaper and long-lasting electricity generation and creates a new pro-peace asset. It would be a broader opportunity for South Sudan to escape its current development path, which depends exclusively on the petroleum sector. Rather than relying solely on the construction of mega-dams and a national grid to electrify the country, a scenario that, given the conflict and economic crisis, seems many years away even in the best-case scenario, solar power offers an easily scaled solution that works on and off the grid, in rural and urban settings.

An investment in renewable energy would provide tangible evidence to civilians and politicians alike of the country's opportunity to leap-frog older technologies and embrace a green development path that takes full advantage of technological developments and broader global political and investment interest in environmentally friendly strategies. Providing basic energy services through PREC investment, then, is a unique opportunity to jumpstart peace-building. Similar efforts include national government investments in trust funds such as the World Bank's Energy Sector Management Assistance Program and NGO campaigns that address landmines or gender equality.

South Sudan is one of the most challenging situations facing the international community today. New approaches are needed to help chart a path out of the crisis and to recapture the hope and optimism that defined South Sudan's future just a few years ago. International humanitarian donors can adapt to this longer-term lens, but doing so calls for new thinking and innovative approaches. Renewable energy presents a rare win-win opportunity, with benefits both in the short term and for years to come.

The following recommendations are intended to help international donors seize this opportunity and exploit it to its fullest:

- Assess current energy spending among UN and humanitarian grantees to create more transparency on energy costs and usage in South Sudan. Encourage relief organisations to publish their actual energy supply and maintenance costs on a standard, levelised cost-of-energy basis.
- Begin donor-level discussions concerning existing or new mechanisms to pool funds to help finance renewable energy systems for humanitarian grantees with multiple donors.
- Implement pilot projects to determine the relative economics and payback periods (length of time for diesel cost savings to equal cost of solar systems) for both small and large relief settings.
- Convene a global summit of humanitarian support groups to share the results of these pilot studies and encourage consideration of a transition to clean energy by the aid and relief community as a whole.
- Explore options and scenarios for transitioning the energy infrastructure for local benefit, to include maintaining donor involvement – including possibly ownership – in the protection and management of newly installed renewable energy systems, as well as planning for new training and capacity-building programmes to support South Sudan's solar sector.
- Commission independent groups to evaluate the planning issues involved in designing solar-plus-storage energy systems to become the new backbone of clean energy infrastructure as IDPs and refugees gradually move back to the towns.

Notes

1   This chapter was first published as 'South Sudan's Renewable Energy Potential: A Building Block for Peace' by David Mozersky and Daniel M. Kammen (2018). Copyright © 2018 by the Endowment of the United States Institute of Peace. It is reprinted with permission of the United States Institute of Peace.

2   According to the International Energy Agency (IEA), South Sudan averaged only 39 kilowatt-hours of electricity consumed per capita for the entire year of 2014. This put South Sudan alongside Haiti at the bottom of the IEA 2016 national rankings. By comparison, Ethiopia averaged 70, Kenya 171, Mexico 2169 and the United States 12962 kilowatt-hours.

3   This figure includes funding for South Sudanese refugees in neighbouring countries (USAID, 2017).

4   Interview with Internews officials, Juba, May 2016. See also Nikolov (2017).

5   The PREC was developed as a new variant of the Renewable Energy Credit (REC) mechanism. RECs represent one megawatt-hour of renewable energy generated and trade successfully in billion-dollar markets in North America and Europe, allowing both public and private sector actors to meet their renewable energy commitments by purchasing these virtual claims. PRECs could be generated from renewable energy projects in South Sudan, for example, sold back into the voluntary renewable energy markets to link existing renewable energy markets to fragile settings, and create a new revenue stream to help promote clean energy in support of peace-building goals. For details, see the work of Energy Peace Partners at www.energypeacepartners.com and RAEL (2017).

References

Akec, John A. (2016), 'South Sudan's economy: Is fuel the new dollar?', *Sudan Tribune*, 11 December, http://www.sudantribune.com/spip.php?article61080.

Alstone, Peter, Dimitry Gershenson and Daniel M. Kammen (2015), 'Decentralised energy systems for clear electricity access', *Nature Climate Change* 5, no. 4: 305–14.

Altai Consulting (2014), 'South Sudan: Mapping the supply chain for solar lighting products', http://www.altaiconsulting.com/wp-content/uploads/2016/03/South-Sudan-Mapping-the-Supply-Chain_July-2014.pdf.

Bazilian, Morgan and Debabrata Chattopadhyay (2015), 'Considering power system planning in fragile and conflict states', *EPRG Working Paper 1518* (Cambridge: University of Cambridge).

Global Humanitarian Assistance (2011), 'Resource flows to Sudan', http://devinit.org/wp-content/uploads/2011/07/gha-Sudan-aid-factsheet-2011-South-Sudan-focus1.pdf.

GRSS (2011), South Sudan Development Plan 2011–2013, http://www.grss-mof.org/wp-content/uploads/2013/08/RSS_SSDP.pdf.

Gueniat, Marc et al. (2016), *Dirty Diesel: How Swiss Traders Flood Africa With Toxic Fuels* (Lausanne, Switzerland: Public Eye).

Hoth Mai, Nyathon J., Augustino T. Mayai and Nhial Tiitmamer (2016), *Sporadic Fuel Crisis in South Sudan: Causes, Impacts, and Solutions*, The Sudd Institute, https://www.suddinstitute.org/assets/Publications/572b7eb2950f7_SporadicFuelCrisisInSouthSudanCausesImpacts_Full.pdf.

IEA (2016), *Key World Energy Statistics 2016*, http://www.oecd-ilibrary.org/energy/key-world-energy-statistics-2016_key_energ_stat-2016-en.

Mansoor, Magdi (2016), 'Civil war spurs spike in solar energy use in Yemen', *Earth Island Journal*, 6 October, http://www.earthisland.org/journal/index.php/elist/eListRead/civil_war_spurs_spike_in_solar_energy_use_in_yemen.

Nikolov, Nikolay (2017), 'How sunshine is bringing radio to remote parts of South Sudan', *Internews*, 12 February, https://www.internews.org/news/how-sunshine-bringing-radio-remote-parts-south-sudan.

Radio Tamazuj (2018), 'South Sudan government scraps expensive fuel subsidies', 11 May, https://radiotamazuj.org/en/news/article/south-sudan-government-scraps-expensive-fuel-subsidies.

RAEL (2017), 'RAEL holds first workshop on the Peace Renewable Energy Credit', Renewable and Appropriate Energy Laboratory, https://rael.berkeley.edu/2017/05/rael-holds-first-experts-workshop-on-the-peace-renewable-energy-credit.

REN21 (2016), *Renewables 2016: Global Status Report*, Renewable Energy Policy Network for the 21st Century, http://www.ren21.net/wp-content/uploads/2016/06/GSR_2016_Full_Report.pdf.

Stalon, Jean-Luc and Biplove Choudhary (2017), 'Confronting climate change in South Sudan: Risks and opportunities', *Sudan Tribune*, 27 June, http://www.sudantribune.com/spip.php?article62844.

Stevis, Matina (2016), 'Kerry threatens to cut aid to South Sudan if peace isn't restored', *Wall Street Journal*, 22 August, https://www.wsj.com/articles/kerry-threatens-to-cut-aid-to-south-sudan-if-peace-isnt-restored-1471881185.

Sudan Tribune (2017a), 'South Sudan hopes oil refinery works in four months', 9 March, http://www.sudantribune.com/spip.php?article61833

— (2017b), 'S. Sudan quietly removes fuel subsidies over hard currency', 3 December, http://www.sudantribune.com/spip.php?article64157.

UN (2014), *Audit of Fuel Management in the United Nations Mission in South Sudan: United Nations Report 2014/146*.

— (2015), *Budget Performance of the United Nations Mission in South Sudan for the Period from 1 July 2014 to 30 June 2015, Report of the Secretary General: UN General Assembly Report A/70/599*.

USAID (2017), 'South Sudan – Crisis fact sheet #5, Fiscal year 2017', *Relief Web*, https://reliefweb.int/report/south-sudan/south-sudan-crisis-fact-sheet-5-fiscal-year-fy-2017.

Wade, Lizzie (2017), 'In Colombia, peace dividend for science proves elusive', *Science* 357, no. 6355: 958.

World Bank (2016), *HFS Market Surveys in South Sudan*, http://www.thepulseofsouthsudan.com/wp-content/uploads/sites/3/2016/08/MPS_v10.pdf.

Conclusion

Luka Biong Deng Kuol and Sarah Logan

There are multiple explanations for what has driven South Sudan into its current crisis. The contributions in this book have shown that, while addressing the dire outcomes of South Sudan's fragility is of immediate urgency, the importance of reflecting on the causes of the country's fragility and recurrent cycles of violence cannot be overemphasised. South Sudan is at a crossroads. A business-as-usual stance could see the country continue to slide into violence. Alternatively, a genuine reflection on what went wrong, a collective search for real and sustainable solutions, and a concerted effort from all national and international stakeholders could make progress towards a more peaceful and democratic future for South Sudan.

This book has provided a number of recommendations to guide thinking around reforming South Sudan's systems and institutions so that they are stronger, more resilient and more representative, inclusive and participatory. Few of these reforms are possible until a permanent ceasefire is reached, and all reforms will require considerable political will and commitment from all national and international stakeholders.

Building institutional and collective leadership: will the SPLM provide it?

Several contributions in this book highlight the centrality of leadership in addressing and transforming the current crisis in South Sudan. Importantly, they emphasise the need for institutional, multi-agent and collective leadership, rather than individual leadership. Reliance on individual leaders does not bring sustained change; indeed, this 'hero orthodoxy' may be a source of development failure (Andrews et al., 2015). Governance in South Sudan relies far too heavily on individuals. Indeed, many South Sudanese believe that the current crisis would have been averted if John Garang were alive and leading the Sudan People's Liberation Movement (SPLM) and the country. More emphasis is instead needed on building strong, resilient institutions that do not depend on individual leaders.

In many ways, the ongoing conflict is the result of a crisis of institutions and a collective SPLM leadership failure. Weak political capacity and undeveloped democratic institutions, both within the SPLM and the state more broadly, were unable to withstand internal SPLM infighting, resulting in political differences escalating into a national crisis.

Although the SPLM waged the liberation war that brought independence to South Sudan, its transition to ruling party was very difficult. Militaristic institutions prevailed in areas under SPLM control, and the Sudanese had nurtured corrupt institutions in areas under their control in an effort to dissuade southern Sudanese from joining the rebellion against Khartoum. This poor institutional base, combined with the SPLM's lack of governance experience, resulted in a rocky post-conflict transition period, with the SPLM becoming increasingly susceptible to the curse of liberation. The curse of liberation refers to the pattern of many liberation movements being ill-equipped to govern a country in a post-conflict period (Clapham, 2012). It manifests in the deterioration of civil and political rights, and high levels of corruption and rent-seeking behaviour, as the liberators are tempted to use state authority and resources to retain power (Clapham, 2012). Indeed, in South Sudan, the liberators appear to have been far more preoccupied with rewarding themselves than serving their citizens.

The SPLM's failure to provide credible political leadership in post-independence South Sudan has resulted in the swift depletion of the significant political capital accrued from the liberation struggle. The weakening of the SPLM could create space for new political parties to articulate a political agenda appealing to the people of South Sudan. Coupled with calls for greater democratisation within the SPLM, the emergence of new political parties could drive the creation of more accountable and competitive political leadership.

Forging a national identity: will customary law and traditional structures provide the basis?

South Sudan's state formation and national narrative have been deeply shaped by the country's history and its continuum of colonisation and oppression by various external authorities prior to independence in 2011. The country's estimated 64 different ethnic groups share a degree of common history. Traditional systems of governance have sustained and nurtured distinct cultures and customs, allowing diversity to endure over time. Indeed, traditional social institutions have proven to be more resilient than formal institutions and, as outlined by Luka Biong Deng Kuol, traditional authorities continue to enhance good governance and conflict resolution, and to be resilient, legitimate and relevant to the socio-economic and political lives of Africans. In contrast, the post-independence adoption of institutions modelled on those of foreign countries further aggravated governance failures as not only were they not tailored to South Sudan's context, but they exceeded the government's capacity to manage (Andrews et al., 2015).

Forging a national identity remains a real challenge in South Sudan. Some argue that what brought southern Sudanese together and differentiated them from the north was their shared history of resistance to colonialism and oppression (Jok, 2011). However, history alone is not adequate for forging a sustainable national identity (Jok, 2011). When the oppressor was removed as a unifying force for the south after independence, the sense of 'being south Sudanese' began to erode and identification with one's ethnic group grew (Kuol, 2018). As the government's legitimacy waned through a failure to perform its core functions, citizens retreated from their national identity and instead associated themselves communally at a level of authority that better provided for their security needs (Ghani et al., 2005). In South Sudan, this trend has been further exacerbated by the close connection between identity and territory and élites' frequent use of identity as a mobilisation strategy for resource conflicts, as explained in the chapter by Peter Hakim Justin and Lotje de Vries.

Little effort was made to build a strong sense of national unity after independence, and the real or perceived dominance of the bigger ethnic groups, particularly the Dinka, in the national government may have sown seeds of dissent. The government's failure to address atrocities committed by the liberation movements during the war likely also undermined a sense of national belonging. The ruling élite's inability or unwillingness to effectively manage South Sudan's ethnic diversity, a stance not unlike that of the Sudanese ruling élites, has been the most significant cause of the breakdown of peace in the country.

Despite the crisis of national identity in South Sudan, South Sudanese still have an opportunity to forge a shared national identity. Frequent daily interaction between different ethnic groups provides exposure that could nurture social capital and social cohesion. The customary law, despite constructing division between ethnic groups in some instances, has also arguably provided a commonality and narrative to imagine a shared South Sudanese national identity, as outlined in the chapter by Naomi Pendle.

Building a unified national identity out of the current fragility and fractured ethnic relations will, however, require a strong visionary, strategic and ethical political leadership.

Managing diversity: can appropriate electoral systems and systems of government help?

Prioritising power-sharing and group autonomy

Inherited colonial systems of governance and constitutionalism lacking in contextual relevance and homegrown legitimacy have not been effective in South Sudan, as demonstrated by Francis M. Deng and Daniel Deng. They have failed, crucially, to provide mechanisms to manage the country's ethnic diversity. This is largely due to its centralised government system, which disrupted and shifted power and resources away from local arrangements that had successfully sustained mutuality of interests over time. As Sarah Logan notes in her chapter, maintaining peace and democracy in diverse and divided societies depends primarily on power-sharing and group autonomy. Electoral systems and systems of government must be adopted based on their ability to achieve these factors. A degree of proportional representation, as well as constituency-based accountability, and a parliamentary system that offers multi-agent executive rule, greater checks on executive power, and longer policymaking horizons could contribute significantly to South Sudan's political stability and long-term development. Additionally, a House of Nationalities along the lines of Ethiopia's House of Federation would be instrumental in ensuring continuous, high-level inter-ethnic dialogue and a dedicated mediation and dispute resolution mechanism for inter-ethnic differences.

Federalism and decentralisation

Much of South Sudan's governance debate has focused on federalism and decentralisation. Since before Sudanese independence, southern élites have called for federalism as the only mechanism able to preserve peace. But what federalism has meant to different people in southern Sudan at different times has varied, as demonstrated by Douglas H. Johnson in his chapter on the history of federalism in South Sudan. Reflecting the southern desire for federalism, the 2005 Interim Constitution put Southern Sudan on a path towards becoming an independent state with a federal system.

There is a growing literature favouring federalism for managing diversity, safeguarding minority interests, and overcoming mistrust and conflict, particularly as a country transitions out of conflict. Although federalism cannot prevent conflict, it can provide the institutional framework within which ethnic diversity can be more effectively managed. Nonetheless, at independence the SPLM reneged on their promise of federalism and the 2011 Transitional Constitution instead favoured a centralised unitary system that has, unsurprisingly, produced an authoritarian government intolerant of discussions of genuine federalism.

In recent years, decentralisation has gained greater prominence in Africa alongside greater recognition of the value of local government and traditional authorities, who were often neglected in the post-independence period. Some argue decentralisation can equally achieve the objectives that federalism hopes to bring about, in terms of offering a path to unity, an instrument for deflecting secessionist tendencies, and a way to achieve local support for central government policies.

Both federalism and decentralisation bring government closer to the people and offer greater efficiency in service delivery. In practice, however, as discussed in the chapter by Alex de Waal and Naomi Pendle, those motivations have tended to be secondary to these systems' value in increasing the reach and discretion of central government's patronage systems, consolidating central power while dividing and weakening regional blocs. Seen in this way, it's not surprising that decentralisation has not led to better governance, economic growth or a deepening of democracy in sub-Saharan Africa. Indeed, in South Sudan the creation of sub-national leadership positions, particularly with the expansion in the number of states, has amounted to little more than granting a licence to loot state resources. Lovise Aalen elaborates on this power calculation, demonstrating in her chapter that a regime will only fully implement decentralisation reforms if it determines that decentralisation will strengthen rather than undermine the regime's survival through consolidating the ruling party's dominance on the local level.

Federalism and decentralisation also claim to potentially reduce conflict and better manage diversity by, for example, establishing a more inclusive government that facilitates minority group representation, and creating flexible institutional mechanisms to accommodate varied interests. However, this may not hold true in diverse, resource-rich countries with weak institutions and central government, and a history of ethnic conflict, such as South Sudan. In such situations, as explained by Joseph Siegle and

Patrick O'Mahony in their chapter, it is thought that decentralisation may in fact increase the likelihood of ethnic strife by growing ethnic divisions and political polarisation, further accentuating inter-group differences and fostering discrimination against minority groups. Similarly, federal systems from elsewhere, including Ethiopia's model of ethnic federalism, as outlined in the chapter by John Young, should not be considered a panacea to addressing ethnic conflict in South Sudan as they are unlikely to be feasible in the country's unique context. Homegrown solutions are needed, and a comprehensive risk analysis focusing particularly on decentralisation's potential to aggravate ethnic divisions and political polarisation should be carried out when considering decentralisation.

If the decentralisation route is chosen, certain conditions are needed for it to be effective. First, it is vital to enhance the capacity of local governments to deliver services. Second, creating a democratic environment and building accountable and legitimate political structures at national and local levels are necessary prerequisites. Third, experience has shown that focusing on local-level revenue expenditure is more important for community cohesion than local tax collection. Fourth, decentralisation is only likely to reduce conflict when the national government has a monopoly on the use of force, otherwise semi-autonomous rule on the sub-national level could foment secession. Fifth, establishing autonomous regions should be avoided as such ethno-federal structures tend to be particularly unstable (Hale, 2004) and are associated with a higher probability of ethnic conflict. Finally, as South Sudan emerges from conflict, the focus should be on creating the conditions needed to prevent a relapse into conflict. These conditions include providing human security, investing in education and other basic services, promoting economic diversification to reduce reliance on oil revenues, reforming structures and systems to ensure inclusive and participatory governance, and creating an open and competitive political environment that includes a role for traditional institutions.

Pursuing macroeconomic stabilisation, poverty reduction and renewable energy

Nora Dihel and Utz Pape demonstrate in their chapter that South Sudan exhibits all the signs of macroeconomic collapse with a bleak economic growth outlook. The economy has contracted drastically as conflict has constrained both oil and agricultural production, leading to a decline in exports and household consumption and significant cuts to basic service delivery. Nevertheless, the government has maintained high levels of recurrent spending in the security sector. This has resulted in soaring inflation, a growing fiscal deficit, and spiralling divergence between the official and black market exchange rates.

How can South Sudan get back onto the path of macroeconomic stability and poverty reduction? Recommendations provided here include the need for the government to limit expenditure and improve its public financial management practices, including transferring revenues from government accounts in commercial banks to national treasury accounts. Investment in public service provision and infrastructure development and, in the longer-term, in social protection programmes, is recommended for economic diversification, job creation and creating resilience against future shocks. For any economic reforms to be feasible, however, peace must first be restored in the country.

On the monetary side, curbing the tide of high inflation is a key priority. Although different paths for macroeconomic stabilisation have been considered, notably Exchange Rate-Based Stabilisation (ERBS) and Money-Based Stabilisation (MBS), the ERBS path with full dollarisation is considered to be the most effective way to address some of the macroeconomic weaknesses present in South Sudan, including high inflation and monetary institutions and policies that lack credibility. However, success will rest on rigorous structural and fiscal reforms that would require political will, strategic leadership and a strong institutional framework.

South Sudan has the opportunity to redesign its economic infrastructure to meet future development needs, leap-frogging technological developments to realise a low-carbon and climate-resilient development outcome. In their chapter, Daniel M. Kammen and David Mozersky outline practical ways in which internationally supported operations could switch to using the country's abundant renewable energy potential rather than generators powered by fossil fuels. Such transition could both cut operational costs and contribute to peace-building efforts in the country.

Diversifying the economy away from oil dependence

South Sudan's extremely high dependence on oil revenues, coupled with weak institutions, has made the country very susceptible to the so-called resource curse. Heavy reliance on oil revenues is antithetical to democracy, as governments tend to be reluctant to account for how oil revenues are spent. Despite enjoying a huge oil revenue windfall at independence, the South Sudanese government has spent little on social service provision, human security or infrastructure development, while increasing security sector spending and enriching themselves at the expense of their citizens.

How oil revenues are collected, accounted for and spent in South Sudan requires a fundamental overhaul. The Petroleum Revenue Management Act (PRMA), which stipulates, among other things, that oil revenue should flow into specific accounts and be utilised through the government budget, was enacted in 2015 but has not been implemented (IMF, 2017). Indeed, Kiir continues to use oil revenues to purchase arms and the loyalty of the militarised élite. Saving and prudent investment of saved funds are also crucial to smoothing expenditure despite fluctuations in oil production and prices.

Diversifying South Sudan's economy is of utmost importance in reducing its economic risk factors for conflict. Building on the macroeconomic stabilisation policies outlined in this book, it is necessary to address constraints to non-oil industry and to private sector growth more broadly. Such challenges require dealing with the country's undeveloped banking sector, lack of rule of law, insufficient infrastructure and endemic corruption (IMF, 2017). Particular attention will need to be paid to revitalising the agricultural sector, which sustains the livelihoods of the majority of South Sudan's population.

Building an effective and capable civil service

South Sudan's long history of colonisation left the post-independence government with very limited experience in developing an effective civil service for state-led service delivery and policymaking. With the conclusion of the 2005 Comprehensive Peace Agreement, the Southern Sudan government came into office with weak and corrupt former Sudanese institutions and militaristic SPLM structures, all of which suffered from significantly low capability. Security sector institutions were particularly weak, and the police and prison services essentially became a dumping ground for absorbing unwanted SPLA officers and untrained and ill-disciplined southern Sudanese militias who had been used by Khartoum against the SPLA. Staffing processes during the 2005–2011 interim period were erratic and motivated by short-term political gains and ethnic patronage. Post-independence, institutions remain characterised by large numbers of former militants and 'ghost workers' on the public payroll, a lack of basic systems and regulations, and low-capacity civil servants unable to manage public affairs. A weak education system produces poor-quality graduates who have few job prospects apart from joining the ineffective civil service.

Reforming the civil service, particularly the security sector, will require strategic thinking. Any overhaul of the national army would need to be supported by the international community, potentially going as far as to outsource security services while security sector institutions and a conducive security environment are established, as done in Liberia. A future South Sudanese national army will likely require equal (rather than proportional) representation of all ethnic groups, as in Burundi. Post-conflict, streamlining the civil service and building its core competency will be essential to improve delivery of basic services. In her chapter, Barbara Nunberg has provided some recommendations in this regard, including reducing the bloated civil service through voluntary and involuntary retrenchment schemes (particularly in the security sector), moving the public payroll onto an electronic system to eliminate 'ghost workers' and improve control of government salary expenditure, and introducing merit-based recruitment for civil servants. As with the other reforms suggested in this book, civil service reforms will require committed, visionary and strategic leadership, supported by a united national vision.

Moving forward

At the time of writing, little implementation of the August 2015 Agreement on the Resolution of the Conflict in the Republic of South Sudan (ARCSS) has taken place. ARCSS was intended to end the conflict and introduce a number of economic, political, security and transitional justice reforms. However, the ARCSS ceasefire obligations, as well as those in the December 2017 Agreement on the Cessation of Hostilities, Protection of Civilians and Humanitarian Access, have been repeatedly violated by both government and opposition forces. The High Level Revitalisation Forum (HLRF), established to restore a permanent ceasefire and bolster ARCSS, is still underway, but has made little progress in securing commitment to end the conflict.

In the event that the HLRF fails and no progress is made in reaching a permanent ceasefire or implementing ARCSS, foreign intervention may be an option of last resort. An international obligation to intervene may be difficult to ignore, with famine and potential genocide sweeping the country. There is precedent for intervention in internal African conflicts, such as the Economic Community of West African States (ECOWAS) military intervention to end the civil war in Sierra Leone in 1997 and French intervention in Mali, Chad and the Central African Republic (Schmidt, 2013). Indeed, Article 4(h) of the Constitutive Act of the African Union (AU) empowers the AU with the right of intervention in a member state in instances of grave circumstances, such as war crimes, genocide and crimes against humanity. The current situation in South Sudan undoubtedly meets the necessary conditions for the AU's intervention.

Other forms of international action are also possible. For example, in early 2018 the United States imposed an arms embargo on South Sudan in an effort to pressurise the government into a ceasefire, with the European Union following suit soon after. For an arms embargo to be effective, South Sudan's neighbours, notably Kenya and Uganda, would need to stop the flow of arms through their countries and into South Sudan. Uganda and Kenya's vested interests in the South Sudanese conflict, as well as minimal progress by the Inter-Governmental Authority on Development (IGAD) in ending the conflict, have led some to question whether IGAD should be allowed to continue to lead the peace talks or whether the AU should instead take over. The AU's greater credibility could inject new life and impetus into the current situation.

Other key issues that remain outstanding include the establishment of an AU–South Sudanese hybrid court to try those accused of perpetrating international crimes during the conflict, and the implementation of a national dialogue. A draft statute for the court and a memorandum of understanding between the AU and the South Sudanese government were submitted to the South Sudanese Council of Ministers in August 2017, but no action has yet been taken. It is reported that several key ministers oppose the establishment of the hybrid court (Human Rights Watch, 2017). There must be consequences for the atrocities committed in South Sudan, and it's crucial that the hybrid court is established. If the South Sudanese government continues to be uncooperative, it will be necessary for the AU to take decisive action and establish the court without South Sudan's cooperation.

There have long been calls for a national dialogue in South Sudan to end the conflict, promote reconciliation, nation-building and the development of a common national identity. In May 2017, Kiir launched the National Dialogue Initiative, a government-led national dialogue effort. Many have questioned whether the national dialogue can be effectively undertaken by the government, or whether a more impartial entity should lead the initiative. Early indications suggest that the National Dialogue Steering Committee appointed by Kiir has been inclusive and credible in the holding of initial plenary debates, however it is uncertain what mechanism will be used for implementation (Deng, 2017). It is also unclear how much progress the national dialogue can make before the guns are silenced.

More broadly, the contributions in this book demonstrate that it will be necessary for South Sudan to embark on reforms in addition to those outlined in ARCSS in order to build strong, independent and durable systems and institutions that achieve the representative, participatory and inclusive power-sharing needed in South Sudan. These reforms should be anchored to a shared national vision. Strong political will, ethical leadership and a concerted effort from all national and international stakeholders will be needed to drive forwards both a ceasefire and the ensuing fundamental reforms.

References

Andrews, Matt et al. (2015), 'Building capability by delivering results: Putting Problem-Driven Iterative Adaptation (PDIA) principles into practice', in Alan Whaites et al. (eds), *A Governance Practitioner's Notebook: Alternative Ideas and Approaches* (Paris: OECD).

Bariyo, Nicholas (2018), 'Hunger woes escalate in war-torn South Sudan', *Wall Street Journal*, 26 February, https://www.wsj.com/articles/hunger-woes-escalate-in-war-torn-south-sudan-1519674389.

Clapham, Christopher (2012), *From Liberation Movement to Government: Past Legacies and the Challenge of Transition in Africa: Discussion Paper 8/2012* (Johannesburg: The Brenthurst Foundation).

Constitutive Act of the African Union of 2000.

Deng, Francis M. (2017), *National Dialogue: A Critical Perspective*, The Sudd Institute, https://reliefweb.int/sites/reliefweb.int/files/resources/5992b5a5aec96_NationalDialoqueACriticalPerspectives_Full.pdf.

Ghani, Ashraf, Clare Lockhart and Michael Carnahan (2005), *Closing the Sovereignty Gap: An Approach to State-Building; Working Paper 253* (London: Overseas Development Institute).

Hale, Henry E (2004), 'Divided we stand: Institutional sources for ethnofederal state survival and collapse', *World Politics* 56, no. 2: 165–93.

Human Rights Watch (2017), 'South Sudan: Stop delays on hybrid court', 14 December, https://www.hrw.org/news/2017/12/14/south-sudan-stop-delays-hybrid-court.

IMF (2017), *South Sudan: 2016 Article IV Consultation; Press Release, Staff Report and Statement by the Executive Director for South Sudan*, 23 March, https://www.imf.org/en/Publications/CR/Issues/2017/03/23/South-Sudan-2016-Article-IV-Consultation-Press-Release-Staff-Report-and-Statement-by-the-44757.

Jok, Jok M. (2011), *Diversity, Unity, and Nation Building in South Sudan* (Washington, DC: US Institute of Peace).

Kuol, Luka B. D., (2018), *What is the Remaining Social Contract Holding South Sudan?* (Denver, CO: Denver University, forthcoming).

Reuters (2018), 'U.S., Britain and Norway warn South Sudan parties over ceasefire violations', 2 January, https://www.reuters.com/article/us-southsudan-unrest/u-s-britain-and-norway-warn-south-sudan-parties-over-ceasefire-violations-idUSKBN1ER0LM.

Schmidt, Elizabeth (2013), *Foreign Intervention in Africa: From the Cold War to the War of Terror* (Cambridge: Cambridge University Press).

Index